"At the right time, Isom's work deliv
political shifts that we are witnessing today. *Gratuitous Angst in White America* is relevant, unapologetically brave, historically grounded, and feisty in its analysis and that is needed now more than ever."

Dr. Zoe Spencer, *Emmy Award Winning Poet, Author, and Scholar*

"This book fills a major gap in the literature by examining the role that whiteness, particularly white privilege and the myth of white supremacy, plays in explaining crime among whites. It is notable for the background information it provides, the many literatures on which it draws, the intersectional approach it takes, and its description of the mechanisms by which whiteness causes crime. The book will stimulate much debate and research, taking criminology in a much needed direction."

Dr. Robert Agnew, *Samuel Candler Dobbs Professor of Sociology, Emeritus, Emory University*

"By offering an innovative analysis of white people's privileged pathways to crime and their privileged exemption from the purview of criminal law, Deena Isom makes one of the most important contributions to a critical criminological understanding of the complex relationship between race/ethnicity, crime, and social control in this current era. It is a tour de force, one that will undoubtedly become a classic piece of intersectionality scholarship. Theoretically sophisticated, Isom's path-breaking offering is a must-read for scholars, activists, practitioners, policymakers, and students seeking a timely, progressive, and unvarnished focus on race, justice, and inequality."

Dr. Walter S. DeKeseredy, *Anna Deane Carlson Endowed Chair of Social Sciences, Director of the Research Center on Violence, and Professor of Sociology, West Virginia University*

"In this book, Dr. Deena Isom has trained her analytical sights upon troubling questions about racial justice. With an unflinching scholarly candor, she asks how it is possible to harness the explanatory lenses and tools of feminist intersectionality theory and critical race theory (among other frameworks) so to understand why the early 21st century witnessed the re-emergence of white nationalist/supremacist rationales for a more punitive American criminal justice system. Readers will be impressed with the breadth of the events and scholarly literature Dr. Isom includes in her cogent argument as to how white racial angst is at the heart of contemporary racist rhetoric, ideals, and policies."

Dr. Todd Shaw, *Distinguished Associate Professor of Political Science and African American Studies, University of South Carolina*

GRATUITOUS ANGST IN WHITE AMERICA

Gratuitous Angst in White America presents a new criminological theory that explains the racialized experiences of white people. Unlike orthodox traditions that assume whiteness as normative or progressive traditions that center the experiences of the marginalized and oppressed, the theory of whiteness and crime flips those perspectives and turns a lens toward white people's lived experiences and the ideologies of whiteness. The theory of whiteness and crime answers two overarching questions: *How does being white impact one's likelihood of engaging in deviant, criminal, and/or violent behaviors?* And, *why are white people treated differently than other racial and ethnic groups by the criminal legal system*? Through the application of a critical whiteness perspective to criminology, the theory of whiteness and crime is an intersectional and integrated framework that explains within (and between) group differences in negative behaviors and entanglements with the criminal legal system.

This book examines the racialized history of America to contextualize the current racial strife in society and inform a more nuanced theoretical approach to explaining disparities. The reader will gain a socio-historical understanding of the depths of the current divides and insight into how such are perpetuated and potentially dismantled. Students will see connections between various theoretical traditions and an application of theory to current social conditions. Researchers will acquire a new theoretical foundation and propositions to ground empirical work that will fill extensive gaps in the criminological literature. And policy makers will see how oversights in understanding the depths of historical significance perpetuate and increase disparities and disadvantages, which are counter to a pursuit of justice.

Written in a compelling and direct way, this book will appeal to those in criminology, sociology, race and ethnic studies, gender and sexuality studies, political science, cultural studies, psychology, criminal justice, law, and beyond. *Gratuitous Angst in White America* is essential for those seeking a more complete understanding of the associations between race and crime and those who want to remedy those disparities. In the end, it is more than a new theory of crime, it is a call to action for all willing to hear.

Deena A. Isom is an Associate Professor of African American Studies and Criminology and Criminal Justice at the University of South Carolina. Her research aims to bring marginalized voices and lived experiences center to the understandings of the causes and consequences of negative and harmful behaviors and entanglement with the criminal legal system through the advancement of criminological theory, critical perspectives, and intersectional methodologies. Her work has appeared in numerous outlets such as the *Race and Justice, Feminist Criminology, Critical Sociology, Journal of Interpersonal Violence, Social Science & Medicine*, and *Youth & Society*. She is a University of South Carolina McCausland Fellow and Garnet Apple Award recipient as well as an Academy of Criminal Justice Sciences Minorities and Women Section's Becky Tatum Excellence in Scholarship Awardee.

Criminology and Justice Studies

Series Editor: Shaun L. Gabbidon, Penn State Harrisburg

Criminology and Justice Studies publishes books for undergraduate and graduate courses that model the best scholarship and innovative thinking in the criminology and criminal justice field today, but in a style that connects this scholarship to a wide audience of students, researchers, and possibly the general public.

Human Trafficking
Interdisciplinary Perspectives, 3rd Edition
Edited by Mary C. Burke

Violence in the Heights
The Torn Social Fabric of Inner-city Neighborhoods
Eileen M. Ahlin

White-Collar Crime
An Opportunity Perspective, 4th Edition
Michael L. Benson and Sally S. Simpson,
with Melissa Rorie and Jay P. Kennedy

Gratuitous Angst in White America
A Theory of Whiteness and Crime
Deena A. Isom

For more information about this series, please visit: https://www.routledge.com/
Criminology-and-Justice-Studies/book-series/CRIMJUSTSTUDIES

GRATUITOUS ANGST IN WHITE AMERICA

A Theory of Whiteness and Crime

Deena A. Isom

Routledge
Taylor & Francis Group

NEW YORK AND LONDON

Designed cover image: Brandon Fountain

First published 2024
by Routledge
605 Third Avenue, New York, NY 10158

and by Routledge
4 Park Square, Milton Park, Abingdon, Oxon, OX14 4RN

Routledge is an imprint of the Taylor & Francis Group, an informa business

© 2024 Deena A. Isom

Library of Congress Cataloging-in-Publication Data
Names: Isom, Deena A., author.
Title: Gratuitous angst in white America : a theory of whiteness and crime / Deena A. Isom.
Description: New York, NY : Routledge, 2024. | Series: Criminology and justice studies | Includes bibliographical references and index. |
Identifiers: LCCN 2023034891 (print) | LCCN 2023034892 (ebook) | ISBN 9780367766436 (hardback) | ISBN 9780367763992 (paperback) | ISBN 9781003167877 (ebook)
Subjects: LCSH: White American criminals. | White American people--Race identity. | White privilege (Social structure)--United States. | Discrimination in criminal justice administration--United States.
Classification: LCC HV6789 .I86 2024 (print) | LCC HV6789 (ebook) | DDC 364.08089/09073--dc23/eng/20230831
LC record available at https://lccn.loc.gov/2023034891
LC ebook record available at https://lccn.loc.gov/2023034892

ISBN: 978-0-367-76643-6 (hbk)
ISBN: 978-0-367-76399-2 (pbk)
ISBN: 978-1-003-16787-7 (ebk)

DOI: 10.4324/9781003167877

Typeset in Times New Roman
by KnowledgeWorks Global Ltd.

This book is dedicated to my soulmate and partner, Brandon; to my supportive and loving parents, Troy and Judy; and to my feline familiar, Douglas.

CONTENTS

FIGURES

SERIES EDITOR'S FOREWORD

It is with great pleasure and excitement that I write this Series Editor's Preface for Dr. Deena Isom's important work, *Gratuitous Angst in White America: A Theory of Whiteness and Crime*. When I learned Dr. Isom was interested in writing a book on the topic of whiteness and crime, I immediately asked Pam Chester from Routledge to contact her. After some brief discourse, Pam and I quickly agreed that signing Dr. Isom was a priority. I was already impressed with her published work and knew she would deliver a path-breaking work. Well, I was right. *Gratuitous Angst* breaks the endless cycle of books (I know there are more on the way) that focus on African American or Latino offending. Many scholars – including myself – have good intentions trying to craft theories and publish books that attempt to both explain racial and ethnic disparities in the criminal legal system with the notable aim to provide a road map to reducing or eliminating them. The reality, however, is that there is – literally – a mountain of reputable scholarship in the area, yet only a small dent has been made in understanding and solving the intricacies of the problem. Notably, there also isn't serious will throughout society to make the necessary changes to ensure fair outcomes in the criminal legal system. Nonetheless, scholars of all racial and ethnic backgrounds continue to devote their entire careers to examining this topic.

Despite the mostly well-intentioned enthusiasm for studying race/ethnicity and crime, few contemporary scholars have considered the reality that there is a serious *white* crime problem in America. While early scholarship by Black scholars such as Du Bois (1896) and Grimke (1915) discuss white criminality, Katheryn Russell-Brown has more recently devoted a pioneering chapter to "White Crime" in her classic, *The Color of Crime* (1998). As she noted then, and remains relevant today, very few criminologists take the topic of white crime seriously. Thus, there is little theoretical or applied research devoted to the topic. The field remains enamored with cross racial/ethnic comparisons that have done little to remedy the problem of racial/ethnic disparities in the criminal legal system. It is encouraging that, in recent years, some scholars have begun to theorize more about whiteness and crime – but largely focusing on elite white-collar offending (Sohoni & Rorie, 2021). Dr. Isom's theoretical work takes an expansive look at white offending and incorporates some important concepts including status dissonance, habitus angst, and aggrieved entitlement. Moreover, the inclusion of intersectional insights adds a dimension that makes the work especially powerful. Thriving largely on fear related to a *perceived* loss of status and power in society, the combination of these concepts provides a comprehensive model for understanding much white offending.

In closing, some scholars have discussed the need for the devotion of more scholarly attention to white criminality (Owusu-Bempah & Gabbidon, 2021; Russell, 1998). Despite this call, with few exceptions (for some examples, see Ahlin, 2023; Jacques & Wright, 2015), the topic has remained a tremendous blind spot in the discipline. Dr. Isom has masterfully filled the blind spot with a seminal book that will one day be among the classics in the field. One can only hope that *Gratuitous Angst* will not only produce tests of Dr. Isom's theory but spark widespread interest in white offending as a core area of study within criminology.

References

Ahlin, E. A. (2023). *Violence in the heights: The torn social fabric of inner-city neighborhoods*. Routledge.

Du Bois, W. E. B. (1896[2007]). *The suppression of the African Slave-Trade to the United States of America, 1638-1870*. Cosimo Classics.

Grimke, A. (1915). *The ultimate criminal*. The American Negro Academy.

Jacques, S., & Wright, R. (2015). *Code of the suburbs: Inside the world of young middle-class drug dealers*. University of Chicago Press.

Owusu-Bempah, A., & Gabbidon, S. L. (2021). *Race, ethnicity, crime, and justice: An international dilemma* (2nd ed.). Routledge.

Russell, K. K. (1998). *The color of crime: Racial hoaxes, white fear, black protectionism, police harassment, and other macroagressions*. New York University Press.

Sohoni, T., & Rorie, M. (2021). The whiteness of white-collar crime in the United States: Examining the role of race in a culture of elite white-collar offending. *Theoretical Criminology, 25*, 66–87.

ACKNOWLEDGMENTS

Nothing is ever achieved alone, and I have a village to thank for bringing this book to fruition. While the deepest seeds of this book were planted long ago (i.e., me learning and understanding my own white privilege within this racially stratified society), its conceptualization began in 2015. Shortly after I moved to South Carolina in the summer of 2015 to begin my career at the University of South Carolina after completing my PhD at Emory University, nine people were murdered at Mother Emanuel AME Church in Charleston, SC and the Confederate flag was finally removed from the State House grounds. That fall, I taught my first course as an Assistant Professor of African American Studies. Over the years that followed, we saw clandestine racial animus explode all over the country and the world. I also experienced much related angst far too close to home. These experiences pulled at my heart and shook me to my core. I saw a way to fight for true justice through my research and teaching. From that, this theoretical framework was born.

I must first thank the editorial staff at Routledge, particularly Pam Chester, Ellen Boyne, Kate Taylor, Deanna Waistell, and Prabhu Chinnasamy, for their encouragement and help through the proposal, planning, and production phases of this book. Also, many thanks to the series editor, Shaun Gabbidon, for this opportunity and encouragement to pursue this line of research. I must thank my coauthors of several previous projects that inspired this theoretical progression – many of them former students, now colleagues, and all friends: Hunter Boehme, Toniqua Mikell, Jessica Grosholz, Deanna Cann, Tia Andersen, Amber Wilson, Stephen Chicoine, and Marion Renner.

Tremendous thanks to Robert Agnew, Walter DeKeseredy, Todd Shaw, Henrika McCoy, Jennifer Wareham, Jessica Grosholz, and Toniqua Mikell, as well as the anonymous reviewers in the proposal phase, for taking the time to carefully read my manuscript and providing such insightful feedback. This book is exponentially better because of you. Also, thank you to my many colleagues and friends – Kate Cartwright, Alicia Girgenti, Karen Hegtvedt, Jason Williams, Michael Mitchell, and Sarah Rogers – among others who I've discussed this work with over the years and have given me feedback on various presentations leading to this book.

Thank you to my Department of African American Studies colleagues and students for teaching me so much and providing me with the space and support to evolve as a progressive, intersectional scholar. Thank you to the University of South Carolina and the Department of Criminology and Criminal Justice for providing me with financial support to collect data to test this theory (forthcoming) and the sabbatical time to produce this book.

Thank you to my parents, Troy and Judy Isom. You have always encouraged me to ask the hard questions, to stand up for what is right, and to use my voice for good. I would not be where I am or who I am without you. Thank you to my loving fur baby and feline familiar, Douglas. He has sat by my side (or in my lap) since the beginning of graduate school. He is the ghost writer of all my work and has been my support system through all the good and bad the past 14 years and for hopefully many more to come.

Thank you to the love of my life, soulmate, and life partner, Brandon Fountain. You have been my sounding board throughout this process – from debating concepts while walking on the beach, to discussing cover art ideas over dinner, to copy editing every revision of every chapter. Every cup of coffee is appreciated. Thank you for all your love and support, in all the ways.

And finally, thank you to all the teachers, mentors, students, scholars, and activists that have inspired me and do the hard work. I stand on the shoulders of giants. Let's keep getting into good trouble.

INTRODUCTION: REMOVING THE CLOAK OF WHITENESS

Our Racialized History Explains Our Racialized Present

Official crime statistics (i.e., arrest and incarceration rates) and self-report data (e.g., surveys and interviews) tell vastly different stories of crime. While official rates suggest people of Color, particularly Blacks, are disproportionately entangled in the criminal legal system (Bureau of Justice Statistics, n.d.; Federal Bureau of Investigation, n.d.), self-report data suggests most people – regardless of race, ethnicity, gender, class, or other statuses – have engaged in some form of criminal or deviant behavior (e.g., Krohn et al., 2010; Miech et al., n.d.). Despite the disparities between such data sources being generally sizable overall, the largest discrepancies are among the white[1] population (e.g., Andersen, 2015). This book provides a new racialized theory of crime that outlines white folks' distinct pathways to crime as well as provides an explanation for why they are less likely to become entangled in the web of the criminal legal system by placing these discrepancies within the historical context of the myth of white supremacy. In the following, I outline the roots of the United States' white supremacist, heteropatriarchal, and imperialist/capitalist structure in the colonization of the Americas by Europeans and use of the African slave trade as the benchmark of the New World's economy. The foundational ideals of the myth of white supremacy are now embedded in our institutions, policies, and practices, as well as impact our everyday interactions and identities. This hierarchal structure has granted those identified as "white" white privilege, yielding them unique entitlements to the American Dream, positions of power, rights and advantages, and the use of others for their own gain. White privilege also emboldens some to engage in crime without fear of prosecution. In other words, white privilege grants

DOI: 10.4324/9781003167877-1

access to deviant and criminal opportunities as well as shields white folks from the full wrath of the system. Thus, whites have distinct privileged pathways *to* crime as well as privileged protections *from* the criminal legal system. Yet, to fully understand these distinct racialized pathways, we must first understand the racialized history of our American criminal legal system.

Liberty and Justice for All Is a Lie

As Americans, we are all taught the same whitewashed history – America is a great democracy; a land created "for the people, by the people"; where all have the right and opportunity to pursue the "American Dream"; and all are "equal under the law." As children, most begin the school day pledging allegiance to a flag that supposedly stands for "liberty and justice for all." Yet, upon closer examination, a realization emerges – these ingrained "truths" are nothing but myths and lies. Walk into most US courtrooms and a color line is abundantly clear; those in the positions of power – judges, prosecutors, even defense attorneys – are mostly white, and those on trial are vastly folks of Color, particularly Black (e.g., Van Cleve, 2016). These distinctions are so normalized – through media portrayals (real and fictionalized, e.g., Jewkes & Linnemann, 2017; Surette, 1992) and official crime statistics (i.e., arrest and incarceration rates) – that many people may not even see it or may mistakenly assume such divisions are how things are "supposed" to be (e.g., Bonilla-Silva, 2018; Bourdieu, 2002). Yet, these depictions of the "criminalblackman" (Russell-Brown, 2009) are by no means natural, innate, or how things should be, but instead are the culmination of the stratified racial structure that is the foundation of America.

Racism as the Roots

America's position as a global superpower, politically and economically, is built on the tyranny of Indigenous Americans and enslaved Africans. "African American enslavement was a major foundation for this country – for its economy, politics, and other societal institutions. If there had been no African American enslavement, there probably would not have been the huge North American wealth generation – and possibly no modern wealth-generating British and American capitalism on the massive scale that developed over the centuries... white Americans 'bought their independence with slave labor'" (Feagin, 2013, p. 28). Such vast oppression was legitimized, institutionalized, and perpetuated over centuries through the assumption and justification of the myth of white superiority morally, religiously, biologically, intellectually, evolutionarily, developmentally, and so forth, that spread throughout the world through imperialist colonization.[2] The perpetual "Othering" of those seen as different from (white) Eurocentric standards justified their domination and exploitation for the gain of

America. Thus, "...modern capitalism *was* systemic racism, and systemic racism *was* modern capitalism" (Feagin, 2013, p. 25).

The domination and exploitation of non-colonizers was the basis of the American legal and criminal justice systems. Some of the first written American "laws" were in reference to how to control those enslaved. The idea of "white" and the racialization of "black" were entrenched in colonial legal code, and primarily linked to fears of those deemed "Other" receiving rights and recognized humanity (see Battalora, 2013; López, 2006). The first police forces were created to capture and control runaway slaves (Hadden, 2001). Furthermore, the inequality of people of Color with whites is embedded in the foundational documents and institutions of the United States. By denying citizenship to enslaved individuals and establishing the three-fifths rule, the US Constitution was essentially a contract of racial hierarchy (Goldstone, 2005; Lively, 1992; Mills, 1997). Through the Electoral College and the frequent redistricting of state's congressional maps (often through gerrymandering), the Founders created a pseudo-democratic system that favors white constituents and more (far) right-leaning candidates, often leading to the election of those that did not win the popular vote (e.g., Presidents George W. Bush and Donald J. Trump, in recent decades), with disparities frequently amplified by voter suppression policies (see Anderson, 2018; Crump, 2019; Glaude, 2016). The creation of various branches of government with immense power that are not democratically determined (i.e., the Senate prior to the ratification of the 17th Amendment and the Supreme Court) further ensured white men remained in positions of power to the service of their own interests (see Feagin, 2013; Mills, 1997). Lifetime presidential appointments to positions such as the Supreme Court could potentially shift the laws and policies of the country away from the will of the people with significant impacts for generations to come, just as we have recently seen with the Trump-era court's ruling in *Dobbs v. Jackson* (2022) that overturned *Roe v. Wade* (1973), despite broad public support for women's rights to choose (Pew Research Center, 2022). Thus, the standard for world democracy – with a hierarchical structure originally established by 55 well-off, white men, many of them slaveowners – is no democracy at all. The ideas of "by the people," "for all," and even "America" for them equated to whites, and particularly men – and for many it still does today. The United States is not now, and has never been, equal and inclusive, just as the Founding Fathers intended.

Systemic institutionalized and legalized inequities have evolved immensely since the signing of the Constitution. Between the end of the Civil War in 1865 and the Civil Rights era of the 1960s, numerous policies and laws were enacted to legally ensure the continued oppression and marginalization of those deemed non-white. From Black Codes and later Jim Crow laws that regulated all the movements and social interactions of people of Color; convict leasing that allowed the government to extract the labor of those incarcerated; poll taxes that required fees for the right to vote; redlining that restricted where Black people could live; to the legal racial segregation established by *Plessy v. Ferguson* (189) (see Anderson, 2016; Kendi, 2016; Wallis, 2016); such policies and rulings reinforced the *Dred Scott* (1856) decision where Justice Roger B. Taney explicitly stated Black people have "no rights which the white man is bound to respect." Thus, the myth of superiority of whites at the cost of the disenfranchisement, marginalization, oppression, and denial of rights of people of Color is blatantly apparent in American history. Free by no means meant equal.

The Civil Rights Movement of the 1960s, and particularly the Civil Rights Acts of 1964 and 1968 and Voting Rights Act of 1965, pushed much overt discrimination underground. Racism, however, did not disappear, but America instead entered an age of color-blind racism (Bonilla-Silva, 2018). In fact, racial segregation persists across social and institutional settings, and when integration does occur, Black people are often expected to navigate such interactions according to orthodox (white) standards of sensibility not to disrupt the stratified status quo (Anderson, 2015). While Blacks are now allowed physical access to white spaces, without systemic changes to policies and institutions that perpetuate inequities, white (male) dominance of powerful positions remains (e.g., gender wage gaps [Aragão, 2023; Bureau of Labor Statistics, 2022]; executive corporate seat holders [U.S. Equal Employment Opportunity Commission, n.d.]; politics [Hansen, 2019; United States Senate, n.d.a.; n.d.b.]). Furthermore, additional covertly racially biased laws and policies were enacted, such as the "war on drugs," that have led to an era of mass incarceration that has been coined the "New Jim Crow" (Alexander, 2010; also see Crump, 2019). Thus, people of Color have always been subjected to heightened scrutiny and have never been treated or seen as equal under the law, and all of such has been in service to the perpetuation of the myth of white supremacy.

The Law as a Tool of the White Man

Because of their historical roots, the law and the legal system, particularly police, are viewed very differently by whites and people of Color. "To protect and serve" is taken to heart by most white folks (at least in terms of *their* lives, properties, and interests), while many people of Color, especially Blacks, are suspect of law enforcement and the criminal legal system (e.g., Kearns et al., 2020; Schuck et al., 2008). One viral example happened in New York City's Central Park, where a white woman illegally had her dog off leash, and when asked to put the dog back on its leash by a Black man, she called the police on him claiming he threatened her life (Hays & Kryska, 2020). When asked later why she called the police, she stated she regarded the police as a "protection agency" (Gruber, 2020).

These racial differences are pervasive and persistent. On May 25, 2020, another unarmed, Black man died at the hands of police,[3] George Floyd, sparking outrage and protests across the country (Westcott et al., 2020). Protesters were met by police in riot gear, shot with pellet guns, and tear gassed. Such aggressive antagonism sparked backlash, and riots[4] erupted in Minneapolis (Helsel, 2020). We were also in the midst of a global pandemic, and anti-lockdown protests had correspondingly broken out all over the country as people (primarily white conservatives, many far-right leaning) pushed to re-open the economy and proclaimed the COVID-19 virus was a political ploy (Bosman et al., 2020; Warren et al., 2020). Many of these protesters were armed and had aggressively berated counter-protesters, lawmakers, and police (Riess, 2020). In Michigan, armed anti-lockdown protesters gathered at the State Capitol numerous times during 2020, brandishing Confederate flags and signs stating, "Tyrants Get the Rope" (Censky, 2020). Three men were even convicted of plotting to kidnap Michigan Governor Gretchen Whitmer with the aims of starting a civil war (The Associated Press, 2022). Yet, these protestors were not met with the same display of force that was enacted upon the racial injustice and police brutality protesters (SBS News, 2020). And, despite law enforcement and far-right counter protesters causing most of the violence associated with the protests of 2020 (Kishi & Jones, 2020; Richer et al., 2020), many armed, far-right protestors were validated by law enforcement as exemplified by one witness in a Seattle, Washington protest stating, "And you could see from the start that the police actually found their own citizens, who they were supposed to be protecting, to be a bigger threat than the people who were there to cause the violence. I remember seeing militiamen helping cops hog-tie antifa protesters in the street..." (Campbell, 2022, p. 88).

Furthermore, in 2020, health officials had called for everyone to wear masks in public to mitigate the spread of COVID-19[5] (Centers for Disease Control and Prevention, 2020), Yet, even masks – a tool to help keep people safe from a deadly virus – were racialized and politicized. Many Blacks, particularly men, were apprehensive about wearing any face covering including a medical mask for fear of being racially profiled (Taylor, 2020), which became a reality in an Illinois Wal-Mart (Toone, 2020). The juxtaposition of racial reckoning and COVID-19 fears vindicated white people using social unrest to invoke terror while weaponizing First Amendment protections to do so (Sweeney, 2020).

These are just some recently relevant examples in the stark differences between how whites and people of Color are viewed by and view the law and social institutions. People of Color, particularly Blacks and especially men, are presumed a threat that must be mitigated and controlled. White folks, on the other hand, are allowed to gratuitously express their attitudes, actions, and behaviors and push the limits of encroaching upon others under the guise that they are within their "rights," and the law will be there to enforce those rights. There is no clearer example of this than the attack on the US Capitol. On January 6, 2021, following a clear loss in the presidential election and a long misinformation campaign to "stop the steal," thousands of Donald Trump supporters, most of whom were white and many of whom were men, breached the US Capitol building in a misguided last-ditch effort to overthrow the certification of the Electoral College vote in favor of Joe Biden (Reilly, 2022; Remnick, 2022). Despite forewarning, security and police presence were sparse, particularly in comparison to the peaceful Black Lives Matter protests against police brutality over the summer (Norwood, 2021; Wamsley, 2021). Beyond gaining access to the Capitol building, the insurrectionists were not maintained for over three hours, despite calls from leaders of Congress for help, leading to chaos, fear, destruction, and death (Leatherby et al., 2021; Lonsdorf et al., 2022). Protestors claimed the Capitol was "their house" as they ransacked the Senate and Congressional Chambers chanting "Hang Mike Pence" and "We're coming for you, Nancy" (Select Committee to Investigate the January 6th Attack on the United States Capitol, 2022). Feeling emboldened following Trump's call to action, many participants live-streamed their participation on social media and justified their actions as an invitation from President Trump (Campbell, 2022; Collier, 2021; Nance, 2022), flouting their perceived entitlement and lack of fear of reprisal. To date at time of authorship, over 1,000 people have been charged in relation to the Capitol siege (Hall et al., 2023; U.S. Department of Justice, n.d.), largely due to their social media posts. Furthermore, the US House of Representative's Select Committee has released their final report and has recommended to the US Department of Justice that criminal charges be brought against former president Donald Trump (Select Committee to Investigate the January 6th Attack on the United States Capitol, 2022); at the time of authorship, history has yet to see who all will be punished for these attacks on American democracy.

As exemplified earlier, whites are often allocated protections – a presumption of innocence, a full respect of inalienable rights – whereas folks of Color are not and are far too often granted the opposite – inescapable assumptions of guilt, disregard of humanity. Therefore, in many ways the Founding Fathers' intentions remain a reality – whites have inalienable rights the law will protect, but people of Color cannot depend on the same.

Due Process as a (White) Privilege

Central elements of the American judicial system are the ideas of "innocent until proven guilty" and the right to due process. Yet, these concepts are also tainted by the myth of white supremacy. As alluded to earlier, before one ever enters a courtroom, people of Color are more likely to acquire the gaze of law enforcement than their white counterparts. Disadvantaged communities, which are largely composed of people of Color, are disproportionately policed (Boehme et al., 2022; Butler, 2017; Rios, 2011). Beyond that, Black folks are more likely to have law enforcement called on them (McNamarah, 2019) and be approached or stopped by police (Pierson et al., 2020), even if they are *not* engaging in criminal activity. Once in contact with the police, Blacks are more likely to be arrested (Schleiden et al., 2020) and convicted (The Sentencing Project, 2018), than whites in the same circumstances. Furthermore, Blacks receive less lenient plea bargains and harsher sentences (Owens et al., 2017), creating misleading official crime statistics (Reiman & Leighton, 2020; Tonry, 2004; 2011) and reinforcing the (white) myth that "crime" is a "Black problem" (e.g., Russell-Brown, 2009).

What is often overlooked in this process are the decisionmakers and power players that influence who enters *and* remains in the criminal legal funnel and who does not. The police, prosecutors, defense attorneys, judges, juries, and even lawmakers – most of whom who are white – all have a hand in who is tagged by the legal system and who remains entangled in its snares.[6] And even if their hands are tied by laws and policies, those parameters were informed by a white racial frame – "the dominant racial frame that has long legitimated, rationalized, and shaped racial oppression and inequality in this country" (Feagin, 2013, p. x) – and the privileges of those holding the dominant social status. Hence, laws are established by white (male) minds through the lens of a white racial frame, thus consciously or unconsciously perpetuating the myth of white supremacy (see Alexander, 2010; Tonry, 2004; 2011). What is deemed "deviant" and "criminal" are deviations from white normative standards and ideals. Consequently, to be a person of Color, especially Black in America, is already a strike against the hegemonic norms, and any further deviations mean one is seen as a true threat to (white) society.[7] Thus, people of Color are not only seen as inherently deviant, but their behaviors and actions are framed and responded to differently than white folks. In the end, folks of Color are not allotted the true protections of the law because the law was never intended to protect them, only control them.

Removing the Cloak

The assumptions of racial equality in America must be disrupted. This is not only true of our laws, policies, and legal system, but even our understandings of criminal behaviors. The leading orthodox theories of crime were developed by white, cisgender men based on (white) men's and boys' experiences. From Shaw and McKay's (1942) dismissiveness of Du Bois' (1899) previous work in their examination of (white) immigrant boys' arrests between neighborhoods, Merton's (1938) focus on "normative" (white) goals and means, Burgess and

Akers' (1966) emphasis on (white) children's interactions with "conventional" (white) others, to Gottfredson and Hirschi's (1990) flippant treatment of racial and gendered variations in control, white and male experiences have been the foundation of the "general" theories of crime. Despite key factors of strain, learning, control, and even social disorganization, theories finding empirical support in various contexts for differing groups (e.g., Broidy, 2001; Pratt & Cullen, 2000; 2005; Pratt et al., 2010), they all fail to fully explain the disparities in deviant behaviors and criminal legal entanglements, particularly within-group differences.[8] This is especially important given that despite marginalized folks having similar criminogenic backgrounds, characteristics, and social standings, the vast majority *do not* engage in serious and violent offending (e.g., Falk et al., 2014; Lurie et al., 2018; Papachristos et al., 2015; Weisburd, 2015). The inadequacies of orthodox approaches are rooted in their lack of acknowledgment of the inherent racism, sexism, and marginalization embedded in American history that established the social structure and still encroaches on our institutions and everyday lives (Anderson, 2016; Gabbidon, 2015; Potter, 2015). Thus, they dismiss the disadvantages, inequities, and injustices faced to various degrees by non-white, non-male, non-cisgender, non-heterosexual, and other marginalized folks every day.

To overcome these inadequacies, we need to not only center the lived experiences of marginalized people but the central role the myth of white supremacy plays in our understanding of crime. To do so means to push back on the arbitrary "normalcy" of whiteness and stop privileging the lived experiences of white people. We must examine their pathways in racialized ways and understand how the myth of white supremacy systemically privileges their interactions with the criminal legal system. We must also aim to not essentialize white privilege. Like other social statuses and identities, whiteness is a complex social construction that operates at the macro-, meso-, and micro-levels (Isom*, 2020).[9] Yet, how it works specifically for an individual is also dependent upon the other status locations and identities they hold (e.g., Potter, 2015), resulting in a unique mix of privilege and marginalization that colors the way individuals interact with the social world (Isom*, 2018, 2020). Incorporating whiteness within an intersectional understanding of crime will disrupt the assumptions of orthodox criminology and enlighten our understandings of diverse pathways to and from criminal behavior for all people, including white folks.

To remove the cloak of whiteness means to acknowledge the existence and perpetual influence of the myth of white supremacy in our society. While white supremacy touches all aspects of our lives, it is most clearly apparent in the racial disparities in our criminal legal system. Despite engaging in deviant and criminal behaviors at similar rates, people of Color, especially Blacks, are more often entangled in and treated worse by the criminal legal system than their white counterparts. Instead of taking a pathological approach and asking, "what is wrong with or different about folks of Color?" (which is far too often the Eurocentric, underlying research question), we should be asking "why are white folks treated differently?" Furthermore, to fully answer this question requires applying a socio-historical lens that centers the significance of the myth of white supremacy historically, structurally, and institutionally in American society. Such a recognition undermines all assumptions of equality – under the law, in access to resources, in presumption of guilt, in distribution of punishments, and so forth. It further dismantles the orthodox understandings of criminal behavior and the role of the criminal legal system. In particular, if all are not treated equally under the law, how may justice ever be achieved? In sum, it cannot.

Acknowledging the myth of white supremacy disrupts our social structure, institutions, and social knowledge. Racism and inequality are not viruses or bad apples that have harmed an otherwise healthy and just society but are pillars of a society characterized by marginalization and oppression. Thus, society and its central institutions, including the criminal legal system, cannot be fixed. Instead, it must be abolished, and new systems grounded in the true application of the concepts for a real democracy "for the people, by the people" and where *all* are fully "equal under the law" must be established in its place. Only then can a criminal *justice* system ever truly be just.

A Roadmap of the Book

In the subsequent chapters, I remove the cloak of whiteness from criminological theory to present a novel, progressive,[10] intersectional theory of whiteness and crime. Chapter 1 provides the socio-historical foundation to ground this new theory by providing an overview of the parallels between racial progress and tensions in America, particularly over the past century and recent decades. Such underpinnings are vital as many Americans only know the whitewashed narratives of history. The strife of the past decade feels new to many, yet it is truly just the latest evolution of our long history of internalized and institutionalized racism. Furthermore, the pillars of critical whiteness studies are discussed, which inform the theory of whiteness and crime. Chapter 2 offers an overview of the concept of status, how social hierarchies are created, perpetuated, and potentially undone, as well as presents a newer idea – status dissonance – that aids in our understanding of variations in feelings of gratuitous angst and entitlement within white folks. I begin the presentation of the central components of the theory of whiteness and crime in Chapter 3. There I build off the extensive threat literature to provide a new concept – habitus angst, or the range of negative feelings evoked in white people due to perceptions of change in orthodox society and the status quo.

Habitus angst is distinct from, but has a reciprocally reinforcing relationship with, aggrieved entitlement, which is discussed at length in Chapter 4. Aggrieved entitlement[11] is a discrete form of strain tied to whiteness that emerges when whites fail to receive what they believe is innately theirs or they are due. The theory of whiteness and crime argues these uniquely racialized strains of habitus angst and aggrieved entitlement distinctively increase whites' likelihood of engaging in deviant, criminal, aggressive, and violent actions; yet, white people also have exclusive protections that mitigate their likelihood of experiencing the harshest wrath of the criminal legal system – their white privilege. Chapter 5 reviews the concept of white privilege and outlines how it idiosyncratically weakens the ties between harmful actions and legal consequences for those with white skin. Chapter 6 presents a comprehensive overview of the theory of whiteness and crime. Chapter 7 reiterates the importance of applying an intersectional lens to all theoretical frameworks, argues for the integration of the new integrative structural identities model to accomplish those aims, and demonstrates how this is achieved in the theory of whiteness and crime. Finally, Chapter 8 resituates the theory of whiteness and crime within the current moment and calls for research and empirically informed policies for social change. So, with that, let's begin to counter the myth of white supremacy to fully understand disparities and find ways to remedy them.

Notes

1 I capitalize *Black*, along with people of Color and other racial and ethnic identifiers, but not *white* citing the explanation offered by the Columbia Journalism Review (Laws, 2020)—that Black reflects (for many) a shared set of experiences in relation to identity. Additionally, the Associated Press (Bauder, 2020) decided not to capitalize white because they have "less shared history and culture" and doing so might "[risk] subtly conveying legitimacy" to white supremacist beliefs (Berkhout & Richardson, 2020; Bauder, 2020; Laws, 2020). Thus, I follow this guidance throughout the book, even in the restatement of quotations from others.

2 Unfortunately, going into the details of these historical tyrannies is beyond the scope of the present work, but see Anderson (2016), Hannah-Jones et al. (2021), Kendi (2016), McGhee (2021), Rothstein (2017), Smith (2021), Wallis (2016) and others for extensive reviews, analyses, and discussion.

3 George Floyd is just one of the many Black lives lost at the hands of police (see Lyn, 2022; National Public Radio [NPR], 2020; The Washington Post, 2023). For discussions of the history and impact of police brutality and the Black Lives Matter movement see Boyles (2019), Butler (2017), Cobbina (2019), and Garza (2020), as well as Ritchie (2017) and Weissinger et al. (2017) for gendered and intersectional takes, among others.

4 Given many, whites especially, ask why people riot, it is best to remember what Dr. Martin Luther King, Jr. once said, "A riot is the language of the unheard."

5 At time of authorship, COVID-19 has killed over 1.1 million people in the United States (Centers for Disease Control and Prevention, n.d.).

6 The criminal legal funnel is a common metaphor for the narrowing of crime statistics as individuals move through the system, e.g., criminal actions (true dark figure of crime), known incidents, arrests, convictions, and incarcerations (see Hansell et al., 2016, as well as Biderman & Reiss, 1967). People are freed or not from the entanglements of the system at all stages of the process due to conscious and unconscious decisions of people in positions of power as well as due to disparities in access to resources (see Tonry, 2004, 2011). The myth of white supremacy is entrenched in this process, amplifying the resulting disparities.

7 Similar to Smart's (1977) idea of "doubly damned," referring to women defying gender norms and engaging in crime, and in turn being judged as more dangerous than their male counterparts.

8 There is extensive research on the associations between race and crime, with much examination occurring at the macro-level (e.g., Crutchfield & Wadsworth, 2013; McNulty, 2001; Peterson & Krivo, 2010; Sampson, 2012; Sampson & Wilson, 1995), with less attention given to micro-level processes. When individual differences have been assessed, it is often from an orthodox theoretical framework, which essentially argue people of Color, particularly Black people, experience more strain, have more deviant peers, and have less control due to their structural position in US society (Agnew, 2006; Akers, 2009; Burgess & Akers, 1966; Hagan et al., 2005; Unnever et al., 2009). Race and other progressive scholars, however, have criticized these orthodox "add and stir" approaches. ("Add and stir" approaches are when theories that were developed on white male experiences are utilized to explain the experiences of others without consideration of varied lived experiences and stratified, intersectional positions in society; thus, aligning with the critique outlined earlier.) Such assessments are often incomplete and distorted. (See Gabbidon [2015] for examples and discussions of the standings and shortcoming of orthodox theoretical perspectives and the associations between race and crime.) Hence, progressive scholars call for race, gender, and other identity-based, as well as intersectional, explanations of deviant and criminal behaviors (e.g., Ball, 2016; Belknap & Holsinger, 2006; Buist & Lenning, 2016; Burgess-Proctor, 2006; Chesney-Lind & Irwin, 2008; Delgado & Stefancic, 2017; Hawkins, 1995; Oliver, 1994; Potter, 2015; Russell, 1992; Woods, 2014). Of the leading orthodox traditions, general strain theory is the only one to attempt to center marginalized and oppressed experiences within specialized articulations of its framework (Agnew, 2006; Broidy & Agnew, 1997; Isom* & Grosholz, 2019; Isom et al., 2023; Kaufman et al., 2008; Pérez et al., 2008). We have also seen distinct identity-based theories emerge in response to these calls, such as the theory of African American offending (Unnever & Gabbidon, 2011). Therefore, this statement just reiterates the need for progressive, inclusive theoretical development to center the unique and distinct lived experiences of all people to provide a fuller and more complete understanding of the nuances of varied pathways to and from criminal and deviant behavior without assuming the "normative" pathway is that of a white, cisgender, heterosexual man.

9 I previously published under the name "Isom Scott," and references to Isom* refer to that time.

10 I use the term *progressive* presently to refer to all critical, feminist, race-and-crime, queer, and other progressive scholars who study inequities and disparities from a non-orthodox perspective that centers the lived experiences of often marginalized and oppressed populations. See Potter (2015) as well as Buist and Lenning (2016) for discussions on the progression and debates around labels of non-orthodox scholarship.

11 Michael Kimmel's *Angry White Men*, originally released in 2013 and re-released in 2017 with a new preface addressing the election of Donald Trump, played a significant part in guiding me down the path of whiteness studies and eventually

writing this book. I have leaned on his qualitative findings and concepts in earlier works – with parts of such appearing here – and one concept in particular – aggrieved entitlement – being a central factor of interest in the theory of whiteness and crime. However, I am also aware of the accusations against Kimmel, including a range of demeaning and predatory behaviors towards women, that cannot be ignored (see Arana et al., 2018; ExposeProfMichaelKimmel, n.d.; Flaherty, 2018; Guckenheimer, 2018; Jensen, 2018; Mangan, 2018; Murphy, 2018; Ratcliffe, 2018). The American Sociological Association as well as Sociologists for Women in Society have revoked or rescinded awards from Kimmel. As an intersectional and interdisciplinary progressive scholar that grounds my research and pedagogy in feminist, Black feminist, and critical race traditions, I cannot ignore these facts. Therefore, following the lead of countless survivor scholars (Cook et al., 2022), and as one myself, I have removed the direct citations of Kimmel within this work. Reference to him will be designated with a ♠ throughout the book.

References

Agnew, R. (2006). *Pressured into crime: An overview of general strain theory.* Roxbury Publishing Company.

Akers, R. L. (2009). *Social learning and social structure: A general theory of crime and deviance.* Transaction Publishers.

Alexander, M. (2010). *The new Jim Crow: Mass incarceration in the age of colorblindness.* The New Press.

Andersen, T. S. (2015). Race, ethnicity, and structural variations in youth risk of arrest: Evidence from a national longitudinal sample. *Criminal Justice and Behavior, 42*(9), 900–916.

Anderson, C. (2016). *White rage: The unspoken truth of our racial divide.* Bloomsbury.

Anderson, C. (2018). *One person, no vote: How voter suppression is destroying our democracy.* Bloomsbury.

Anderson, E. (2015). "The white space". *Sociology of Race and Ethnicity, 1*(1), 10–21.

Aragão, C. (2023). *Gender pay gap in U.S. hasn't changed much in two decades. Pew Research Center.* https://www.pewresearch.org/fact-tank/2023/03/01/gender-pay-gap-facts/

Arana, J., Barker, G., Bathrick, D., Botkin, S., Derry, C., Donaldson, C., Ehrmann, J., Flood, M., Heisterkamp, A., Idibouo, C., Kaufman, M., Katz, J., Keith, T., Lemmon, P., Messner, M., Molano, S., Montoya, O., Norberg-Bohm, C., Messerschmidt, J., O'Brien, J., & Okun, R. (2018, August 31). Profeminist men respond to allegations about Michael Kimmel. *Voice Male.* https://voicemalemagazine.org/profeminist-men-respond-toallegations-about-michael-kimmel/

Ball, M. (2016). *Criminology and queer theory: Dangerous bedfellows?* Springer Publishing.

Battalora, J. (2013). *Birth of a white nation: The invention of white people and its relevance today.* Strategic Book Publishing.

Bauder, D. (2020, July 20). AP says it will capitalize Black but not white. *Associated Press.* https://apnews.com/article/7e36c00c5af0436abc09e051261fff1f

Belknap, J., & Holsinger, K. (2006). The gendered nature of risk factors for delinquency. *Feminist Criminology, 1*(1), 48–71.

Berkhout, S. G., & Richardson, L. (2020). Identity, politics, and the pandemic: Why is COVID-19 a disaster for feminism (s)? *History and Philosophy of the Life Sciences*, *42*(4), 1–6.

Biderman, A., & Reiss, A. (1967). On exploring the "dark figure" of crime. *The ANNALS of American Academy of Political and Social Science*, *374*(1), 1–15.

Boehme, H. M., Cann, D., & Isom, D. A. (2022). Citizens' perceptions of over- and under-policing: A look at race, ethnicity, and community characteristics. *Crime & Delinquency*, *68*(1), 123–154.

Bonilla-Silva, E. (2018). *Racism without racists: Color-blind racism and the persistence of racial inequality in America* (5th ed.). Rowman & Littlefield.

Bosman, J., Tavernise, S., & Baker, M. (2020, April 23). Why these protesters aren't staying home for coronavirus orders. *The New York Times*. https://www.nytimes.com/2020/04/23/us/coronavirus-protesters.html

Bourdieu, P. (2002). Habitus. In J. Hillier, & E. Rooksby (Eds.), *Habitus: A sense of place* (pp. 27–34). Ashgate.

Boyles, A. S. (2019). *You can't stop the revolution: Community disorder and social ties in post-Ferguson America*. University of California Press.

Broidy, L. M. (2001). A test of general strain theory. *Criminology*, *30*(1), 9–35.

Broidy, L., & Agnew, R. (1997). Gender and crime: A general strain theory perspective. *Journal of Research in Crime and Delinquency*, *34*(3), 275–306.

Buist, C. L., & Lenning, E. (2016). *Queer criminology*. Routledge.

Bureau of Justice Statistics. (n.d.). *Correctional populations in The United States series*, Washington, DC, Department of Justice. https://www.bjs.gov/index.cfm?ty=tp&tid=1

Bureau of Labor Statistics. (2022, January 24). *Median earning of women in 2021 were 83.1 percent of the median for men*, Washington, DC, Department of Labor. https://www.bls.gov/opub/ted/2022/median-earnings-for-women-in-2021-were-83-1-percent-of-the-median-for-men.htm

Burgess, R. L., & Akers, R. L. (1966). A differential association-reinforcement theory of criminal behavior. *Social Problems*, *14*, 128–147.

Burgess-Proctor, A. (2006). Intersections of race, class, gender, and crime: Future directions for feminist criminology. *Feminist Criminology*, *1*(1), 27–47.

Butler, P. (2017). *Chokehold: Policing black men*. The New Press.

Censky, A. (2020, May 14). Heavily armed protesters gather again at Michigan capitol to decry stay-at-home order. *NPR*. https://www.npr.org/2020/05/14/855918852/heavily-armed-protesters-gather-again-at-michigans-capitol-denouncing-home-order

Campbell, A. (2022). *We are Proud Boys: How a right-wing street gang ushered in a new era of American extremism*. Hachette Books.

Centers for Disease Control and Prevention. (n.d.). *COVID data tracker*. Atlanta, GA, Centers for Disease Control and Prevention. Accessed March 3, 2023. https://covid.cdc.gov/covid-data-tracker/#datatracker-home

Centers for Disease Control and Prevention. (2020, May 23). *Use of cloth face coverings to help slow the spread of COVID-19*. Atlanta, GA, Centers for Disease Control and Prevention. Available at https://www.cdc.gov/coronavirus/2019-ncov/prevent-getting-sick/diy-cloth-face-coverings.html

Chesney-Lind, M., & Irwin, K. (2008). *Beyond bad girls: Gender, violence and hype*. Routledge.

Cobbina, J. (2019). *Hands up, don't shoot: Why the protests in Ferguson and Baltimore matter, and how they changed America.* New York University Press.

Collier, K. (2021, January 16). Selfies, social media posts making it easier for FBI to track down Capitol riot suspects. *NBC News.* https://www.nbcnews.com/tech/social-media/selfies-social-media-posts-making-it-easier-fbi-track-down-n1254522

Cook, K. J., Williams, J. M., Lamphere, R. D., Mallicoat, S. L., & Ackerman, A. R. (Eds.). (2022). *Survivor criminology: A radical act of hope.* Rowman & Littlefield.

Crump, B. (2019). *Open season: Legalized genocide of colored people.* Amistad/HarperCollins Publishers.

Crutchfield, R. D., & Wadsworth, T. (2013). Aggravated inequality: Neighborhoods, school, and juvenile delinquency. In R. Rosenfeld (Ed.), *Macro economic effects on youth violence* (pp. 152–180). New York University Press.

Delgado, R., & Stefancic, J. (2017). *Critical race theory: An introduction* (3rd ed.). New York University Press.

Dobbs v. Jackson Women's Health Organization, No. 19-1392, 597 U.S. ___ (2022)

Dred Scott v. Sandford: 60 US 393 (1856)

Du Bois, W. E. B. (1899). *The Philadelphia negro: A social study.* University of Pennsylvania.

ExposeProfMichaelKimmel [@ExposeProf]. (n.d.). *Tweets* [Twitter profile]. Retrieved May 27, 2023, from https://twitter.com/ExposeProf

Falk, O., Wallinius, M., Lundström, S., Frisell, T., Anckarsäter, H., & Kerekes, N. (2014). The 1% of the population accountable for 63% of all violent crime convictions. *Social Psychiatry and Psychiatric Epidemiology, 49,* 559–571.

Feagin, J. R. (2013). *The white racial frame* (2nd ed.). Routledge.

Federal Bureau of Investigation (n.d.). *Crime data explorer.* Washington, DC, Department of Justice. Accessed March 3, 2023. https://cde.ucr.cjis.gov/LATEST/webapp/#/pages/home

Flaherty, C. (2018, August 9). More than rumors. *Inside Higher Ed.* https://www.insidehighered.com/news/2018/08/10/michael-kimmels-former-student-putting-name-and-details-those-harassment-rumors

Gabbidon, S. L. (2015). *Criminological perspectives on race and crime* (3rd ed.). Routledge.

Garza, A. (2020). *The purpose of power: How we come together when we fall apart.* One World.

Glaude, E. S. Jr. (2016). *Democracy in black: How race still enslaves the American soul.* Crown Publishers.

Goldstone, L. (2005). *Slavery, profits, and the struggle for the constitution.* Walker and Company.

Gottfredson, M. R., & Hirschi, T. (1990). *A general theory of crime.* Stanford University Press.

Gruber, A. (2020, May 27). Why Amy Cooper felt the police were her personal "protection agency. *Slate.* https://slate.com/news-and-politics/2020/05/amy-cooper-white-women-policing.html

Guckenheimer, D. (2018, August 3). What we need from accused perpetrators like Michael Kimmel #metoosociology. *Medium.* https://medium.com/@debraguckenheimer/what-we-need-from-accused-perpetrators-like-michael-kimmel-metoosociology-979a8102547f

Hadden, S. (2001). *Slave patrols: Law and violence in Virginia and the Carolinas.* Harvard University Press.

Hagan, J., Shedd, C., & Payne, M. R. (2005). Race, ethnicity, and youth perceptions of criminal injustice. *American Sociological Review, 70*(3), 381–407.

Hall, M., Gould, S., Harrington, R., Shamsian, J., Haroun, A., Ardrey, T., & Snodgrass, E. (2023, February 16). At least 1,003 people have been charged in the Capitol insurrection so far. This searchable table shows them all. *Insider.* https://www.insider.com/all-the-us-capitol-pro-trump-riot-arrests-charges-names-2021-1

Hannah-Jones, N., Roper, C., Silverman, I., & Silverstein, J. (Eds.). (2021). *The 1619 project: A new origin story.* One World.

Hansell, E., Bailey, C., Kamath, N., Corrigan, L., & Bessette, J. M. (2016). *The crime funnel.* Claremont McKenna College, Rose Institute of State and Local Government. Available at https://s10294.pcdn.co/wp-content/uploads/2016/05/28-April-Crime-Funnel-Natl-Report.pdf

Hansen, C. (2019, December 19). 116th Congress by party, race, gender, and religion. *U.S. News & World Report.* https://www.usnews.com/news/politics/slideshows/116th-congress-by-party-race-gender-and-religion

Hawkins, D. F. (1995). Ethnicity, race, and crime: A review of selected studies. In D. F. Hawkins (Ed.), *Ethnicity, race, and crime: Perspectives across time and place* (pp. 11–45). State University of New York Press.

Hays, T., & Kryska, R. (2020, May 27). Bird-watcher on woman who called the cops on him over viral Central Park dog dispute: 'I wasn't having it'. *USA Today.* https://www.usatoday.com/story/news/nation/2020/05/27/central-park-dog-viral-video-christian-cooper-comments-amy-cooper/5265010002/

Helsel, P. (2020, May 28). George Floyd protest turns deadly; Minneapolis mayor requests National Guard. *NBC News.* https://www.nbcnews.com/news/us-news/conflict-erupts-minneapolis-l-protests-over-george-floyd-death-n1216096

Isom*, D. A. (2018). Understanding white Americans' perceptions of "reverse" discrimination: An application of a new theory of status dissonance. In S. R. Thye & E. J. Lawler (Eds.), *Advances in group processes* (vol. 35, pp. 129–157). Emerald Insight.

Isom*, D. A. (2020). Status, socialization, and identities: Central Factors to understanding disparities in crime. *Sociology Compass, 14*(9), e12825.

Isom*, D. A., & Grosholz, J. M. (2019). Unpacking the racial disparity in crime from a racialized general strain theory perspective. *Deviant Behavior, 40*(12), 1445–1463.

Isom*, D. A., Whiting, S., & Grosholz, J. M. (2023). Examining and expanding Latinx general strain theory. *Race and Justice, 13*(2), 231–255.

Jensen, R. (2018, August 6). What are the responsibilities of pro-feminist men in the Michael Kimmel case? *Feminist Current.* https://www.feministcurrent.com/2018/08/06/responsibilities-pro-feminist-men-michael-kimmel-case/

Jewkes, Y., & Linnemann, T. (2017). *Media and crime in the. U.S*: Sage.

Kaufman, J. M., Rebellon, C. J., Thaxton, S., & Agnew, R. (2008). A general strain theory of racial differences in criminal offending. *The Australian and New Zealand Journal of Criminology, 41*(3), 421–37.

Kearns, E. M., Ashooh, E., & Lowrey-Kinberg, B. (2020). Racial differences in conceptualizing legitimacy and trust in police. *American Journal of Criminal Justice, 45*, 190–214.

Kendi, I. X. (2016). *Stamped from the beginning.* Bold Type Books.

♠Kimmel, M. (2017). *Angry white men: American masculinity at the end of an era.* Nation Books.

Kishi, R., & Jones, S. (2020, September 3). *Demonstrations and political violence in America: New data from summer 2020.* Armed Conflict Location & Event Data Project (ACLED). https://acleddata.com/2020/09/03/demonstrations-political-violence-in-america-new-data-for-summer-2020/

Krohn, M. D., Thornberry, T. P., Gibson, C. L., & Baldwin, J. M. (2010). The development and impact of self-report measures of crime and delinquency. *Journal of Quantitative Criminology, 26,* 509–525.

Laws, M. (2020, June 16). Why we capitalize 'Black'(and not 'white'). *Columbia Journalism Review.* https://www.cjr.org/analysis/capital-b-black-styleguide.php

Leatherby, L., Ray, A., Singhvi, A., Triebert, C., Watkins, D., & Willis, H.. (2021, January 12). How a presidential rally turned into a capitol rampage. *The New York Times.* https://www.nytimes.com/interactive/2021/01/12/us/capitol-mob-timeline.html

Lively, D. E. (1992). *The constitution and race.* Praeger.

Lonsdorf, K., Dorning, C., Isackson, A., Kelly, M. L., & Chang, A. (2022, June 9). A timeline of how the Jan. 6 attack unfolded – including who said what when. *NPR.* https://www.npr.org/2022/01/05/1069977469/a-timeline-of-how-the-jan-6-attack-unfolded-including-who-said-what-and-when

López, I. H. (2006). *White by law: The legal construction of race.* New York University Press.

Lurie, S., Acevedo, A., & Ott, K. (2018). *The less than 1%: Groups and the extreme concentration of urban violence* [Paper presentation]. American Society of Criminology Annual Meeting, Atlanta, GA, United States.

Lyn, D. (2022, May 25). Timeline of black Americans killed by police: 2014-2022. *Anadolu Agency.* https://www.aa.com.tr/en/americas/timeline-of-black-americans-killed-by-police-2014-2022/2596913

Mangan, K. (2018, August 1). 'I want to hear the charges': Noted sociologist defers award until he can 'make amends'. *The Chronicle of Higher Education.* https://www.chronicle.com/article/i-want-to-hear-those-charges-noted-sociologist-defers-award-until-he-can-make-amends/

McGhee, H. (2021). *The sum of us: What racism cost everyone and how we can prosper together.* One World.

McNamarah, C. T. (2019). White caller crime: Racialized police communication and existing while black. *Michigan Journal of Race and Law, 24,* 335–415.

McNulty, T. L. (2001). Assessing the race-violence relationship at the macro level: The assumption of racial invariance and the problem of restricted distributions. *Criminology, 39,* 467–90.

Merton, R. K. (1938). Social structure and anomie. *American Sociological Review, 3,* 672–682.

Miech, R. A., Schulenberg, J. E., Johnston, L. D., Bachman, J. G., & O'Malley, P. M. (Principal Investigators) (n.d.). *Monitoring the future: A continuing study of American youth.* Ann Arbor, MI, University of Michigan. http://www.monitoringthefuture.org/

Mills, C. (1997). *The racial contract.* NY, Cornell University Press.

Murphy, M. J. (2018, August 6). The two Kimmels. *Medium.* https://emjaymurphee.medium.com/the-two-kimmels-7b695ce5ebda

Nance, M. (2022). *They want to kill Americans: The militias, terrorists, and deranged ideology of the Trump insurgency.* St. Martin's Press.

National Public Radio [NPR]. (2020, May 29). Code switch: A decade of watching Black people die. *NPR*. https://www.npr.org/2020/05/29/865261916/a-decade-of-watching-black-people-die

Norwood, C. (2021, January 12). How was a violent mob able to breach the U.S. Capitol? Activists see double standard in police response. *PBS News Hour*. https://www.pbs.org/newshour/politics/how-was-a-violent-mob-able-to-breach-the-u-s-capitol-activists-see-double-standard-in-police-response

Oliver, W. (1994). *The violent social world of black men*. Lexington Books.

Owens, E., Kerrison, E. M., & Da Silveira, B. S. (2017). *Examining racial disparities in criminal case outcomes among indigent defendants in San Francisco*. Philadelphia, PA, University of Pennsylvania Law School, Quattrone Center for the Fair Administration of Justice. https://www.law.upenn.edu/live/files/6793-examining-racial-disparities-may-2017-full

Papachristos, A. V., Wilderman, C., & Roberto, E. (2015). Tragic, but not random: The social contagion of nonfatal gunshot injuries. *Social Science & Medicine, 125*, 139–150.

Pérez, D. M., Jennings, W. G., & Gover, A. R. (2008). Specifying general strain theory: An ethnically relevant approach. *Deviant Behavior, 29*(6), 544–78.

Peterson, R. D., & Krivo, L. J. (2010). *Divergent social worlds: Neighborhood crime and the racial-spatial divide*. Russell Sage Foundation.

Pew Research Center. (2022, July 6). Majority of public disapproves of Supreme Court's decision to overturn *Roe v. Wade*. https://www.pewresearch.org/politics/2022/07/06/majority-of-public-disapproves-of-supreme-courts-decision-to-overturn-roe-v-wade/

Pierson, E., Simoiu, C., Overgoor, J., Corbett-Davies, S., Jenson, D., Shoemaker, A., Ramachandran, V., Barghouty, P., Phillips, C., Shroff, R., & Goel, S. (2020). A large-scale analysis of racial disparities in police stops across the United States. *Nature Human Behavior, 4*, 736–745.

Plessy v. Ferguson, 163 U.S. 537; 16 S. Ct. 1138; 41 L. Ed. 256 (1856)

Potter, H. (2015). *Intersectionality and criminology: Disrupting and revolutionizing studies of crime*. Routledge.

Pratt, T. C., & Cullen, F. T. (2000). The empirical status of Gottfredson and Hirschi's general theory of crime: A meta-analysis. *Criminology, 38*, 931–964.

Pratt, T. C., & Cullen, F. T. (2005). Assessing macro-level predictors and theories of crime: A meta-analysis. *Crime & Justice, 32*, 373–450.

Pratt, T. C., Cullen, F. T., Sellers, C. S., Winfree, L. T. Jr., Madensen, T. D., Daigle, L. E., Fearn, N. E., & Gau, J. M. (2010). The empirical status of social learning theory: A meta-analysis. *Justice Quarterly, 27*(6), 765–802.

Ratcliffe, R. (2018, August 15). US women's rights campaigner accused of sexual harassment. *The Guardian*. https://www.theguardian.com/global-development/2018/aug/15/us-womens-rights-campaigner-accused-of-sexual-harassment

Reilly, R. J. (2022, June 20). For Jan. 6 rioters who believed Trump, storming the Capitol made sense. *NBC News*. https://www.nbcnews.com/politics/donald-trump/jan-6-rioters-believed-trump-storming-capitol-made-sense-rcna33125

Reiman, J., & Leighton, P. (2020). *The rich get richer and the poor get prison: Thinking critically about class and criminal justice* (12th ed.). Routledge.

Remnick, D. (2022, December 22). The devastating new history of the January 6th insurrection. *The New Yorker*. https://www.newyorker.com/news/american-chronicles/the-devastating-new-history-of-the-january-sixth-insurrection

Richer, A. D., Long, C., & Balsamo, M. (2020, October 20). AP finds most arrested in protests aren't leftist radicals. *AP News*. https://apnews.com/article/virus-outbreak-race-and-ethnicity-suburbs-health-racial-injustice-7edf9027af1878283f3818d96c54f748

Riess, R. (2020, April 30). Protesters in Michigan demonstrate against stay-at-home order. *CNN*. https://www.cnn.com/us/live-news/us-coronavirus-update-04-30-20/h_e90047bd263620ce7d71d643aba02ed0

Rios, V. M. (2011). *Punished: Policing the lives of black and Latino boys*. New York University Press.

Ritchie, A. J. (2017). *Invisible no more: Police violence against Black women and women of color*. Beacon Press.

Roe v. Wade, 410 U.S. 113 (1973).

Rothstein, R. (2017). *The color of law*. Liveright Publishing Company/W.W. Norton & Company.

Russell, K. K. (1992). Development of a black criminology and the role of the black criminologist. *Justice Quarterly, 9*(4), 667–83.

Russell-Brown, K. K. (2009). *The color of crime: Racial hoaxes, white fear, black protectionism, police harassment, and other microaggressions* (2nd ed.). New York University Press.

Sampson, R. J. (2012). *Great American city: Chicago and the enduring neighborhood effect*. University of Chicago Press.

Sampson, R. J., & Wilson, W. J. (1995). Toward a theory of race, crime, and urban inequality. In J. Hagan, & R. D. Peterson (Eds.), *Crime and inequality* (pp. 37–54). Stanford University Press.

SBS News. (2020, May 28). How US police responded differently to protester demanding justice for George Floyd and anti-lockdown rallies. *SBS News*. https://www.sbs.com.au/news/how-us-police-responded-differently-to-protesters-demanding-justice-for-george-floyd-and-anti-lockdown-rallies

Scott v. Sandford, 60 U.S. 19 How. 393 393 (1856)

Schleiden, C., Soloski, K. L., Milstead, K., & Rhynehart, A. (2020). Racial disparities in arrests: A race specific model explaining arrest rates across black and white young adults. *Child and Adolescent Social Work Journal, 37*, 1–14.

Schuck, A. M., Rosenbaum, D. P., & Hawkins, D. F. (2008). The influence of race/ethnicity, social class, and neighborhood context on residents' attitudes toward the police. *Police Quarterly, 11*(4), 496–519.

Select Committee to Investigate the January 6th Attack on the United States Capitol. (2022, December 22). *Final Report*. 117th Congress Second Session, House Report 117-663. Washington, DC. https://www.govinfo.gov/content/pkg/GPO-J6-REPORT/pdf/GPO-J6-REPORT.pdf

Shaw, C. R., & McKay, H. D. (1942). *Juvenile delinquency and urban areas*. University of Chicago Press.

Smart, C. (1977). *Women, crime, and criminology: A feminist critique*. Routledge.

Smith, C. (2021). *How the word is passed: A reckoning with the history of slavery across America*. Little, Brown and Company.

Surette, R. (1992). *Media, crime, and criminal justice: Images and realities*. Books/Cole Publishing Co.

Sweeney, D. (2020, May 12). 'Frustrated' man who wore KKK-style hood to grocery won't be charged, CA cops say. *The Sacramento Bee*. https://www.sacbee.com/news/coronavirus/article242669336.html

The Associated Press. (2022, October 26). Three men are convicted or support-ing a plot to kidnap Michigan Gov. Gretchen Whitmer. *NPR*. https://www.npr.org/2022/10/26/1131607112/michigan-governor-gretchen-whitmer-kidnapping-convictions

The Sentencing Project. (2018, April 19). *Report to the United Nations on racial disparities in the U.S. criminal justice system*. Washington, DC. https://www.sentencingproject.org/publications/un-report-on-racial-disparities/

The Washington Post. (2023). Police shooting database. Retrieved March 3, 2023. https://www.washingtonpost.com/graphics/investigations/police-shootings-database/

Taylor, D. B. (2020, April 14). For black men, fear that masks will invite racial profiling. *The New York Times*. https://www.nytimes.com/2020/04/14/us/coronavirus-masks-racism-african-americans.html

Tonry, M. (2004). *Thinking about crime: Sense and sensibility in American penal culture*. Oxford University Press.

Tonry, M. (2011). *Punishing race: A continuing American dilemma*. Oxford University Press.

Toone, S. (2020, April 7). Black men wearing COVID-19 masks at store reportedly booted out for not removing. *The Atlanta Journal-Constitution*. https://www.ajc.com/news/black-men-wearing-covid-masks-store-reportedly-booted-out-for-not-removing/zqrswyCI6Sn4DjxpXz0FjN/

U.S. Department of Justice. (n.d.). *Capitol breach cases.* https://www.justice.gov/usao-dc/capitol-breach-cases (Accessed 3 March 2023).

U.S. Equal Employment Opportunity Commission. (n.d.). *Job patterns for minori-ties and women in private industry*. Washington, DC, U.S. Equal Employment Opportunity Commission. https://www.eeoc.gov/statistics/job-patterns-minorities-and-women-private-industry-eeo-1

United States Senate. (n.d.a.). *Ethnic diversity in the Senate*. Washington, DC, Senate Historical Office. https://www.senate.gov/senators/EthnicDiversityintheSenate.htm

United States Senate. (n.d.b.) *Women Senators*. Washington, DC, Senate Historical Of-fice. https://www.senate.gov/senators/ListofWomenSenators.htm

Unnever, J. D., Cullen, F. T., Mathers, S. A., McClure, T. E., & Allison, M. C. (2009). Racial discrimination and Hirschi's criminological classic: A chapter in the sociology of knowledge. *Justice Quarterly, 26*(3), 377–409.

Unnever, J. D., & Gabbidon, S. L. (2011). *A theory of African American offending: Race, racism, and crime*. Routledge.

Van Cleve, N. G. (2016). *Crook county: Racism and injustice in America's largest crimi-nal court*. Stanford University Press.

Wallis, J. (2016). *America's original sin: Racism, white privilege, and the bridge to a new America*. Brazos Press.

Wamsley, L. (2021, January 15). What we know so far: A timeline of security re-sponse at the Capitol on Jan 6. *NPR*. https://www.npr.org/2021/01/15/956842958/what-we-know-so-far-a-timeline-of-security-at-the-capitol-on-january-6

Warren, M., Marquez, M., Scannell, K., & Perez, E. (2020, April 20). Conservative groups boost anti-stay-at-home protests. *CNN*. https://www.cnn.com/2020/04/20/politics/stay-at-home-protests-conservative-groups-support/index.html

Weisburd, D. (2015). The law of crime concentration and the criminology of place. *Crim-inology, 53*(2), 133–157.

Weissinger, S. E., Mack, D. A., & Watson, E. (Eds.). (2017). *Violence against black bodies: An intersectional analysis of how black lives continue to matter*. Routledge.

Westcott, B., McKeehan, B., Smith-Spark, L., & Alfonso, F. III. (2020, May 30). George Floyd protests spread nationwide. *CNN*. https://www.cnn.com/us/live-news/george-floyd-protests-05-30-20/index.html

Woods, J. B. (2014). Queering criminology': Overview of the state of the field. In D. Peterson, & V. R. Panfil (Eds.), *Handbook of LGBT communities, crime, and justice* (pp. 15–41). Springer Publishing.

1

OVER A DECADE OF TURMOIL WITHIN A HISTORY OF STRIFE

We've Reached a New Boiling Point

Since the early 2010s, America has seen renewed racial strife. During the tenure of America's first Black president on February 26, 2012, Trayvon Benjamin Martin, a Black teenaged boy, was brutally killed by a vigilante neighborhood watchman for supposedly looking "suspicious" for wearing a hoodie and walking home from a convenience store with his hands in his pockets. In the wake of Trayvon's murder, President Obama stated, "…this could have been my son… Trayvon Martin could have been me 35 years ago" (The White House, 2013).[1] Over a year later, following extensive media coverage and a grueling trial, Trayvon's killer was acquitted for his murder (Alverez & Buckley, 2013; CNN Editorial Research, 2022). The outcry over Trayvon's death and the handling of his case sparked the modern Black Lives Matter (BLM) movement[2] (Lebron, 2017). On July 17, 2014, Eric Garner, a 43-year-old Black man and father of six, was killed after an officer placed him in a chokehold for illegally selling cigarettes. While officers had him pinned to the ground, he repeatedly uttered, "I can't breathe" until he lost consciousness and died due to suffocation. "I Can't Breathe" became an additional rallying cry against police brutality and for racial justice (Associated Press, 2019b). A few weeks after the tragic death of Garner on August 9, 2014, Michael Brown, an 18-year-old Black man days away from starting college and the next chapter of his young life, was confronted by Ferguson, Missouri police for not walking on the sidewalk. An altercation ensued, and Brown, who was unarmed, was shot and killed by police. His body remained on display in the street for several hours in the heat of summer. Protests erupted over numerous nights calling for police accountability

DOI: 10.4324/9781003167877-2

(Associated Press, 2019a). Poignantly, a few months later, on November 22, 2014, 12-year-old Tamir Rice was killed by a Cleveland, Ohio police officer as he was playing with a toy gun in a public park. Tamir's untimely death at the hands of police brought further national and international attention to law enforcement's excessive use of force, particularly against Black and Brown people, and solidified the BLM movement (Dewan & Oppel, 2015).

The year 2015 brought several more deaths of Black and Brown men and women at the hands of police that made national and international headlines – Eric Harris, Walter Scott, Freddie Gray, and Sandra Bland (Lyn, 2022) – as well as numerous others that did not garner as much media attention (The Washington Post, n.d.).[3] In the midst of racial strife, on June 16, 2015, Donald Trump announced his presidential run, riding down the golden escalator of Trump Tower (Gabbatt, 2019). His opening statements to the country were the racist remarks:

> When Mexico sends its people, they're not sending their best. They're not sending you… They're sending people that have lots of problems… They're bringing drugs. They're bringing crime. They're rapists. And some, I assume, are good people.
>
> (TIME Staff, 2015)

This was only the beginning of his derogatory, offensive, and divisive rhetoric that he brought not only to the national political stage but also into the White House and beyond (Lopez, 2020; Montanaro, 2022). On June 17, 2015, the day following Trump's announced presidential bid, Dylann Roof shot and killed nine Black Americans during a Bible study session at Mother Emanuel African Methodist Episcopal Church in Charleston, South Carolina. The federal investigation into Roof found evidence he held white supremacist ideologies, including photos of Roof draping himself with a Confederate flag, his admission to wanting to start a race war, and his statement that the Ku Klux Klan was not "doing enough" (Love, 2017; Norris, 2017).

Following the massacre at Mother Emmanuel AME and throughout Trump's 2016 presidential campaign, Black and Brown people continued to die at the hands of law enforcement and the chants of BLM grew louder and went global (Armitage, 2016; Lyn, 2022; The Washington Post, n.d.). We also saw Donald Trump gain popularity among conservatives and the far-right, with many of his supporters feeling emboldened to spew racist rhetoric and counter BLM and other progressive movements (e.g., LGBTQ rights [Jones, 2018], abortion access [Andaya, 2019], voting access [Minnite & Piven, 2021], healthcare [Sides et al., 2018], immigration [Hooghe & Dassonneville, 2018]), with some going as far as engaging in violence (Morrison et al., 2018). Trump's blatant disparagement of certain groups through anti-immigrant, anti-Muslim, anti-disability, and misogynistic rhetoric (Crandall et al., 2018) ultimately garnered support from white supremacist ideologies and groups (Barnett, 2018; Taylor, 2018). Smith and Hanley (2018) examined the American National Election Study from the 2016 election and found that Trump supporters voted for him largely due to his racist and misogynist beliefs. Overall, it was the appeal of an authoritarian, dominant, and intolerant leader that attracted many to vote for Donald Trump.

Given far-right groups' sense of victimhood and disdain for political correctness and social justice (Berbrier, 2000; Southern Poverty Law Center, n.d.b.), it is no wonder they quickly rallied around Trump's presidential campaign. Trump's campaign slogan, "Make America Great Again," quickly dubbed "Make America White Again" (Barnett, 2018; Eddington, 2018), spoke to the nostalgia touted by the far-right, signaling his own belief that the country should re-embrace its white supremacist, patriarchal roots (Boehme & Isom*, 2020; Isom et al., 2021). Trump's overtly racist remarks reinforced the far-right's own notions of white supremacy by emitting hate speech and peddling his own opposition to "political correctness" (Barkun, 2017). Trump allowed white America's deep-rooted racism to surface, as he made recent history's unsayable, sayable again.

August 11 and 12, 2017 brought the violent "Unite the Right" rally in Charlottesville, Virginia where a large gathering of neo-Nazi, white supremacists, white nationalists, Ku Klux Klan members, and counterprotesters collided at the Robert E. Lee statue in response to the city council's decision to remove the Confederate monument and ended with the death of counterprotester Heather Heyer (Heim, 2017; Schragger, 2018). The "Unite the Right" rally was also an unmasking for far-right groups such as the Proud Boys, as touted by some as "A pivotal moment for the pro-white movement in America" (Campbell, 2022, p. 100), and where they received their first (supposed) public support from Donald Trump when he said there were "very fine people on both sides" (Kessler, 2020), further provoking extremist groups.

The presidential tenure of Trump brought a rise in the number of active hate groups and their memberships and affiliations, such as the Proud Boys, the Oath Keepers, and the Boogaloo Bois, among others (Nance, 2022; Tenold, 2018; Southern Poverty Law Center, n.d.b.) as well as a significant rise in hate crimes against marginalized groups (Southern Poverty Law Center, n.d.c.). Furthermore, many of these extremists entered the mainstream ranks of the Republican Party earning their support and allyship (Campbell, 2022; Gais & Hayden, 2022; Nance, 2022), including when Trump said, "Proud Boys – stand back and stand by" in a presidential debate against Joe Biden when asked if he condemned white supremacist and militia groups (Frenkel & Karni, 2021).

The year 2020 also brought America, and truly the world, to a new boiling point. On February 23, 2020, Ahmaud Arbery, a 25-year-old Black man, was brutally hunted down and murdered by three white men while on a jog in southern Georgia. The men claimed to be attempting to make a "citizen's arrest" because they believed Arbery had potentially stolen from a construction site. The men were arrested and, in time, convicted of murder and hate crime charges, but not before first triggering indignation against laws that protected vigilante "justice" (Fausset et al., 2022). Shortly after, on March 13, 2020, Louisville, Kentucky police executed a no-knock warrant in the middle of the night and errantly killed Breonna Taylor, a 26-year-old Black woman, sparking further protests and outrage (Waldrop et al., 2022). On May 25, 2020, George Floyd, a 46-year-old Black man, was arrested by three white police officers in Minneapolis, Minnesota for allegedly using a counterfeit US$20 bill. Officers wrestled him to the ground and Derek Chauvin, who was later arrested and convicted for Floyd's murder, knelt on his neck for 9 minutes and 29 seconds ultimately killing him (Levenson & Cooper, 2021; The Associated Press, 2022). Their deaths ignited worldwide protests for racial justice and the end of police brutality, despite the health risks due to the global COVID-19 pandemic (Silverstein, 2021).

The year 2020 ended with the presidential defeat of Donald Trump to Joe Biden, but not without Trump and his supporters spreading the "Big Lie" of widespread election fraud (Clark et al., 2022). Trump was still aiming to "Stop the Steal" and had not conceded his loss on the day Congress was set to meet to certify the election. On January 6, 2021, from the Ellipse in Washington, DC, Trump urged his supporters – most of whom were white men and many of whom who were openly armed – to march on the US Capitol, saying, "We fight like hell. And if you don't fight like hell, you're not going to have a country anymore" (Naylor, 2021). Thousands marched on the Capitol building, not only forcing access onto the grounds but also breaching both chambers and raiding officials' offices. The insurrectionists were left unrestrained for over three hours, leading to turmoil, terror, devastation, and death (Leatherby et al., 2021). The insurrection on January 6 led to Trump's second impeachment (Cai, 2021) and calls to the Justice Department to bring criminal charges against Trump and others from the Congressional Select Committee (Select Committee to Investigate the January 6th Attack on the United States Capitol, 2022; also see Barak, 2022).

The attack on the US Capitol at the bidding of Trump, however, was far from the end. On May 14, 2022, a 19-year-old white man motivated by racist hatred entered a Tops Friendly Markets in a predominantly Black neighborhood of Buffalo, New York killing ten and wounding others (Morales et al., 2022). This was just one of the numerous other incidents of hate-inspired violence since January 6, 2021. Events such as these bring the remaining prominence of the myth of white supremacy in America back into the limelight (Futrell & Simi, 2017) and demonstrate the depth of racial tensions still haunting the United States; so much so Congress is investigating the rising threat of domestic terrorism (Committee on Homeland Security, 2021). And regrettably, analysts and researchers believe more violence is on the horizon (Campbell, 2022; Kaufman, 2022; Nance, 2022).

However, this is not a book about Donald Trump, the re-emergence and mainstreaming of far-right extremism, or even the insurrection of January 6, 2021. I lay out some central events of the past decade as a reminder of the perpetual racial tensions weighing on America, and arguably the world (Kaufmann, 2019). Yet, while the past decade seems unusual, it was in fact, far from new. Instead, the events over the past decade were only the latest iteration of the poisonous myth of white supremacy embedded within our society. The progressive criminological theory I propose within this book does provide insight into Trump's election and popularity, the rise of the far-right extremist ideologies, particularly the Alt-Right – "a set of far-right ideologies, groups, and individuals whose core belief is that 'white identity' is under attack by multicultural forces using 'political correctness' and 'social justice' to undermine white people and 'their' civilization" (Southern Poverty Law Center, n.d.a.) – and its integration into the mainstream Republican party, as well as the violent insurrection on the US Capitol following Trump's 2020 loss to Joe Biden, but it's not specifically about them. It's about something much larger. In the coming chapters, I outline a distinctly racialized pathway to violent and deviant behaviors, as well as potential protections from legal entanglement, for white people that accounts for the internalized norms and resultant perceptions that influence behaviors due to America's white supremacist roots. But first, to best accomplish this aim, I place this present moment in a more historical context, as a means of applying a critical whiteness lens and highlighting the continued significance of history for understanding the present and to hopefully change the future.

Critical Whiteness: The Lasting Impact of the Myth of White Supremacy

In 2005, McDermott and Sampson called for more intricate studies of whiteness, stating "Navigating between the long-term staying power of white privilege and the multifarious manifestations of the experience of whiteness remains the task of the next era of research on white racial and ethnic identity" (p. 256). A decade later, the progressive, intersectional, Black feminist criminologist, Hillary Potter, put forth a similar call saying, "Researchers typically include the demographics of their research samples in their publications, yet, often the race of white is deemed a default and regularly goes unexamined, as though 'white' is not a race … Certainly, white is a race. Consequently, criminologists should, at least, contemplate how being white may influence individuals' experiences compared with those of other races" (2015, pp. 149–150; also see Russell, 1998; Carbado, 2013).

As a progressive, intersectional scholar, I often aim to center the lived experiences of marginalized and oppressed people, particularly those too-oft harmed by the criminal legal system. So, I too, particularly in my early work, often engaged in such comparisons of people of Color from varied backgrounds and ethnicities to whites, or women and nonbinary folks to men, or even taking an intersectional approach of how various others were distinct from whites and (white) men. And while this work is important, necessary, and informative, Potter is correct in that it is not enough, especially in the wake of the past decade, and truly all our history. Thus, when I came across the aforementioned quote in Potter's (2015) *Intersectionality and Criminology* in the aftermath of numerous deaths of people of Color at the hands of police, the mass killing of the Mother Emanuel Nine in Charleston, South Carolina, and the Trump presidential election campaign, I was stirred to my core. To fully understand disparities, we must question the true roots of what causes differences, and that means disrupting the orthodox and normative. Thus, that means questioning whiteness, investigating the hold of the myth of white supremacy, and bringing it into the fold of criminology.

What Is Critical Whiteness Studies?

Scholars such as W.E.B. Du Bois (1920) have long called for the critical assessment of white supremacy and whiteness for over a century. Critical whiteness (or white) studies emerged from the critical race tradition, itself an evolution from critical legal studies from the 1970s, inspired by the works of Derrick Bell, Alan Freeman, and others (Delgado & Stefancic, 1997). Critical race theory is rooted in progressive scholarship that centers the lived experiences of people of Color by recognizing the historical, systemic, and institutionalized reach of racism and the social construction of race, the strategic purpose of racial stratification and differential racialization, as well as acknowledging the varied and intersectional identities and voices of individuals (Delgado & Stefancic, 2017). Much like the parallel movements of Latine[4] critical studies and critical race feminism, critical whiteness studies seek to put whiteness under a critical microscope. Critical whiteness studies ask questions about what it means to "be white" as well as examines the historical creation and preservation of the myth of white supremacy. They explore white privilege, or "the invisible bundle of expectations and courtesies that go along with membership in the dominant race" (Delgado & Stefancic, 1997, p. xvi). Furthermore, given its legal roots, it examines the role of the law in the formation and perpetuation of hegemonic white power (Delgado & Stefancic, 1997). Thus, critical whiteness studies move beyond exploring white nationalism and extremism to critically exploring the continued impacts of the myth of white supremacy on our society, institutions, social relationships, and norms, as well as individuals.

Questions about power, society, and their use of the concept of "race" link such critical perspectives. While critical race theory, and relatedly intersectionality and Black feminist thought (Collins, 2008; Crenshaw, 1991), have been more substantially integrated (though not always welcomed) into criminology and other fields (see Potter, 2015 for discussion), critical whiteness studies remain on the fringe or largely nonexistent. The past few years, in the wake of the re-awakening of far-right ideologies, the Trump era, the BLM movement, and other racial reckonings, have spawned new interests in white extremism (e.g., Jasko et al., 2022; Latif et al., 2020; Perry et al., 2022; Windisch et al., 2022). Yet, little still exists exploring the links between whiteness and crime for a more general white population (though see Boehme & Isom*, 2020; Isom*, 2018b; Isom* & Andersen, 2020; Isom* & Grosholz, 2019; Isom et al., 2021). The theory provided within this book fills that gap. However, we must first understand our racialized history to best explain our racialized present. The following section provides this foundation for the theory to come.

The Perpetual 30%–40% of White Folks

Given much of my race and crime research focuses on the impacts of discrimination experiences (i.e., Isom*, 2016, 2018a, 2020; Isom* & Mikell, 2019; Isom* & Seal, 2019; Isom et al., 2021, 2022; Isom* et al., 2023), that's where I began my critical look at whiteness and crime. Despite white folks' privileged position at the top of the US racial hierarchy, therefore prohibiting their *true* oppression, many still *feel* like they face discrimination (Anderson, 2016; Hammon, 2013). And, unfortunately, these feelings potentially have real consequences. For decades now, opinion polls and survey research have found approximately 30%–40% of white people believe white folks are discriminated against, either generally or personally. In the late 1990s, Kessler and colleagues found around 30% of whites reported experiencing discrimination from various sources (Kessler et al., 1999). Similarly, a 2008 Gallup poll revealed 42% of white adults believed racism against whites was a significant problem in America (Jones, 2008). A 2011 study by Norton and Sommers made national headlines when they found whites believe they face more discrimination presently than their Black counterparts. That same year, a Public Religion Research Institute report found whites were equally likely to say discrimination against whites was as critical an issue as discrimination against Blacks, with their perceptions of "reverse discrimination" increasing with their conservative media consumption (Jones et al., 2011).

Such feelings were exacerbated following Trump's entrance on the political scene and the mainstreaming of more extremist beliefs. A 2016 poll revealed 24% of whites generally felt whites face a lot of discrimination and 45% of white Trump supporters reported the same (Edwards-Levy, 2016). Furthermore, a 2017 national survey by psychologists Forscher and Kteily found nearly 78% of self-identified white Alt-Righters voted for Trump and nearly 60% of them saw Trump as an ally of the Alt-Right movement. Relatedly, in a more recent study of white's political identity, Jardina (2019) found between 30% and 40% of whites feel a strong sense of racial solidarity. In a 2018 national survey, nearly 40% of whites reported experiencing at least some racial discrimination as well as over 25% reporting being worried about whites losing the statistical majority of the American population (Isom* & Andersen, 2018). Furthermore, a 2019 poll of active military found 36% hold white supremist beliefs or racist ideologies (Nance, 2022). And, the election of 2020 found die-hard Trump supporters, many of whom support him because of his racist ideologies, made up 40% of the American electorate (Nance, 2022).

Such sentiments have implications beyond political leanings and harnessing racist prejudices. For instance, Gabbidon and Higgins (2010) conducted a descriptive analysis of self-reported white victims of consumer racial profiling (i.e., shoppers feeling profiled or discriminated against in retail settings). About 22% of their sample reported experiencing such anti-white bias, and most reported a person of Color being the perpetrator (Gabbidon & Higgins, 2010). Relatedly, using a nationally representative sample of white Americans, Isom* (2018b) found men, the least educated, and self-identified lower-class were the most likely to believe racial inequality was no longer an issue in America, that anti-white bias is a problem generally in America, as well as claim to have experienced anti-white bias personally. Furthermore, Boehme and Isom* (2020) revealed perceptions of anti-white bias to be the strongest predictor of affiliation with the Alt-Right for white men and women, and these associations were significantly amplified if one held heteronormative gender beliefs. Isom, Boehme, et al. (2021) found believing discrimination against whites is a major problem in America was significantly associated with feelings of status threat and both factors significantly increased the odds of affiliation with the Alt-Right among their sample of white adults. And, in an assessment of racialized general strain theory, Isom* and Grosholz (2019) found both perceived anti-white bias and anger were significantly associated with serious offending in their comparison sample of white youth. Isom* and Andersen (2020) also found perceptions of anti-white bias are a racialized strain for white youth that is significantly associated with their likelihood of engaging in serious and violent offending. Furthermore, the degree of the revealed associations varied by gender, with the association being the strongest for young white men. And finally, a 2022 nationally representative survey of white Americans revealed over 30% reported not only supporting initiatives to bolster the white race but also being willing to resort to violence to protect their rights if needed (Isom, 2022). This sentiment aligns with the 29% of respondents who agreed that "If elected leaders will not protect America, the people must do it themselves, even if it requires violent actions" in a 2020 American Enterprise Institute survey (Nance, 2022).

Unfortunately, as work such as this reveals, "extreme" views are much more commonplace with the distance between white supremacist extremists and the "Average Joe" being shorter than most want to admit. While much of the polls and research highlighted focus of Trump and the infiltration of far-right extremism into the (conservative) mainstream since 2015 or so, it also demonstrates these are not solely a Trump effect and such sentiments are far from new. The following section outlines just how old these divides are in America as well as how such ebb and flow in coordination with racial progress and strife.

Again, This Is Nothing New...

"The sociocultural expressions of the contradictions of patriarchy, neocolonialism, and capitalism have been around since this nation's inception. Today's Proud Boys are the contemporary versions of New England churchmen of the 1700s, the Klan riders of the 1800s, or the fervent followers of Joseph McCarthy in the 1950s."

(Barak, 2022, p. 2).

As Barak (2022) demonstrates in this quote, tensions between the oppressed and marginalized and those in power – especially between Blacks and whites – are not modern occurrences. As Anderson (2016), Alexander (2010), Baptist (2014), Kendi (2016), Feagin (2013), McGhee (2021), Smith (2021), Wallis (2016), Wilkerson (2020), among others, eloquently demonstrate, racial strife rooted in white supremacist ideologies have *always* been around and persist still today. Despite what many whites want to believe, racism did not disappear with the 1960s Civil Rights Movements, it just evolved into a more covert form (e.g., Bonilla-Silva, 2018). I demonstrate this in the following, utilizing data from the American National Elections Studies (ANES).

Beginning in 1948, researchers at the University of Michigan began surveying the American electorate. Over time, these surveys collected every mid-term and presidential election year became the ANES (Burns, 2006). Since 1966, the ANES has utilized a thermometer scale to assess public opinion on various groups, organizations, movements, ideologies, and political parties. Questions are typically as follows: "On the feeling thermometer scale from 0 to 100, how would you rate _____?", with stronger, positive feelings receiving a higher number score. The ANES collects cross-sectional as well as panel data each election year and employs probability sampling to ensure a representative sample of all those within the US (ANES, n.d.). Using the thermometer question about Black Americans between 1966 and 2020, I assessed the percentage of white Americans with positive feelings toward Black people for each election year.[5] These are presented in Figure 1.1. Additionally, to highlight how white people's feelings

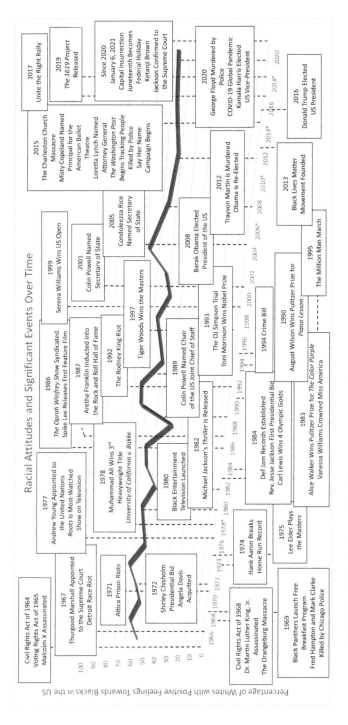

FIGURE 1.1 Whites' racial attitudes and significant events over time

toward Blacks have ebbed and flowed in relation to significant racial events in American history, some significant moments are also highlighted.

As theoretically expected, there are ups and downs that somewhat correspond to varied historical moments of racial unity and strife, such as the election of Barak Obama following a high (e.g., 69.1% of white respondents reporting positive feelings in 2004) and a there being a low in the late 1980s (e.g., 40.2% of whites reporting positive feelings toward Blacks in 1988) following a rise in prominence and recognition of Black people in popular culture throughout the decade prior. What is more telling, however, is the overall consistency of whites' perceptions of Blacks no matter what is happening in America during those moments. Across this nearly six-decade time span, white folks with positive feelings toward Blacks averages 57%. This reveals that around 40% of white people on average have negative feelings toward Black people at any given time, regardless the larger cultural or political climate. It also must be remembered these are self-reported feelings and a conservative indicator of "positive" (see note 4), thus likely are an underestimate of whites' biases and abhorrence toward Blacks. While unable to unpack the nuances behind white people's reported aversions over time with these data, this trend contextualizes the findings discussed earlier within the history of the past 60 years and further reiterates the current racial strife is not solely a recent event. Racial progress is often met with backlash, and white supremacist ideologies are tenacious over time. Hence, what is novel now is that clandestine animus is coming out of hiding and into the light, and their boldness to do so is greatly facilitated by modern technology.

What Has Changed Is Technology and the Reach of Media

The media may be no more influential than in the realm of politics (Newton, 2006). Yet, with the increasing divisiveness among media outlets, where one gets their news reinforces their political ideology and influences their perspectives (Messing & Westwood, 2014). Moreover, 24-hour media coverage and extended exposure to politically biased media outlets only strengthens the polarized beliefs of viewers (Martin & Yurukoglu, 2017). This is particularly important given the integration of our racial, religious, regional, cultural, and ideological identities into our political selves over the past 50 years (Klein, 2020). What modern technology provides is not just more access to information, but a choice in the information individuals consume, including polarized media, which "doesn't emphasize commonalities, it weaponizes differences" (Klein, 2020, p. 149). "The political media is biased, but not toward the Left or the Right so much as toward the loud, outrageous, colorful, inspirational, confrontational" (Klein, 2020, p. 170). For instance, the propagation of such divisive rhetoric has perpetuated Trump's campaign against "fake news" (Pickard, 2017).

"Fake news," or factually incorrect news stories, is not a new phenomenon (Burkhardt, 2017). However, the concept of fake news was most recently popularized by Donald Trump during the 2016 presidential election. His 2016 presidential campaign rested on "calling out" "fake" news; and his tirades against "the liberal media" consistently labeled news stories and outlets that do not match his storyline as "fake news." In reality, most news stories he deems as fake news are indeed factual, and it is *his* words that are false, making him one of the biggest creators of "fake news" (Kessler et al., 2021; Polletta & Callahan, 2019; including in relation to his current legal difficulties at the time of authorship [Date, 2023; Savage, 2023]). Ironically, a fact checker database beginning January 20, 2017—the day Trump assumed office—reports that he made over 30,000 false or misleading claims throughout his tenure (Kessler et al., 2021) as "Disruptor-in-Chief" (Wade, 2018). Similarly, the far-right depends upon conspiracy theories that stem from fake news while simultaneously proliferating fake news stories to gain followers and dispel their beliefs, relying heavily on the internet and social media (Daniels, 2018; Johnson, 2018; Persily, 2017).

The conservative media proliferation of fake news has perpetuated the expansion and presence of extremist ideologies, such as the far-right, within orthodox media outlets. People self-select certain news outlets, aligning their political beliefs with the political slant of their news organization of choice while ignoring opposing news outlets who offer a different political angle (Iyengar & Hahn, 2009). Networks such as *Fox News* emerged out of conservative protests of mainstream media's liberal biases, thus further facilitating American polarization (Klein, 2020). Thus, consistent exposure to slanted rhetoric normalizes the information received (Rosenberg & Feldman, 2008). This phenomenon, in turn, intensifies the divisiveness currently seen in America (Ash et al., 2017). Consuming such messaging pushes people toward more polarized others, likely increasing associations with loosely defined extremist and other far-right ideologies.

The technology proclaimed to keep us informed and bring people together (i.e., social media and 24-hour cable news) in reality fosters antagonism and division instead of substantive and respectful discourse (e.g., Vaidhyanathan, 2018). No influencer has possibly capitalized on this social phenomenon more so than Donald Trump. His (former) use of Twitter and other social media platforms, and the endless coverage of such by the political news channels, over the years means he is the perpetual point of conversation, and the more provocative, the greater the coverage (Zelizer, 2019). As a result, the more mainstream and left-leaning outlets criticize and counter Trump, the more emboldened his base becomes, reinforcing their distrust in less conservative news sources. Moreover, too many in the conservative audience take Trump and right-wing outlets at face value and are uncritical of the grandiloquence purported (e.g., Peters, 2019).

Furthermore, Trump granting extreme right-wing outlets, such as the Heritage Foundation and Claremont Institute, White House press passes, and invitations to a social media summit, to the exclusion of Facebook and Twitter, further legitimized fringe political rhetoric (Darcy, 2019; Rosenwald, 2019). As just one example, in July 2019 Trump attacked four freshman Democratic congress-women of Color on Twitter saying they should "go back" to their home countries inciting chants of "send her back" from his supporters at a political rally a few days later (Rummler, 2019). Hence, social media far too often serves as a catalyst and propagator of hate narratives (Kaufman, 2022).

We saw tensions further escalate through the Trump presidential tenure, during the COVID-19 pandemic, and following Trump's defeat in 2020. This time saw a rise in not only those adhering to far-right ideologies but also those having affiliation with their militant wings – Oath Keepers, Three-Percent Militia, Boogaloo Bois, Proud Boys – among others, generally labeled TITUS (Trump Insurgency in the United States) (Nance, 2022). Many of these folks were brought together through message boards, such as 8chan, 8kun, 4chan, Discord, and Endchan (Gonzalez, 2019; Wendling, 2019; Wong, 2019) and social media platforms such as Parler (Newhouse, 2020) and now Donald Trump's Truth Social (Forman-Katz & Stocking, 2022; founded following his removal from Twitter [Allyn & Keith, 2021]), that promote lies and conspiracy theories, such as those spouted by QAnon believers and Trump's stolen election falsehoods (Campbell, 2022; Nance, 2022).

While many want to write these off as outliers, data and events in recent years have again shown how prevalent – and dangerous – these perceptions and beliefs are. For instance, inspired by QAnon posts, in 2018, a man from North Carolina attacked Comet Ping Pong pizzeria in Washington, DC based on falsified claims of Democrats abusing children in the basement (Miller, 2021). On Christmas day in 2020, a white man set off a bomb in downtown Nashville, Tennessee because he believed a QAnon conspiracy that cell towers were controlling people's minds (Tucker & Balsamo, 2021). And most horrifically to date, the January 6, 2021 US Capitol Insurrection was promoted and coordinated through similar online channels (Nance, 2022). Thus, the media – in all its forms – creates an echo chamber that amplifies strife and division, as well as the potential for violence.

A New Theory for a Deeper Understanding

Consequently, we are in an era of amplified division, but the divides are far from unique. As the examples described earlier, research, and data support, the messaging perpetuated through conservative and far-right media (e.g., traditional American [white] way of life is under attack) influences viewers' and users' (primarily white Americans) perceptions of social issues. The sentiments evoked are associated with feelings of victimization and oppression, affiliation with more far-right ideologies, and potentially dangerous behaviors. It's the extensive spread and influence of this messaging and resultant negative outcomes that are novel to the current age and amplifies the real threat of crime and violence. As FBI director Christopher Wray testified to the January 6th Committee, the attack in the US Capitol "was not an isolated event" (Tucker & Jalonick, 2021). As he stated in previous testimony to Congress, "Within the domestic terrorism bucket, the category as a whole, racially motivated violent extremism is, I think, the biggest bucket within that larger group. And within the racially motivated violent extremist bucket, people subscribing to some kind of white supremist-type ideology is certainly the biggest chunk of that" (Beavers, 2020).

Yet, it is not just far-right extremists that warrant attention. White men make up the majority of the arrested population for violence (Federal Bureau of Investigation, n.d.). White men possess the most firearms in the country (Parker et al., 2017), with the number of guns in the United States outnumbering the American population (Ingraham, 2018; Karp, 2018). Yet, when we hear the word "criminal" a Black man most likely comes to mind (Russell-Brown, 2009). As discussed earlier, many white "Average Joes" hold some degree of racist, misogynistic, xenophobic, or other marginalizing, prejudiced, or derogatory beliefs, even if not uttered in public. And, research suggests holding such animus makes it all the more likely someone will accept falsehoods, particularly toward "Others" (Benegal & Motta, 2022), further reinforcing the dangers of far-right narratives. White men also still hold most positions of economic and political power (Brown & Atske, 2021; Zweigenhaft, 2021), thus making true change even harder. The theory of whiteness and crime (TWC) provides a framework for understanding why these are so. Taking a critical whiteness perspective, TWC argues white people, and particularly men, are distinctly impacted by the socialization into the myth of white supremacy embedded within American history, culture, and institutions that then frames how they perceive and interact with the social world. This lens makes it more likely that they experience feelings of habitus angst and aggrieved entitlement (see Chapters 3 and 4) related to their social status as whites (and men) that may inspire acts of deviance, aggression, and violence. Yet, due to their inherent white privilege (see Chapter 5), they are also likely to escape entanglements with the criminal legal system. In other words, TWC presents a distinctly racialized pathway to criminal and violent behaviors as well as protections from entanglement in the criminal legal system for white people. Instead of accepting white people's behaviors as individual deviations from "normative" behaviors, TWC questions the orthodox understandings of whiteness, white privilege, and the myth of white supremacy to understand the variations in deviant and criminal behaviors, particularly violence, and involvement with the legal system within the white population as well as between whites and other groups. The remaining chapters in this book will present the central elements of TWC as well as how they are theorized to operate together. Up first, the concept of status dissonance.

Notes

1 Some elements of this chapter appeared in or were revised from my earlier works, including Boehme and Isom* (2020) https://www.tandfonline.com/doi/full/10.1080/15564886.2019.1679308; Isom* (2018); Isom* & Andersen (2020) 'Whitelash?'status threat, anger, and white America: A general strain theory approach. *Journal of Crime and Justice, copyright ©Midwestern Criminal Justice Association, reprinted by permission of Taylor & Francis Ltd*, https://www.tandfonline.com/doi/full/10.1080/0735648X.2019.1704835 on behalf of Midwestern Criminal Justice Association; Isom, Boehme, et al. (2021) and Isom, Mikell, et al. (2021) https://www.tandfonline.com/doi/full/10.1080/02732173.2021.1885531. All used with permission.

2 The Black Live Matter (BLM) movement is an inclusive, de-centralized movement against the racial injustices and police brutality faced by many Black Americans. It was started by three female anti-racist activists of Color and has grown to include over 30 chapters internationally (Banks, 2018; Carney, 2016; Clayton, 2018). BLM is often a target of politicized media and (far-right) conservatives (Banks, 2018; Taylor, 2018).

3 The police violence against Black women and other women of Color, including against those that are nonbinary and transgender, also warrant acknowledgment and discussion as the association between policing and race and further complicated by gender, sexuality, and other identities. For discussions of these complexities and nuances, see Crenshaw et al. (2015), Ritchie (2017), and Weissinger et al. (2017).

4 The term "Latine" refers to those who classify themselves as persons of Cuban, Mexican, Puerto Rican, Central American, South American, or other Spanish cultural origin. While the term "Latinx" is prominent in the scholarly literature (including in my own previous work) due to its gender neutrality, it is still highly debated. Thus, in the spirit of evolving best praxis and inclusivity, I presently use "Latine" as a more culturally accepted gender-neutral term (see Ochoa, 2022 for discussion).

5 Specifics of the ANES methodology may be found within each year's study description available through the ANES Data Center (https://electionstudies.org/datacenter/). Additionally, the race thermometer question was not asked in 1978, and data was not collected in 2006, 2010, 2014, or 2018. Thus, responses for the 2 years prior and two years after each of these missing years were averaged to provide consistent spacing between data points in Figure 1.1. These years are designated with an asterisk. Furthermore, "positive" is define as any rating greater than 50, thus is a conservative estimate of positive feelings. The white respondents from each data set were selected for assessment. The number of those with a positive response to the race thermometer question was divided by the total number of white people in the sample to determine the percentage of whites with positive feelings toward Blacks for each year. Additional information on the specific data utilized and assessment conducted are available upon request.

References

Alexander, M. (2010). *The new Jim Crow: Mass incarceration in the age of colorblindness*. The New Press.

Allyn, B., & Keith, T. (2021, January 8). Twitter permanently suspends Trump, citing 'risk of further incitement of violence'. *NPR*. https://www.npr.org/2021/01/08/954760928/twitter-bans-president-trump-citing-risk-of-further-incitement-of-violence

Alvarez, L., & Buckley, C. (2013, July 13). Zimmerman is acquitted in Trayvon Martin killing. *The New York Times*. https://www.nytimes.com/2013/07/14/us/george-zimmerman-verdict-trayvon-martin.html

American National Election Studies. (ANES). (n.d.). *Data Center*. https://electionstudies.org/data-center/

Andaya, E. (2019). "I'm building a wall around my uterus": Abortion politics and the politics of othering in Trump's America. *Cultural Anthropology, 34*, 10–17.

Anderson, C. (2016). *White rage: The unspoken truth of our racial divide*. Bloomsbury.

Armitage, S. (2016, December 8). 2016 was the year Black Lives Matter went global. *BuzzFeed*. https://www.buzzfeednews.com/article/susiearmitage/2016-was-the-year-black-lives-matter-went-global

Ash, E., Morelli, M., & Van Weelden, R. (2017). Elections and divisiveness: Theory and evidence. *The Journal of Politics, 79*(4), 1268–1285.

Banks, C. (2018). Disciplining Black activism: Post-racial rhetoric, public memory and decorum in news media framing of the Black Lives Matter movement. *Continuum, 32*(6), 709–720.

Baptist, E. E. (2014). *The half has never been told*. Basic Books.

Barak, G. (2022). *Criminology on Trump*. Routledge.

Barkun, M. (2017). President Trump and the "fringe. *Terrorism and Political Violence, 29*(3), 437–443.

Barnett, B. A. (2018). The Trump effect: The 2016 presidential campaign and the racist right's internet rhetoric. *Journal of Hate Studies, 14*(1), 77–96.

Beavers, O. (2020, September 17). Wray: Racially motivated violent extremism makes up most of FBI's domestic terrorism cases. *The Hill*. https://thehill.com/policy/national-security/516888-wray-says-racially-motivated-violent-extremism-makes-up-most-of-fbis/

Benegal, S., & Motta, M. (2022). Overconfident, resentful, and misinformed: How racial animus motivates confidence in false beliefs. *Social Science Quarterly*. Advance online publication. https://doi.org/10.1111/ssqu.13224

Berbrier, M. (2000). The victim ideology of white supremacists and white separatists in the United States. *Sociological Focus, 33*(2), 175–191.

Boehme, H. M., & Isom*, D. A. (2020). Alt-white? A gendered look at "victim" ideology and the alt-right. *Victims and Offenders, 15*(2), 174–196.

Bonilla-Silva, E. (2018). *Racism without racists: Color-blind racism and the persistence of racial inequality in America* (5th ed.). Rowman & Littlefield.

Brown, A., & Atske, S. (2021, January 22). *Black Americans have made gains in U.S. political leadership, but gaps remain*. Pew Research Center. https://www.pewresearch.org/fact-tank/2021/01/22/black-americans-have-made-gains-in-u-s-political-leadership-but-gaps-remain/

Burkhardt, J. M. (2017). History of fake news. *Library Technology Reports, 53*(8), 5–9.

Burns, N. (2006). *The Michigan, then National, then American National Elections Studies*. American National Election Studies. https://electionstudies.org/wp-content/uploads/2018/07/20060815Burns_ANES_history.pdf

Cai, W. (2021, February 13). A step-by-step guide to the second impeachment of Donald J. Trump. *The New York Times*. https://www.nytimes.com/interactive/2021/02/08/us/politics/trump-second-impeachment-timeline.html

Campbell, A. (2022). *We are Proud Boys: How a right-wing street gang ushered in a new era of American extremism*. Hachette Books.

Carbado, D. W. (2013). Colorblind intersectionality. *Signs*, *38*(4), 811–845.

Carney, N. (2016). All Lives Matter, but so does race: Black Lives Matter and the evolving role of social media. *Humanity and Society*, *40*(2), 180–199.

Clark, D. B., Berzon, A., & Berg, K. (2022, April 26). Building the "big lie": Inside the creation of Trump's stolen election myth. *ProPublica*. https://www.propublica.org/article/big-lie-trump-stolen-election-inside-creation

Clayton, D. M. (2018). Black Lives Matter and the Civil Rights movement: A comparative analysis of two social movements in the United States. *Journal of Black Studies*, *49*(5), 448–480.

CNN Editorial Research. (2022, February 14). Trayvon Martin shooting fast facts. *CNN*. https://www.cnn.com/2013/06/05/us/trayvon-martin-shooting-fast-facts/index.html

Collins, P. H. (2008). *Black feminist thought: Knowledge, consciousness, and the politics of empowerment*. Routledge.

Committee on Homeland Security. (2021, February 4). *Examining the domestic terrorism threat of the wake of the attack on the U.S. Capitol*. House of Representatives, Serial No. 117-1. https://www.congress.gov/117/chrg/CHRG-117hhrg44243/CHRG-117hhrg44243.pdf

Crandall, C. S., Miller, J. M., & White, M. H. (2018). Changing norms following the 2016 U.S. presidential election: The Trump effect on prejudice. *Social Psychological and Personality Science*, *9*(2), 186–192.

Crenshaw, K. (1991). Mapping the margins: Intersectionality, identity politics, and violence against women of color. *Stanford Law Review*, *43*(6), 1241–1299.

Crenshaw, K. W., Ritchie, A. J., Anspach, R., Gilmer, R., & Harris, L. (2015). *Say her name: Resisting police brutality against black women*. Center for Intersectionality and Social Policy Studies, Columbia Law School. https://scholarship.law.columbia.edu/faculty_scholarship/3226

Daniels, J. (2018). The algorithmic rise of the "Alt-Right. *Contexts*, *17*(1), 60–65.

Darcy, O. (2019, July 11). Trump invites right-wing extremists to White House 'social media summit'. *CNN*. https://www.cnn.com/2019/07/10/tech/white-house-social-media-summit/index.html

Date, S. V. (2023, March 15). Trump keeps crying 'witch hunt' – but what happens when a witch is actually indicted? *HuffPost*. https://www.huffpost.com/entry/trump-potential-indictment_n_6412136fe4b0a3902d2e5528

Delgado, R., & Stefancic, J. (Eds.). (1997). *Critical white studies*. Temple University Press.

Delgado, R., & Stefancic, J. (2017). *Critical race theory: An introduction* (3rd ed.). New York University Press.

Dewan, S., & Oppel, R. A. Jr. (2015, January 22). In Tamir Rice case, many errors by Cleveland police, then a fatal one. *The New York Times*. https://www.nytimes.

com/2015/01/23/us/in-tamir-rice-shooting-in-cleveland-many-errors-by-police-then-a-fatal-one.html

Du Bois, W. E. B. (1920/1999). *Darkwater: Voices from within the veil*. Dover Publications, Inc.

Eddington, S. M. (2018). The communicative constitution of hate organizations online: A semantic network analysis of "make America great again. *Social Media & Society*, *4*(3), 2056305118790763.

Edwards-Levy, A. (2016, November 21). Nearly half of Trump voters think whites face a lot of discrimination. *HuffPost*. https://www.huffpost.com/entry/discrimination-race-religion_n_5833761ee4b099512f845bba

Fausset, R., Levenson, M., Mervosh, S., & Taylor, D. B. (2022, August 8). Ahmaud Arbery shooting: A timeline of the case. *The New York Times*. https://www.nytimes.com/article/ahmaud-arbery-timeline.html

Feagin, J. R. (2013). *The white racial frame* (2nd ed.). Routledge.

Federal Bureau of Investigation. (n.d.). *Crime data explorer*. https://cde.ucr.cjis.gov/LATEST/webapp/#/pages/home

Forman-Katz, N., & Stocking, G. (2022, November 18). *Key facts about truth social*. Pew Research Center. https://www.pewresearch.org/fact-tank/2022/11/18/key-facts-about-truth-social-as-donald-trump-runs-for-u-s-president-again/

Forscher, P. S., & Kteily, N. S. (2017). *A psychological profile of the alt-right*. [Data set]. https://osf.io/xge8q/

Frenkel, S., & Karni, A. (2021, January 20). Proud boys celebrate Trump's 'stand by' remark about them at the debate. *The New York Times*. https://www.nytimes.com/2020/09/29/us/trump-proud-boys-biden.html

Futrell, R., & Simi, P. (2017, August 18). The [un] surprising alt-right. *Contexts*. https://contexts.org/articles/the-unsurprising-alt-right/

Gabbatt, A. (2019, June 14). Golden escalator ride: The surreal day Trump kicked off his bid for president. *The Guardian*. https://www.theguardian.com/us-news/2019/jun/13/donald-trump-presidential-campaign-speech-eyewitness-memories

Gabbidon, S. L., & Higgins, G. E. (2010). Profiling white Americans: A research note of "shopping while white. In M. J. Lynch, E. B. Patterson, & K. K. Childs (Eds.), *Racial divide: Racial and ethnic bias in the criminal justice system* (pp. 197–209). Lynne Rienner Publishers.

Gais, H., & Hayden, M. E. (2022, December 11). *White nationalists, other republicans brace for 'total war'*. Southern Poverty Law Center. https://www.splcenter.org/hatewatch/2022/12/11/white-nationalists-other-republicans-brace-total-war

Gonzalez, O. (2019, November 7). 8chan, 8kun, 4chan, Endchan: What you need to know. *CNET*. https://www.cnet.com/news/politics/8chan-8kun-4chan-endchan-what-you-need-to-know-internet-forums/

Hammon, B. (2013). Playing the race card: White Americans' sense of victimization in response to affirmative action. *Texas Hispanic Journal of Law and Policy*, *19*, 95–120.

Heim, J. (2017, August 14). Recounting a day of rage, hate, violence and death. *The Washington Post*. https://www.washingtonpost.com/graphics/2017/local/charlottesville-timeline/

Hooghe, M., & Dassonneville, R. (2018). Explaining the Trump vote: The effect of racist resentment and antiimmigrant sentiments. *PS: Political Science and Politics*, *51*(3), 528–534.

Ingraham, C. (2018, June 19). There are more guns than people in the United States, according to a new study of global firearm ownership. *The Washington Post*. https://www.washingtonpost.com/news/wonk/wp/2018/06/19/there-are-more-guns-than-people-in-the-united-states-according-to-a-new-study-of-global-firearm-ownership/

Isom, D. (2016). Microaggressions, injustices, and racial identity: An empirical assessment of the theory of African American offending. *Journal of Contemporary Criminal Justice*, *32*(1), 27–59.

Isom, D. A. (2022). *Whiteness and crime* [Unpublished data set]. University of South Carolina.

Isom*, D. (2018a). Latina fortitude in the face of disadvantage: Exploring the conditioning effects of ethnic identity and gendered ethnic identity on Latina offending. *Critical Criminology*, *26*, 49–73.

Isom*, D. A. (2018b). Understanding White Americans' perceptions of "reverse" discrimination: An application of a new theory of status dissonance. In E. J. Lawler (Ed.), *Advances in group processes* (pp. 129–157). Emerald Publishing Limited.

Isom*, D. A. (2020). The new Juan Crow? Unpacking the links between discrimination and crime for Latinxs. *Race and Justice*, *10*(1), 20–42.

Isom*, D. A., & Andersen, T. S. (2018). *Aggrieved entitlement and discrimination* [Unpublished data set]. University of South Carolina.

Isom*, D. A., & Andersen, T. S. (2020). 'Whitelash?'status threat, anger, and white America: A general strain theory approach. *Journal of Crime and Justice*, *43*(4), 414–432.

Isom*, D. A., & Grosholz, J. M. (2019). Unpacking the racial disparity in crime from a racialized general strain theory perspective. *Deviant Behavior*, *40*(12), 1445–1463.

Isom*, D. A., & Mikell, T. (2019). "Gender" and general strain theory: Investigating the impact of gender socialization on young women's criminal outcomes. *Journal of Crime and Justice*, *42*(4), 393–413.

Isom*, D. A., & Seal, Z. T. (2019). Disentangling the roles of negative emotions and racial identity in the theory of African American offending. *American Journal of Criminal Justice*, *44*(2), 277–308.

Isom*, D. A., Whiting, S., & Grosholz, J. M. (2023). Examining and expanding Latinx general strain theory. *Race and Justice*, *13*(2), 231–255.

Isom, D. A., Boehme, H. M., Mikell, T. C., Chicoine, S., & Renner, M. (2021). Status threat, social concerns, and conservative media: A look at white America and the alt-right. *Societies*, *11*, 72. https://doi.org/10.3390/soc11030072

Isom, D. A., Cann, D., & Wilson, A. (2022). Discrimination, emotions, and identity: Unpacking Latinx pathways to crime. *Criminal Justice and Behavior*, *49*(3), 432–450.

Isom, D. A., Grosholz, J. M., Whiting, S., & Beck, T. (2021). A gendered look at Latinx general strain theory. *Feminist Criminology*, *16*(2), 115–146.

Isom, D. A., Mikell, T. C., & Boehme, H. M. (2021). White America, threat to the status quo, and affiliation with the alt-right: A qualitative approach. *Sociological Spectrum*, *41*(3), 213–228.

Iyengar, S., & Hahn, K. S. (2009). Red media, blue media: Evidence of ideological selectivity in media use. *Journal of Communication*, *59*(1), 19–39.

Jardina, A. (2019). *White identity politics*. Cambridge University Press.

Jasko, K., LaFree, G., Piazza, J., & Becker, M. H. (2022). A comparison of political violence by left-wing, right-wing, and Islamist extremists in the United States and the world. *PNAS, 119*(30), e2122593119.

Johnson, J. (2018). The self-radicalization of white men: "Fake news" and the affective networking of paranoia. *Communication Culture & Critique, 11*(1), 100–115.

Jones, J. M. (2008). *Majority of Americans say racism against blacks widespread.* Gallup. https://news.gallup.com/poll/109258/majority-americans-say-racism-against-blacks-widespread.aspx

Jones, T. (2018). Trump, trans students and transnational progress. *Sex Education, 18*(4), 479–494.

Jones, R. P., Cox, D., Galston, W. A., & Dionne, E. J. Jr. (2011). *What it means to be American: Attitudes towards increasing diversity in America ten years after 9/11.* Public Religion Research Institute. https://www.prri.org/research/what-it-means-to-be-american/

Karp, A. (2018, June). *Estimating global civilian-held firearms numbers.* Small Arms Survey. https://www.smallarmssurvey.org/sites/default/files/resources/SAS-BP-Civilian-Firearms-Numbers.pdf

Kaufman, S. J. (2022). Is the US heading for a civil war? Scenarios for 2024-2025. *Studies in Conflict & Terrorism*, Advance online publication. https://doi.org/10.1080/1057610X.2022.2137892

Kaufmann, E. (2019). *Whiteshift: Populism, immigration, and the future of white majorities.* Abrams Press.

Kendi, I. X. (2016). *Stamped from the beginning.* Bold Type Books.

Kessler, G. (2020, May 8). The 'very fine people' at Charlottesville: Who are they? *The Washington Post.* https://www.washingtonpost.com/politics/2020/05/08/very-fine-people-charlottesville-who-were-they-2/

Kessler, R. C., Mickelson, K. D., & Williams, D. R. (1999). The prevalence, distribution, and mental health correlates of perceived discrimination in the United States. *Journal of Health and Social Behavior, 40*(3), 208–230.

Kessler, G., Rizzo, S., & Kelly, M. (2021, January 24). Trump's false or misleading claims total 30,573 over 4 years. *The Washington Post.* https://www.washingtonpost.com/politics/2021/01/24/trumps-false-or-misleading-claims-total-30573-over-four-years/

Klein, E. (2020). *Why we're polarized.* Avid Reader Press.

Latif, M., Blee, K., DeMichele, M., & Simi, P. (2020). Do white supremacist women adopt movement archetypes of mother, whore, and fighter? *Studies in Conflict & Terrorism.* Advance online publication. https://doi.org/10.1080/1057610X.2020.1759264

Leatherby, L., Ray, A., Singhvi, A., Triebert, C., Watkins, D., & Willis, H. (2021, January 12). How a presidential rally turned into a capitol rampage. *The New York Times.* https://www.nytimes.com/interactive/2021/01/12/us/capitol-mob-timeline.html

Lebron, C. J. (2017). *The making of Black Lives Matter: A brief history of an idea.* Oxford University Press.

Levenson, E., & Cooper, A. (2021, April 21). *Derek Chauvin found guilty of all three charges for killing George Floyd.* CNN. https://www.cnn.com/2021/04/20/us/derek-chauvin-trial-george-floyd-deliberations/index.html

Lopez, G. (2020, August 13). Donald Trump's long history of racism, from the 1970s to 2020. *Vox.* https://www.vox.com/2016/7/25/12270880/donald-trump-racist-racism-history

Love, N. S. (2017). Back to the future: Trendy fascism, the trump effect, and the alt-right. *New Political Science, 39*(2), 263–268.

Lyn, D. (2022, May 25). *Timeline of black Americans killed by police: 2014-2022.* Anadolu Agency. https://www.aa.com.tr/en/americas/timeline-of-black-americans-killed-by-police-2014-2022/2596913

Martin, G. J., & Yurukoglu, A. (2017). Bias in cable news: Persuasion and polarization. *American Economic Review, 107*(9), 2565–2599.

McDermott, M., & Samson, F. L. (2005). White racial and ethnic identity in the United States. *Annual Review of Sociology, 31,* 245–261.

McGhee, H. (2021). *The sum of us: What racism cost everyone and how we can prosper together.* One World.

Messing, S., & Westwood, S. J. (2014). Selective exposure in the age of social media: Endorsements Trump partisan source affiliation when selecting news online. *Communication Research, 41*(8), 1042–1063.

Miller, M. E. (2021, February 16). Pizzagate's violent legacy. *The Washington Post.* https://www.washingtonpost.com/dc-md-va/2021/02/16/pizzagate-qanon-capitol-attack/

Minnite, L. C., & Piven, F. F. (2021). Voter suppression: The attack on rights. In L. Chorbajin (Ed.), *Power and inequality,* 2nd ed. (pp. 125–138). Routledge.

Montanaro, D. (2022, February 1). Trump escalates racist rhetoric and plays on white grievance at recent rallies. *NPR.* https://www.npr.org/2022/02/01/1077166847/trump-escalates-racist-rhetoric-plays-on-white-grievance-at-recent-rallies

Morales, M., Levenson, E., & Sgueglia, K. (2022, November 28). Buffalo grocery store mass shooter pleads guilty to terrorism and murder charges in racist attack. *CNN.* https://www.cnn.com/2022/11/28/us/buffalo-tops-grocery-shooting-payton-gendron-plea/index.html

Morrison, C. N., Ukert, B., Palumbo, A., Dong, B., Jacoby, S. F., & Wiebe, D. J. (2018). Assaults on days of campaign rallies during the 2016 US presidential election. *Epidemiology, 29*(4), 490–493.

Nance, M. (2022). *They want to kill Americans: The militias, terrorists, and deranged ideology of the Trump insurgency.* St. Martin's Press.

Naylor, B. (2021, February 10). Read Trump's Jan. 6 speech, a key part of impeachment trial. *NPR.* https://www.npr.org/2021/02/10/966396848/read-trumps-jan-6-speech-a-key-part-of-impeachment-trial

Newhouse, A. (2020, December 3). Right-wing users flock to Parler as social media giants rein in misinformation. *PBS NewsHour.* https://www.pbs.org/newshour/nation/right-wing-users-flock-to-parler-as-social-media-giants-rein-in-misinformation

Newton, K. (2006). May the weak force be with you: The power of The mass media in modern politics. *European Journal of Political Research, 45*(2), 209–234.

Norris, J. J. (2017). Why Dylann Roof is a terrorist under federal law, and why it matters. *Harvard Journal on Legislation, 54,* 259–298.

Norton, M. I., & Sommers, S. R. (2011). Whites see racism as a zero-sum game that they are now losing. *Perspectives on Psychological Science, 6*(3), 215–218.

Ochoa, M. K. (2022, September 9). Stop using 'Latinx' if you really want to be inclusive. *The Conversation.* https://theconversation.com/stop-using-latinx-if-you-really-want-to-be-inclusive-189358

Parker, K., Horowitz, J. M., Igielnik, R., Oliphant, J. B., & Brown, A. (2017, June 22). *The demographics of gun ownership.* Pew Research Center. https://www.pewresearch.org/social-trends/2017/06/22/the-demographics-of-gun-ownership/

Perry, B., Gruenewald, J., & Scrivens, R. (Eds.) (2022). *Right-wing extremism in Canada and the United States.* Springer.

Persily, N. (2017). The 2016 US election: Can democracy survive the internet? *Journal of Democracy, 28*(2), 63–76.

Peters, J. W. (2019, June 18). Michael Savage has doubts about Trump. His conservative radio audience does not. *The New York Times.* https://www.nytimes.com/2019/06/18/us/politics/michael-savage-trump.html

Pickard, V. (2017). Media failures in the age of Trump. *The Political Economy of Communication, 4*(2), 118–122.

Polletta, F., & Callahan, J. (2019). Deep stories, nostalgia narratives, and fake news: Storytelling in the Trump era. In *Politics of meaning/meaning of politics* (pp. 55–73). Palgrave Macmillan.

Potter, H. (2015). *Intersectionality and criminology: Disrupting and revolutionizing studies of crime.* Routledge.

Ritchie, A. J. (2017). *Invisible no more: Police violence against Black women and women of color.* Beacon Press.

Rosenberg, H., & Feldman, C. S. (2008). *No time to think: The menace of media speed and the 24-hour news cycle.* A&C Black.

Rosenwald, B. (2019, July 13). Trump just launched the newest phase of the GOP's romance with right-wing media. *The Washington Post.* https://www.washingtonpost.com/outlook/2019/07/13/trump-just-launched-newest-phase-gops-romance-with-right-wing-media/?utm_term=.92ec6eea1f48

Rummler, O. (2019, July 17). Trump supporters echo his racist tweets, chanting 'send her back'. *Axios.* https://www.axios.com/trump-supporters-chant-send-her-back-rally-echoing-racist-tweets-274f0261-f69b-4755-906d-3da7f06582fb.html

Russell, K. K. (1998). *The color of crime: Racial hoaxes, white fear, black protectionism, police harassment, and other macroagressions.* New York University Press.

Russell-Brown, K. K. (2009). *The color of crime: Racial hoaxes, white fear, black protectionism, police harassment, and other microaggressions* (2nd ed.). New York University Press.

Savage, C. (2023, June 9). The Trump classified documents indictment, annotated. *The New York Times.* https://www.nytimes.com/interactive/2023/06/09/us/trump-indictment-document-annotated.html

Schragger, R. C. (2018). When white supremacists invade a city. *Virginia Law Review, 104*, 58–73.

Select Committee to Investigate the January 6th Attack on the United States Capitol. (2022, December 22). *Final Report.* 117th Congress Second Session, House Report 117-663. Washington, DC. https://january6th.house.gov/

Sides, J., Tesler, M., & Vavreck, L. (2018). Hunting where the ducks are: Activating support for Donald Trump in the 2016 Republican primary. *Journal of Elections, Public Opinion and Parties, 28*(2), 135–156.

Silverstein, J. (2021, June 4). The global impact of George Floyd: How Black Lives Matter protests shaped movements around the world. *CBS News.* https://www.cbsnews.com/news/george-floyd-black-lives-matter-impact/

Smith, C. (2021). *How the word is passed: A reckoning with the history of slavery across America*. Little, Brown and Company.

Smith, D. N., & Hanley, E. (2018). The anger games: Who voted for Donald Trump in the 2016 election, and why? *Critical Sociology, 44*(2), 195–212.

Southern Poverty Law Center. (n.d.a.). *Alt-Right*. https://www.splcenter.org/fighting-hate/extremist-files/ideology/alt-right

Southern Poverty Law Center. (n.d.b.). *Extremist files*. https://www.splcenter.org/fighting-hate/extremist-files

Southern Poverty Law Center. (n.d.c.). *Hate map*. https://www.splcenter.org/hate-map

Taylor, K. Y. (2018). The white power presidency: Race and class in the trump era. *New Political Science, 40*(1), 103–112.

Tenold, V. (2018). *Everything you love will burn: Inside the rebirth of white nationalism in America*. Nation Books.

The Associated Press. (2022, January 2). Timeline of events since George Floyd's arrest and murder. *AP News*. https://apnews.com/article/george-floyd-death-timeline-2f9abbe6497c2fa4adaebb92ae179dc6

The Associated Press. (2019a, August 8). Timeline of events in shooting of Michael Brown in Ferguson. *AP News*. https://apnews.com/article/shootings-police-us-news-st-louis-michael-brown-9aa32033692547699a3b61da8fd1fc62

The Associated Press. (2019b, August 20). From Eric Garner's death to firing of NYPD officer: A timeline of key events. *USA Today*. https://www.usatoday.com/story/news/2019/08/20/eric-garner-timeline-chokehold-death-daniel-pantaleo-fired/2059708001/

The Washington Post. (n.d.). Police shootings database. Retrieved December 5, 2022. https://www.washingtonpost.com/graphics/investigations/police-shootings-database/

The White House (2013, July 19). *Remarks by the President on Trayvon Martin* [Press release]. https://obamawhitehouse.archives.gov/the-press-office/2013/07/19/remarks-president-trayvon-martin

TIME Staff. (2015, June 16). Here's Donald Trump's presidential announcement speech. *TIME*. https://time.com/3923128/donald-trump-announcement-speech/

Tucker, E., & Balsamo, M. (2021, March 15). Christmas day bomber in Nashville driven by conspiracies, paranoia, FBI says. *PBS NewsHour*. https://www.pbs.org/newshour/nation/fbi-says-nashville-bomber-driven-by-conspiracies-paranoia

Tucker, E., & Jalonick, M. C. (2021, March 2). FBI chief warns violent 'domestic terrorism' growing in the US. *AP News*. https://apnews.com/article/fbi-chris-wray-testify-capitol-riot-9a5539af34b15338bb5c4923907eeb67

Vaidhyanathan, S. (2018). *Antisocial media: How Facebook disconnects us and undermines democracy*. Oxford University Press.

Wade, Z. (2018, September 17). Disruptor in chief: How Trump is changing world order. *CNN*. https://www.cnn.com/2018/09/16/world/world-order-under-president-trump/index.html

Waldrop, T., McLaughlin, E. C., Moghue, S., & Rabinowitz, H. (2022, August 4). Breonna Taylor killing: A timeline of the police raid and its aftermath. *CNN*. https://www.cnn.com/2022/08/04/us/no-knock-raid-breonna-taylor-timeline/index.html

Wallis, J. (2016). *America's original sin: Racism, white privilege, and the bridge to a new America*. Brazos Press.

Weissinger, S. E., Mack, D. A., & Watson, E. (Eds.). (2017). *Violence against black bodies: An intersectional analysis of how black lives continue to matter*. Routledge.

Wendling, M. (2019, August 5). What is 8chan? *BBC News*. https://www.bbc.com/news/blogs-trending-49233767

Wilkerson, I. (2020). *Caste: The origins of our discontents*. Random House.

Windisch, S., Simi, P., Blee, K., & DeMichele, M. (2022). Measuring the extent and nature of adverse childhood experiences (ACE) among former white supremacists. *Terrorism and Political Violence*, *34*(6), 1207–1228.

Wong, J. C. (2019, August 4). 8chan: The far-right website linked to the rise in hate crimes. *The Guardian*. https://www.theguardian.com/technology/2019/aug/04/mass-shootings-el-paso-texas-dayton-ohio-8chan-far-right-website

Zelizer, J. (2019, July). Trump is a dangerous media mastermind. *CNN*. https://www.cnn.com/2019/07/21/opinions/trump-racist-tweet-mastery-media-coverage-zelizer/index.html

Zweigenhaft, R. L. (2021). Diversity among Fortune 500 CEOs from 2000 to 2020: White women, hi-tech South Asians, and economically privileged multilingual immigrants from around the world. *Who rules America?* Blog Post. https://whorulesamerica.ucsc.edu/power/diversity_update_2020.html

2
STATUS DISSONANCE AND WHITE AMERICAN OFFENDING

A surprising trend has emerged in the past few decades. Many in the power majority (i.e., white folks) now believe white Americans face as much or more racial discrimination than people of Color, particularly Black Americans (Jones, 2008; Jones et al., 2011).[1] These perceptions are surfacing in a time gaps have been decreasing (Anderson, 2016; Thernstrom & Thernstrom, 1998), with the gender wage gap the smallest in history (Bureau of Labor Statistics, 2021) and Black college enrollment on the rise (National Center for Education Statistics, 2022). However, white men still earn more than their similarly situated female and Black and Latine counterparts (Miller, 2020), and are still the majority seat holders in the corporate sector (U.S. Equal Employment Opportunity Commission, n.d.; Zweigenhaft, 2021). Yet, the advances of marginalized populations toward equality leave some white Americans, about 30%–40% (e.g., Isom* & Andersen, 2018; Jones et al., 2017; Pew Research Center, 2016),[2] feeling as if they are "the victims of government-sponsored racial discrimination" (2017*, p. 40).

Scholars argue that for some whites, progress toward racial equality is perceived as a threat to their dominant status as the racial majority (Outten et al., 2012; Sidanius & Pratto, 1999), and often times whites believe equality for marginalized populations may only be achieved at their expense (Eibach & Keegan, 2006; Norton & Sommers, 2011).* In other words, many whites think racial equality is a zero-sum game (Wilkins et al., 2015).[3] Many whites, particularly men, perceive the steps taken to remedy social inequality are taking away resources *they* are entitled to and are in turn *unfair to them*, leading to anger toward women and people of Color and feelings of loss and victimhood.* Thus, some white Americans appear to believe their social status is not only threatened, but already lost, and *they* are now the victims of a racially biased society.

DOI: 10.4324/9781003167877-3

My recent status dissonance theory (SDT) (Isom*, 2018) provides insight into the mechanisms that lead to habitus angst (see Chapter 3), such as perceiving anti-white bias, and aggrieved entitlement (see Chapter 4), both distinctly racialized drivers of white offending. Status dissonance theory builds on status construction theory to highlight significant factors and pathways that impact white Americans' likelihood of feeling their dominant social position is under attack. Status construction theory (Ridgeway, 1991; Ridgeway & Balkwell, 1997; Ridgeway & Correll, 2006; Ridgeway & Erickson, 2000; Ridgeway & Glasgow, 1996; Ridgeway et al., 1998; with elaborations by Hysom, 2009; Webster & Hysom, 1998) generally posits the arbitrary associations between nominal characteristics, such as race/ethnicity and gender, and the distribution of resources, goal objects, power, and prestige are reinforced and perpetuated through confirming social interactions until the value of some characteristics, such as being white and male, over others, such as being Black and female, becomes a cultural norm. Status construction theory and its extensions provide sufficient mechanisms for the creation, dissemination, and even de-generalization of status beliefs. Yet, how do we explain when some of those holding high status, such as white men, feel oppressed and targeted? Building upon the mechanisms proposed by status construction theory, SDT posits a sufficient process for understanding the disconnect between one's view of deserved status value in social structure and how one perceives others to actually value people similar to themselves. In other words, how one believes things *ought* to be compared to how one thinks things *actually are*. This status dissonance then provides a lens through which the individual perceives and interacts with and behaves within the social world. Thus, while SDT is not exclusive to whites, it provides a framework for understanding variations in the social lens that impacts the likelihood of manifesting habitus angst and aggrieved entitlement and resulting behaviors within the white race. Thus, this is where the theory of whiteness and crime (TWC) begins – understanding deviations in feelings of status dissonance.

Status Construction Theory

Drawing upon an expectation states tradition (Berger & Conner, 1974; Berger et al., 1980; Ridgeway & Berger, 1986), status construction theory (Ridgeway, 1991) posits sufficient mechanisms by which structural conditions influence social interactions and in turn affect cultural norms and beliefs. A nominal characteristic is an attribute that is commonly distinguishable and professed to categorize people, such as gender, race, or ethnicity. A characteristic has status value when cultural norms and beliefs suggest one category (i.e., white skin or men) is more worthy than another (i.e., black skin or women).

Ridgeway (1991) makes four assumptions about the structural conditions of society, based on structuralist theory (Blau, 1977), which are sufficient, but not necessary, for a culture of status value to emerge. First, exchange-able resources must be unequally distributed across the population; thus, at the least, there is a dichotomous distinction in the population between those with abundant resources and those without. Second, this distinction between the resource rich and poor must be socially meaningful, so that individuals associate most with similar others. Third, the population is distinguishable on a characteristic which is socially salient (i.e., easily noticeable in society, such as race/ethnicity or gender), but does not have status value.[4] And finally, there must be a correlation between the resource distribution and the nominal characteristic. Consequently, there is a structure of inequality in society such that resources are disproportionately associated with different categories of the nominal characteristic (Ridgeway, 1991). Thus, according to status con-struction theory, because the resource distribution of a society and the nomi-nal characteristics of color are associated, the links between status, resources, and race/ethnicity are conditional. Race and ethnicity, therefore, along with resources, become categorical cues for performance expectations,[5] and thus, status (Berger & Conner, 1974; Ridgeway, 1991; Ridgeway et al., 1985).

Status value beliefs are reinforced through repeated interaction with dis-similar others, particularly with those that differ in both resources and nominal characteristics. Beliefs gained in such interactions will be transferred to similar others and will be reinforced by similar outcomes, therefore the status value of race/ethnicity, for example, becomes increasingly salient and categorically meaningful. Race/ethnicity acquires independent status value, and categorical referential structures emerge (Ridgeway, 1991; Ridgeway & Berger, 1986). Referential structures are widely held, socially endorsed beliefs about what is assumed to be the relationship between remunerative distribution of resources and a nominal characteristic. As racialized referential structures are more com-monly applied over time, they become legitimized rationales for racial inequal-ity (Ridgeway & Berger, 1986).

Status construction theory has been extensively examined with experimen-tal methods supporting the posited mechanisms for the creation of status value (Ridgeway & Erickson, 2000; Ridgeway & Glasgow, 1996; Ridgeway et al., 1998) and their diffusion into social norms (Ridgeway & Correll, 2006; Ridge-way & Erickson, 2000; Ridgeway et al., 2009). The posited processes have also been generalized beyond the lab with nationally representative (Brezina & Winder, 2003) and international (Brashears, 2008) survey data. Furthermore, scholars have expanded the mechanisms of status construction theory finding the distribution of other valued things, such as honors, a better office, or praise (i.e., "goal objects"), create status value in addition to exchangeable resources, and things such as personal characteristics and behaviors may gain status value as well (Webster & Hysom, 1998). Much empirical work on status construction theory focuses on how the lower status actor comes to internalize status value beliefs about themself and others and behave in accordance with these norms. For instance, in an experiment, Ridgeway and Erickson (2000) found repeatedly witnessing those like themselves treated as unworthy led subjects to believe those like themselves have low status value, though subjects resisted evaluating themselves as such. Hysom (2009) also found those arbitrarily given goal objects, such as an honorary title, were more resistant to influence from others and evaluated themselves as the most competent in the task group. Together these findings reinforce how referential structures differentially influence individuals' perceptions of self and their beliefs about how others view people similar to themselves based on status value.

De-generalization of Status Value

Ridgeway suggests "for the status value of a nominal characteristic to be undermined in a sustainable way, resource differences between those who differ on the characteristics must be eliminated" (1991, p. 382), and one must have numerous disconfirming interactions with dissimilar others to counteract assumptions and stereotypes about status value (Ridgeway, 1997). Extensive work has focused on decreasing status generalizations by countering normative referential structures, particularly in terms of race. For instance, in a review of status generalization research, Webster and Driskell (1978) outlined the work of Katz, Cohen, and colleagues attempting to neutralize performance expectations in mixed-race task groups. Their interventions intended to promote equality but were largely ineffective and arguably counterproductive. As Webster and Driskell summarized, "from the whites' point of view, the blacks behaved inappropriately, considering their low abilities; from the blacks' point of view the whites, refusing to acknowledge the blacks' equal abilities, behaved inappropriately" (1978, p. 227). Beyond the status struggle and increased hostility[6] (see Webster & Driskell, 1978), this quote also implies a racial variance in acceptance of normative referential structures. In other words, whites believing in their supposed superior abilities and competence generally over Blacks, and Blacks not internalizing the referential status beliefs about their assumed inferior status.

More recent work advancing these traditions finds racial inequality can be reduced in task-oriented groups. Using similar experimental designs, Goar and Sell (2005) found how a task is framed influenced Black women's group participation, and Walker et al. (2014) found increased participation by Black women increased their group influence. Neither experimental manipulation, however, completely eliminated white control in the groups. Building upon their previous work, Cohen and colleagues (see Webster & Driskell, 1978) did achieve racial equality in interactions only by counteracting normative referential structures through teaching the Black participants to be assertive, giving the Black participants positive feedback during the task, designating the Black participants as leaders in the group, and providing the group with information on Blacks' superior knowledge for the task at hand. Thus, equality was only achieved when Blacks' superiority was demonstrated and reinforced. In support of Ridgeway's claims (1991, 1997), these findings emphasize the notion that people of Color, particularly Blacks, must work harder to neutralize normative referential structures in order to achieve the same respect and status as whites.

Such extreme demonstrations of ability and worthiness are likely needed to surmount normative referential structures because they challenge the legitimated social order. In other words, the status equality of Blacks with whites contradicts orthodox cultural norms. "Given that individuals form expectations for valued status positions on the basis of these referential beliefs, this leads them to treat individuals who occupy high-status positions differently depending on their external status. Specifically, those with low external status may often be treated as normatively inappropriate occupants of high-status positions" (Berger & Webster, 2006, p. 281). Resistance is most likely from those in the highest status positions because they have the most to lose for legitimizing the rise in status of someone from a lower social order. Yet, *not all* of those holding the highest status positions resist or feel threatened by the advancement of lower status others. Furthermore, while everyone in society generally *knows* the normative referential structures, there is a large variation in the degree of influence status value beliefs have on individuals. Following a status construction theory tradition, status dissonance theory (SDT) attempts to explain why and how those with similar status characteristics respond differently to changes in social inequality.

Status Dissonance Theory

Status dissonance is the degree of discrepancy between where one believes those with similar characteristics should be positioned on the social hierarchy and where one believes others actually position people similar to themselves (Isom*, 2018). In other words, where one believes they *ought to be* compared to where they believe they *truly are*. Similar to reflected appraisals[7] (Cooley, 1902; Felson, 1985; Mead, 1934), status dissonance gauges individual's perceptions about orthodox cultural norms and their social positions in relations to others, but not actually other's beliefs. SDT (Isom*, 2018) generally posits one's overall projected status value influences the degree they internalize normative referential structures. The salience of normative referential structures frames an individual's justice perceptions, which creates status dissonance that manifests as a positional lens through which individuals perceive and interact with the social world. How these factors function together is outlined in the following sections.

Differential Roles of Status Characteristics

While other characteristics beyond the "big two" of gender and race, such as sexuality or being a doctor, may possess status value (e.g., Berger & Fisek, 2006; Walker et al., 2011; Webster & Hysom, 1998), the degree and salience of the given characteristic often varies with context (Berger et al., 1977). Despite variations in significance across situations, every individual still has a fundamental self that is the combination of all their characteristics. People do not experience any characteristic in insolation, thus all individual understanding of any one characteristic is conditioned by all other embodied characteristics – in other words, everyone has an intersectional self (Collins & Bilge, 2016). SDT argues the combination of one's status characteristics determines one's overall status value – based on orthodox cultural norms. Considering the known variation in the salience of given status characteristics, SDT further posits all status characteristics do not contribute equally to an individual's overall status value, but instead operate on a graduated scale.

Given the significance of easily recognizable differences to form fundamental schemas of self and others[8] (Fiske & Taylor, 2017), race and gender are posited to carry the most weight and operate as level one status characteristics. Other characteristics have intrinsic value, and these make up the second level of status characteristics. For instance, social class is fundamentally ordinal. At the foundation of a class structure is the difference between those with resources and those without, the bourgeoisie and the proletariat, and the struggles for power that comes with such divides (Marx, 1867). Yet, social class is not solely about economic divisions, but about culture, values, and morals (Bourdieu, 1987; Lamont, 1992). While there are reasonably established objectives based upon wealth, income, educational attainment, and occupation of who classifies as upper, middle, working, and lower class (Newman, 2010), most Americans do not classify themselves in these terms. Instead, they see themselves as some degree of "middle" class, either out of modesty or self-promotion (Ortner, 1998). Thus, objective and subjective, as well as frontstage and backstage (Goffman, 1959; also see Houts Picca & Feagin, 2007), determinates of social class (i.e., how one dresses, the car they drive, or their professional title) are relevant as second level status characteristics. The third level of status characteristics are those that are more concealable in some way to others. One's sexuality or nonbinary gender identity are prime examples. All these characteristics vary in importance to any individual's identity, but they also vary in significance for social standing and their degree of privateness. For instance, one may choose to disclose their sexuality or not, but one cannot easily hide their race or ethnicity in social settings (though their socially ascribed race may not align with their racial identity). Thus, SDT posits one's combination of status characteristics, with each providing varying degrees of significance, determines one's overall status value in society.

Referential Structures

Building upon status construction theory, status dissonance theory posits individuals understand their overall relative status in the social hierarchy based on normative referential structures determined by the combined status value of their held characteristics. For instance, a white woman knows orthodox society does not value her as much as a white man, but society does value her more than a Black woman. Furthermore, it is posited one's combination of status value will impact the likelihood people generally internalize the normative referential structure, with the "big two" of race and gender being the primary drivers, followed by the other levels of status characteristics. Thus, white men should be more likely to internalize normative referential structures because these beliefs reinforce their high-status value in society. The impact of other status characteristics will follow the expected associations, with the higher valued status state being most likely to internalize normative referential structures. The degree of this association, however, is contingent upon one's racial and gender status. For instance, a working-class white man is still likely to internalize traditional status generalization because he has high-status value based on his race and gender. An upper-class Black woman, however, is unlikely to internalize such normative beliefs to the same degree as her white male counterpart because despite her economic success, she still faces disadvantages based on her race and gender. Thus, SDT recognizes the impact of understanding and operating within the orthodox cultural and social structure as well as how such may impact one's identity and sense of self, particularly through the likelihood of internalizing normative beliefs.

Contact With Dissimilar Others and "Broadcast Processes"

Normative beliefs or referential structures, however, are posited to be conditioned by two factors: contact with dissimilar others and the "broadcast process" (Ridgeway & Balkwell, 1997). Ridgeway (1991) argues status value spreads most rapidly through interactions with doubly dissimilar others. While such interactions spread normative referential structures, counter-normative interactions also de-generalize status beliefs (e.g., Goar & Sell, 2005; Ridgeway & Correll, 2006; Walker et al., 2014). Furthermore, interactions between dissimilar others reduces prejudicial beliefs, with the largest reduction occurring when people choose to interact with people of different races or statuses (Pettigrew & Tropp, 2006). Research also finds forced encounters, such as at work, sometimes increase discriminatory beliefs and behaviors (Pettigrew et al., 2011). Thus, interaction with dissimilar others could dismantle or reinforce conventional referential structures depending upon the nature of the interaction.

Moreover, referential structures may be spread through other means besides face-to-face interactions. Ridgeway and Balkwell (1997) argue a "broadcast process" of cultural diffusion may spread normative referential structures through means such as media consumption, interactions with institutions, and observing others' public social interactions. Therefore, the social messages one consumes will condition the degree they internalize normative referential structures. For instance, white Americans are consistently receiving messages about their dwindling status and value in American society, especially from conservative media (Mitchell et al., 2014; Resnick, 2017; Stern, 2016). With repeated messages about the advances of people of Color, particularly at what they perceive to be their expense, white Americans are more likely to believe not only that racial equality has been achieved, but that they are now the disadvantaged. Thus, as discussed in Chapter 1, the advances in technology, particularly in terms of the media, are a vital conditioning factor (exacerbating or mitigating) in understanding the cultural tensions in America – especially the anger and violence in white America.

Justice Perceptions

The degree of internalization of orthodox referential structures in turn impacts one's perceptions of fair outcomes. Status construction theory (Ridgeway, 1991) posits referential structures emerge due to the correlation between the distribution of resources and a nominal characteristic. Furthermore, this distribution is evaluated as just based on normative expectations of competence and worthiness. SDT argues one's referential structure provides the framework for evaluating the fairness of an outcome. Status construction theory assumes status value is granted based on expectations and outcomes, following the distributive justice principle of equity[9] (e.g., Adams, 1965; Cook & Hegtvedt, 1983; Folger, 1986; Jasso, 1980). Therefore, a fair outcome is based on one's status value. Thus, if one has internalized the normative referential structure, then they should believe whites, men, and the middle and upper classes rightfully *deserve* their place in the social structure because they are more worthy and qualified for the position, and in turn social inequalities are justified. If one has not internalized the normative referential structures, they are likely to have a different justice framework and think changes are needed in terms of social policies and institutions to reduce social inequality. Thus, one's status value and resultant degree of internalization of normative referential structures impact one's likelihood of believing in a just world (Furnham, 2003; Lerner, 1980).

Status Dissonance and a Positional Lens

One's justice perceptions then lead to the degree one experiences status dissonance. Status dissonance is the discrepancy between one's beliefs about how people with similar status characteristics to one's self should fall on the status hierarchy compared to how one believes others actually value similarly situ-ated others generally (Isom*, 2018). Such status dissonance arises from percep-tions of injustice toward self or similar others based on one's held referential structure. Status dissonance provides a lens through which one interacts with the world. In other words, it shapes their perceptions of world events as well as interpersonal interactions and guides one's behaviors. Figure 2.1 presents a nomological depiction of status dissonance theory.

Status Dissonance and Whites' Perceptions and Outlook

Due to its recency, SDT has yet to garner much theoretical or empirical atten-tion. However, a few studies lend it some empirical merit. First, in an empirical accompaniment to the original presentation of SDT, I found some support for status dissonance theory's general propositions (Isom*, 2018). Following a SDT framework, I posited that white, lower-class men are likely to believe enough has been done to give Blacks equal rights with whites in America due to their internalization of normative orthodox referential structures and resulting jus-tice framework. In turn, these beliefs were posited to create status dissonance increasing their likelihood of perceiving anti-white bias. Using a nationally rep-resentative sample of white Americans (Pew Research Center, 2017), I assessed the associations between status characteristics, perceptions of racial equality (i.e., resource/opportunity distribution), and perceptions of anti-white bias. Results suggested that among whites, men, those who self-identified as lower-class, and the least educated had the highest odds of perceiving racial equality, and in turn all these factors increased the odds of perceiving anti-white bias generally and personally, lending modest support to SDT.

Using a nationally representative sample (Isom* & Andersen, 2018), I directly assessed the existence of status dissonance and its association to various correlates of habitus angst (Chapter 3) and aggrieved entitlement (Chapter 4). Participants were asked two questions – "How important are people like you in American society?" and "How important should people like you be in American society?" responding on a scale of 1 = not important at all to 10 = absolutely essential. The difference between responses served as an indication of status dissonance, with higher scores indicating a greater feeling of being undervalued by society. Results suggest greater feelings of status dissonance are associated with belief in the American Dream (i.e., "that anyone can rise as high as their aspirations, talents, discipline, and dedicated hard work can take them" (2017*, p. 14)), perceptions of anti-white bias, and fear of whites' lost numerical majority in the decades to come for white Americans. Using the same indicator of status dissonance, in a recent repre-sentative survey of white Americans (Isom, 2022), those with greater feelings of status dissonance were less likely to report beliefs in Blacks experiencing

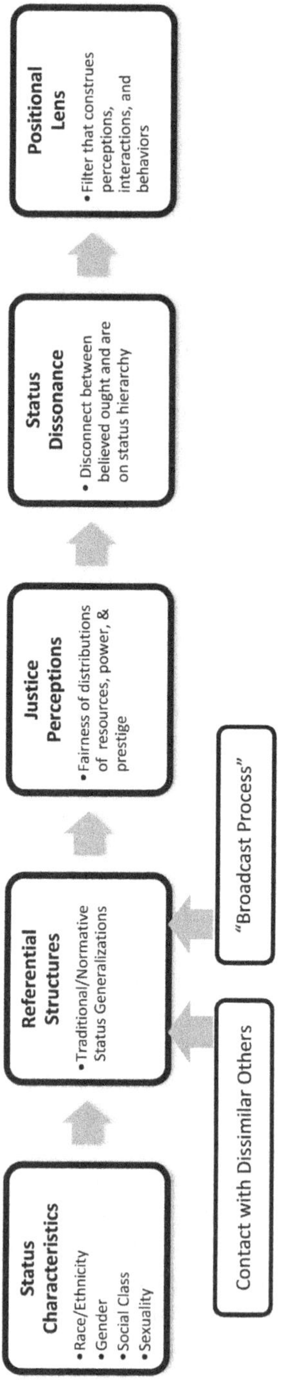

FIGURE 2.1 A nomological depiction of status dissonance theory

Status Characteristics
- Race/Ethnicity
- Gender
- Social Class
- Sexuality

Referential Structures
- Traditional/Normative Status Generalizations

Justice Perceptions
- Fairness of distributions of resources, power, & prestige

Status Dissonance
- Disconnect between believed ought and are on status hierarchy

Positional Lens
- Filter that construes perceptions, interactions, and behaviors

Contact with Dissimilar Others

"Broadcast Process"

discrimination in various context (except in encounters with police), were more likely to feel they are losing out on the American Dream, and were marginally more likely to report being willing to resort to violence to defend their rights. Together these findings lend credence to SDT, particularly as a framework for understanding why similarly situated individuals may perceive and respond differently to shifts in the social hierarchy.

SDT as a Gateway to White Crime

Thus, SDT purports feelings of status dissonance arise when individuals' believed status value based on the combination of their status characteristics and degree of internalization of orthodox referential structures does not align with how individuals believe society values people like themselves. These feelings of dissonance can lead to perceptions of injustice and provide a positional lens through which people perceive and interact with the social world. SDT, while not exclusively developed to explain whites' perceptions and behaviors (see Isom*, 2018 for a full discussion), does fill a void in the status literature, particularly in regard to understanding variations within high-status groups. Extensive research on status threat (Blalock, 1967; Blumer, 1958; Bobo, 1999; Bobo & Hutchings, 1996) finds perceptions of increases in the proportion of people of Color and/or their influence impacts whites' voting behaviors, political alignment, and racial attitudes (Abascal, 2015; Andrews & Seguin, 2015; Craig & Richeson, 2014a, 2014b; Enos, 2014; 2016; Outten et al., 2012; Willer et al., 2016) as well as increased use of direct social control, such as arrests rates of people of Color (Eitle et al., 2002; Parker et al., 2005). Yet, "status threat" is always assumed, leaving the underlying social psychological processes that lead to these perceptions and feelings and their potential outcomes unassessed. SDT provides a bridge between these literatures and lays a foundation for additional investigations into unpacking the causes and consequences of perceptions of anti-white bias, in addition to other forms of "status threat" (or habitus angst, see Chapter 3), and aggrieved entitlement (see Chapter 4) as well as mechanisms to counter status hierarchies. In the next chapters, the paths between status dissonance and the resultant habitus angst and aggrieved entitlement, as well as the subsequent likelihood of criminal and deviant behaviors, especially violence, for white Americans are further explored.

Notes

1 Much of this chapter first appeared in Isom* (2018); used by permission.
2 Each of these studies finds 30%–36% of their white respondents report experiencing racial discrimination.
3 Zero-sum beliefs are the perspective that gains of one group can only come at the expense of another (see Wilkins et al. (2015) for a detailed discussion).

4 Race has never been without status value in America (see Anderson (2016) for a critique of America's racial history). The argument presented by status construction theory (Ridgeway, 1991), however, is that the theorized conditions are sufficient, but only one potential mechanism of how status value may be attached to a nominal characteristic.

5 Status construction theory (Ridgeway, 1991) draws upon reward expectations theory (Ridgeway & Berger, 1986) to provide the method by which a nominal characteristic gains status value initially. Reward expectations theory suggests when people differ in resources, these differences are used to form performance expectations (Berger et al., 1980; Ridgeway & Berger, 1986). Performance expectations are generalized beliefs about one's and other's ability to meaningfully contribute to a task. Performance expectations may be based on assumptions about one's specific capability on a given task or general stereotypes about one's group affiliation (Berger et al., 1980; Ridgeway & Berger, 1986). Thus, a resource rich actor is assumed to be more competent and capable of performing a task than a resource poor actor. This assumption is made even if the actors are equal on all fronts (e.g., both are white) except for resource allocation. Resources, thus, act as a categorical cue that informs performance expectations (Ridgeway et al., 1985). Higher resources lead to higher performance expectations for the resource rich by the resource poor and the actor themself. In turn, the opposite is also true in relation to the resource poor. The performance expectations influence each actor to either participate more or less and in turn affects the perceptions of each actor as competent and/or influential. In the end, the resource rich are viewed as a worthy and competent member responsible for the accomplishment of the task. The resource poor are judged as less competent and worthy, but likely a likeable supporter of the group. The resource rich, therefore, gain high status and the resource poor gain low status in a specific social interaction (Berger & Conner, 1974; Ridgeway, 1991; Ridgeway & Berger, 1986). For a thorough overview of status construction theory, see Ridgeway (2015).

6 For instance, Katz and Cohen (1962) put their Black participants through assertion training to try to reduce white dominated mixed-race group interaction. While the intervention did increase Blacks' participation, it also evoked hostility and derogatory behavior from whites. See Webster and Driskell (1978) for a review of this research agenda and related works as well as their citations.

7 Reflected appraisals are a concept from symbolic interactionism and suggest our sense of self is based on how we believe others see us. See Cooley (1902) and Mead (1934) for foundational works as well as Felson (1985).

8 Research on social cognition demonstrates people use easily recognizable differences between people, such as race, to categorize people and formulate schemas about themselves and others. See Fiske and Taylor (2017) for a comprehensive overview of these processes.

9 Distributive justice is perceived fairness of outcomes based on the principles of equality, equity, and need. See Adams (1965), Cook and Hegtvedt (1983), Folger (1986), and Jasso (1980) as examples of foundational work in this expansive literature. Furthermore, see Hegtvedt and Isom (2014) for an overview for the relationship between justice and inequality.

References

Abascal, M. (2015). Us and them: Black-white relations in the wake of Hispanic population growth. *American Sociological Review, 80,* 789–813.

Adams, J. S. (1965). Inequity in social exchange. *Advances in Experimental Social Psychology, 2,* 267–299.

Anderson, C. (2016). *White rage: The unspoken truth of our racial divide.* Bloomsbury.

Andrews, K. T., & Seguin, C. (2015). Group threat and policy change: The spatial dynamics of prohibition politics, 1890–19191. *American Journal of Sociology, 121,* 475–510.

Berger, J., & Conner, T. L. (1974). Performance expectations and behavior in small groups: A revised formulation. In J. Berger, T. L. Conner, & M. H. Fisek (Eds.), *Expectation states theory: A theoretical program* (pp. 85–109). Wintrhrop.

Berger, J., & Fisek, M. H. (2006). Diffuse status characteristics and the spread of status value: A formal theory. *The American Journal of Sociology, 111,* 1038–1079.

Berger, J., Fisek, M. H., Norman, R. Z., & Zelditch, M. Jr. (1977). *Status characteristics and social interaction: An expectation states approach.* Elsevier.

Berger, J., Rosenholtz, S., & Zelditch, M. Jr. (1980). Status organizing process. *Annual Review of Sociology, 6,* 479–508.

Berger, J., & Webster, M. Jr. (2006). Expectations, status, and behavior. In P. J. Burke (Ed.), *Contemporary social psychological theories* (pp. 268–300). Stanford University Press.

Blalock, H. M. (1967). *Toward a theory of minority-group relations.* Wiley.

Blau, P. M. (1977). A macrosociological theory of social structure. *The American Journal of Sociology, 83*(1), 26–54.

Blumer, H. (1958). Race prejudice as a sense of group position. *The Pacific Sociological Review, 1,* 3–7.

Bobo, L. D. (1999). Prejudice as group position: Microfoundations of a sociological approach to racism and race relations. *Journal of Social Issues, 55,* 445–472.

Bobo, L., & Hutchings, V. L. (1996). Perceptions of racial group competition: Extending Blumer's theory of group position to a multiracial social context. *American Sociological Review, 61,* 951–972.

Bourdieu, P. (1987). What makes a social class? On the theoretical and practical existence of groups. *Berkeley Journal of Sociology, 32,* 1–17.

Brashears, M. E. (2008). Sex, society, and association: A cross-national examination of status construction theory. *Social Psychology Quarterly, 71*(1), 72–85.

Brezina, T., & Winder, K. (2003). Economic disadvantage, status generalization, and negative racial stereotyping by white Americans. *Social Psychology Quarterly, 66*(4), 402–418.

Bureau of Labor Statistics. (2021). *Highlights of women's earnings in 2020.* https://www.bls.gov/opub/reports/womens-earnings/2020/home.htm

Collins, P. H., & Bilge, S. (2016). *Intersectionality.* Polity Press.

Cook, K. S., & Hegtvedt, K. A. (1983). Distributive justice, equity, and equality. *Annual Review of Sociology, 9,* 217–241.

Cooley, C. H. (1902[1922]). *Human nature and social order.* Scribner.

Craig, M. A., & Richeson, J. A. (2014a). More diverse yet less tolerant? How the increasingly diverse racial landscape affects White Americans' racial attitudes. *Personality and Social Psychology Bulletin, 40,* 750–761.

Craig, M. A., & Richeson, J. A. (2014b). On the precipice of a "majority-minority" America: Perceived status threat from the racial demographic shift affects White Americans' political ideology. *Psychological Science, 25,* 1189–1197.

Eibach, R. P., & Keegan, T. (2006). Free at last? Social dominance, loss aversion, and white and Black Americans' differing assessments of progress towards racial equality. *Journal of Personality and Social Psychology, 90,* 453–467.

Eitle, D., D'Alessio, S., & Stolzenberg, L. (2002). Racial threat and social control: A test of the political, economic, and threat of Black crime hypotheses. *Social Forces*, *81*(2), 557–576.

Enos, R. D. (2014). Causal effect of intergroup contact on exclusionary attitudes. *Proceedings of the National Academy of Sciences*, *111*, 3699–3704.

Enos, R. D. (2016). What the demolition of public housing teaches us about the impact of racial threat on political behavior. *American Journal of Political Science*, *60*, 123–142.

Felson, R. B. (1985). Reflected appraisal and the development of self. *Social Psychology Quarterly*, *48*(1), 71–78.

Fiske, S. T., & Taylor, S. E. (2017). *Social cognition: From brains to culture* (3rd ed.). edition). Sage.

Folger, R. (1986). Re-thinking equity theory: A referent cognitions model. In H. Bierhoff, R. L. Cohen, & J. Greenberg (Eds.), *Justice in social relations* (pp. 145–163). Plenum Press.

Furnham, A. (2003). Belief in a just world: Research progress over the last decade. *Personality and Individual Differences*, *34*(5), 795–817.

Goar, C., & Sell, J. (2005). Using task definition to modify racial inequality within task groups. *The Sociological Quarterly*, *46*, 525–543.

Goffman, E. (1959). *The presentation of self in everyday life.* Anchor Books.

Hegtvedt, K. A., & Isom, D. (2014). Inequality: A matter of justice? In J. D. McLeod, M. Schwalbe, & E. Lawler (Eds.), *Handbook of the social psychology of inequality* (pp. 65–94). Springer.

Houts Picca, L., & Feagin, J. R. (2007). *Two-faced racism: Whites in the backstage and frontstage.* Routledge.

Hysom, S. J. (2009). Status valued goal objects and performance expectations. *Social Forces*, *87*(3), 1623–1648.

Isom*, D. A. (2018). Understanding white Americans' perceptions of "reverse" discrimination: An application of a new theory of status dissonance. In E. J. Lawler (Ed.), *Advances in group processes* (pp. 129–157). Emerald Publishing Limited.

Isom, D. A. (2022). *Whiteness and crime* [Unpublished data set]. University of South Carolina.

Isom*, D. A., & Andersen, T. S. (2018). *Aggrieved entitlement and discrimination* [Unpublished data set]. University of South Carolina.

Jasso, G. (1980). A new theory of distributive justice. *American Sociological Review*, *45*, 3–32.

Jones, J. M. (2008, August 4). *Majority of Americans say racism against Blacks widespread.* Gallup. http://www.gallup.com/poll/109258/Majority-Americans-Say-Racism-Against-Blacks-Widespread.aspx

Jones, R. P., Cox, D., Cooper, B., & Lienesch, R. (2017). *Majority of Americans oppose transgender bathroom restrictions.* Washington, DC: Public Religion Research Institute. http://www.prri.org/research/lgbt-transgender-bathroom-discrimination-religious-liberty/

Jones, R. P., Cox, D., Galston, W. A., & Dionne, E. J. Jr. (2011). *What it means to be American: Attitudes towards increasing diversity in America ten years after 9/11.* Washington, DC: Public Religion Research Institute. https://www.prri.org/research/what-it-means-to-be-american/

Katz, I., & Cohen, M. (1962). The effects of training Negros upon cooperative problem solving in biracial teams. *Journal of Abnormal and Social Psychology, 64*, 319–325.

♠Kimmel, M. (2017). *Angry white men: American masculinity at the end of an era.* Nation Books.

Lamont, M. (1992). *Money, morals and manners: The culture of the French and the American upper-middle class.* The University of Chicago Press.

Lerner, M. (1980). *The belief in a just world: A fundamental delusion.* Plenum.

Marx, K. (1867[2017]). *Capital (volume 1: A critique of the political economy).* Digireads.com Publishing.

Mead, G. H. (1934[1967]). *Mind, self, and society from the standpoint of a social behaviorist.* The University of Chicago Press.

Miller, S. (2020, June 11). *Black workers still earn less than their white counterparts.* Society for Human Resource Management. https://www.shrm.org/resourcesandtools/hr-topics/compensation/pages/racial-wage-gaps-persistence-poses-challenge.aspx

Mitchell, A., Gottfried, J., Kiley, J., & Masta, K. E. (2014). *Political polarization & media habits: From Fox News to Facebook, how liberals and conservatives keep up with politics.* Pew Research Center. http://www.journalism.org/2014/10/21/political-polarization-media-habits/

National Center for Education Statistics. (2022). *Table 306.20: Total fall enrollment in degree-granting postsecondary institutions, by level and control of institution and race/ethnicity or nonresident status of student: Selected years, 1976 through 2021.* Washington, DC: National Center for Education Statistics. https://nces.ed.gov/programs/digest/d22/tables/dt22_306.20.asp

Newman, D. M. (2010). *Sociology: Exploring the architecture of everyday life.* Pine Forge Press.

Norton, M. I., & Sommers, S. S. (2011). Whites see racism as a zero-sum game that they are now losing. *Perspectives on Psychological Science, 6*(3), 215–218.

Ortner, S. B. (1998). Identities: The hidden life of class. *Journal of Anthropological Research, 54*, 1–17.

Outten, H. R., Schmitt, M. T., Miller, D. A., & Garcia, A. L. (2012). Feeling threatened about the future: Whites' emotional reactions to anticipated ethnic demographic changes. *Personality and Social Psychology Bulletin, 38*, 14–25.

Parker, K. F., Stults, B. J., & Rice, S. K. (2005). Racial threat, concentrated disadvantage and social control: Considering the macro-level sources of variation in arrests. *Criminology, 43*(4), 1111–1134.

Pettigrew, T. F., & Tropp, L. R. (2006). A meta-analytic test of intergroup contact theory. *Journal of Personality and Social Psychology, 90*(5), 751–783.

Pettigrew, T. F., Tropp, L. R., Wagner, U., & Christ, O. (2011). Recent advances in intergroup contact theory. *International Journal of Intercultural Relations, 35*, 271–280.

Pew Research Center. (2016, June 27). *On views of race and inequality, Blacks and whites are worlds apart.* http://assets.pewresearch.org/wp-content/uploads/sites/3/2016/06/ST_2016.06.27_Race-Inequality-Final.pdf

Pew Research Center. (2017). *2016 racial attitudes in America iii survey* [Data file]. http://www.pewsocialtrends.org/dataset/2016-racial-attitudes-in-america-survey/

Resnick, B. (2017, January 28). White fear of demographic change is a powerful psychological force: Increasing diversity could make America a more hostile place. *Vox.*

https://www.vox.com/science-and-health/2017/1/26/14340542/white-fear-trump-psychology-minority-majority

Ridgeway, C. (1991). The social construction of status value: Gender and other nominal characteristics. *Social Forces, 70,* 367–386.

Ridgeway, C. (1997). Interaction and the conservation of gender inequality: Considering employment. *American Sociological Review, 62,* 218–235.

Ridgeway, C. L. (2015). Status construction theory. *The Blackwell Encyclopedia of Sociology.* https://doi.org/10.1002/9781405165518

Ridgeway, C. L., Backor, K., Li, Y. E., Tinkler, J. E., & Erickson, K. G. (2009). How easily does a social difference become a status distinction? Gender matters. *American Sociological Review, 74,* 44–62.

Ridgeway, C. L., & Balkwell, J. W. (1997). Group processes and the diffusion of status beliefs. *Social Psychology Quarterly, 60*(1), 14–31.

Ridgeway, C., & Berger, J. (1986). Expectations, legitimation and dominance in task groups. *American Sociological Review, 51,* 603–17.

Ridgeway, C., Berger, J., & Smith, L. (1985). Nonverbal cues and status expectation states account. *American Journal of Sociology, 90,* 955–78.

Ridgeway, C. L., Boyle, E. H., Kuipers, K. J., & Robinson, D. T. (1998). How do status beliefs develop? The role of resources and interactional experience. *American Sociological Review, 63,* 331–50.

Ridgeway, C., & Correll, S. J. (2006). Consensus and the creation of status beliefs. *Social Forces, 85*(1), 431–453.

Ridgeway, C., & Erickson, K. G. (2000). Creating and spreading status beliefs. *American Journal of Sociology, 106,* 579–615.

Ridgeway, C. L., & Glasgow, K. (1996). Creating and spreading status beliefs. *American Journal of Sociology, 106,* 579–615.

Sidanius, J., & Pratto, F. (1999). *Social dominance: An intergroup theory of social hierarchy and oppression.* Cambridge University Press.

Stern, K. (2016, November 23). My descent into the right-wing media vortex. *Vanity Fair.* https://www.vanityfair.com/news/2016/11/my-descent-into-the-right-wing-media-vortex

Thernstrom, A., & Thernstrom, S. (1998). *Black progress: How far we've come, and how far we have to go.* Washington, DC: Brookings Institution. https://www.brookings.edu/articles/black-progress-how-far-weve-come-and-how-far-we-have-to-go/

U.S. Equal Employment Opportunity Commission. (n.d.). *Job Patterns for Minorities and Women in Private Industry (EEO-1).* Washington, DC: U.S. Equal Employment Opportunity Commission. https://www.eeoc.gov/data/job-patterns-minorities-and-women-private-industry-eeo-1-0

Walker, L. S., Doerer, S. C., & Webster, M. Jr. (2014). Status, participation, and influence in task groups. *Sociological Perspectives, 57*(3), 364–381.

Walker, L. S., Webster, M. Jr., & Bianchi, A. J. (2011). Testing the spread of status value. *Social Science Research, 40,* 1652–1663.

Webster, M. Jr., & Driskell, J. E. Jr. (1978). Status generalization: A review and some new data. *American Sociological Review, 43,* 220–236.

Webster, M. Jr., & Hysom, S. (1998). Creating status characteristics. *American Sociological Review, 63,* 351–378.

Wilkins, C. L., Wellman, J. D., Babbitt, L. G., Toosi, N. R., & Schad, K. D. (2015). You can win but I can't lose: Bias against high-status groups increases their zero-sum beliefs about discrimination. *Journal of Experimental Social Psychology, 57,* 1–14.

Willer, R., Feinberg, M., & Watts, R. (2016). Threats to racial status promote tea party support among white Americans. Published online at http://dx.doi.org/10.2139/ssrn.2770186

Zweigenhaft, R. L. (2021). Diversity among Fortune 500 CEOs from 2000 to 2020: White women, hi-tech South Asians, and economically privileged multilingual immigrants from around the world. *Who rules America?* Blog Post. https://whorulesamerica.ucsc.edu/power/diversity_update_2020.html

3

HABITUS ANGST AND WHITE AMERICAN OFFENDING

Dismay and Antipathy in White America

As alluded to in Chapter 2, there is extensive research, particularly out of social psychology, that investigates the creation, perpetuation, and at times dismantling, of the concepts of "status," "value," "norms," and "frames."[1] In general, this literature argues these concepts are all social constructions that reinforce and maintain the status quo of social relations, that serve the interest of those in positions of power, and that fabricate and distort individuals' perceptions of self and others (e.g., Berger & Conner, 1974; Blau, 1977; Fiske & Taylor, 2017; Goar & Sell, 2005; Isom*, 2018; Ridgeway, 1991, 1997; Ridgeway & Correll, 2006; Ridgeway & Erickson, 2000; Ridgeway et al., 2009). In the United States – as well as other parts of the world touched by European colonization – the myth of white supremacy, along with patriarchal notions, underlies the hierarchical social structure that is upheld by orthodox beliefs and normative referential structures. American society was founded on the philosophies of racial oppression as a core component of society (Anderson, 2016; Feagin, 2013; Kendi, 2016; Wallis, 2016), from enslaving people of Africa for their labor to the taking of land from the Indigenous people of the Americas (Dunbar-Ortiz, 2015; 2021; Hannah-Jones et al., 2021; Smith, 2021). From these myths of superiority and entitlement came laws and institutional practices (e.g., Battalora, 2013; Glaude, 2016; López, 2006; Mills, 1997), as well as referential structures and frames that rationalize, legitimize, and reinforce racial (and other forms of) marginalization and inequity (Anderson, 2016; Feagin, 2013; McGhee, 2021; also see Introduction).

Feagin states, "The white racial frame includes a broad and persisting set of racial stereotypes, prejudices, ideologies, interlinked interpretations and

DOI: 10.4324/9781003167877-4

narratives, and visual images. It also includes racialized emotions and reactions that imbed inclinations to discriminate. This white racial frame, like most social frames, operates to assist people in defining, interpreting, conforming to, and acting in their everyday social worlds" (2013, p. xi). This white racial frame – or normative referential structure (see Chapter 2) – provides the hegemonic ideals that are woven into American society – from notions of success and the American Dream,* masculinity and manhood (Messerschmidt, 2000),*^ ideal femininity and beauty (Ridgeway, 2011; Wade & Ferree, 2015), to who is a criminal, what is a crime, and who deserves to be punished (Reiman & Leighton, 2020; Russell-Brown, 2009; Tonry, 1995, 2004, 2011) – all through a white lens that *all* people are socialized to believe. The internalization of historically rooted notions of self, culture, and society – or again, normative referential structures – is what Bourdieu (1977, 1990) dubbed "habitus" (see Lizardo (2004) for a fuller discussion of the complexity of this concept). More recently, Bonilla-Silva asserted *white habitus* is "a racialized, uninterrupted socialization process that conditions and creates whites' racial taste, perceptions, feelings, and emotions and their views of racial matters" (2018, p. 121). Thus, through socialization – from family, social networks, institutions, and media – we all learn, but particularly whites learn, the myths of whites' superiority engrained in all aspects of our society that inform our orthodox referential structures that reflect the white racial frame and create a white habitus for those (whites) who internalize it. Thus, differentiation in the internalization of white habitus impacts variations in feelings of status dissonance and the positional lens (or depth of the white racial fame) through which white folks see and interact with the world.

This positional lens or white racial frame, therefore, colors the way white people perceive, interpret, and interact with society, including their assessments of supposed "threats." Significant research and theorizing exist on various social threats – such as status threat (e.g., Feldman & Stenner, 1997; Jost et al., 2003; Nagi, 1963), intergroup conflict and social identity threat (e.g., Tajfel & Turner, 1979), and racial threat (e.g., Blalock, 1967; Bobo, 1983). While each of these are distinct, they are not necessarily mutually exclusive, and they do share a common theme: *fear*. Underlying all threat literature is a fear of things changing by those in advantaged positions. I argue these "threats" are not actual threats, but solely perceptions, and truly represent a fear of change – of norms, the status quo, orthodox beliefs, and so forth – in other words, the white habitus. This fear results in anxiety and uncertainty – or angst – that may spark a range of unruly coping mechanisms, including violence. Thus, the all-encompassing negative feelings evoked by perceptions of change to orthodox society represent what I call *habitus angst*. In this chapter, I provide an overview of the extant threat literature which supplies the empirical foundation for the concept of habitus angst and its ties to white deviant and violent behavior.

"Threats" to the White Status Quo

Theories and research on racial threat and status provide insight into white Americans' perceived threat to the status quo and their majority position. Substantial social psychological and sociological literature purports individuals gain their identity and self-worth through interactions with and self-comparisons to others (e.g., Goffman, 1959; Mead, 1934[1967]). Thus, people are motivated to establish and uphold their relative social position through such comparisons (e.g., Bobo, 1983; Tajfel & Turner, 1979). Beyond individuals holding intergroup biases (Hewston et al., 2002), racial threat theory posits that as racial minority populations increase, the racial majority (i.e., whites) use their political power and influence to increase state sanctioned control over minority groups (Blalock, 1967). Together, this literature generally argues that as whites perceive challenges to their power and privilege from holding the dominant status position—whether economically, politically, or sheer numbers—they tend to respond to such believed "threats" with increased social control of marginalized others (e.g., Blalock, 1967; Blumer, 1958; Bobo, 1999; Bobo & Hutchings, 1996), greater conservative ideological affiliation and political partisan divides (e.g., Blalock, 1967; Craig & Richeson, 2014; Willer et al., 2016), as well as increased implicit and explicit biases (e.g., Outten et al., 2012; Tajfel & Turner, 1979). Research finds whites' perceptions of racial threat are associated with increased police size and expenditures (Liska, 1992; Stults & Baumer, 2007), more arrests of people of Color (Eitle et al., 2002; Parker et al., 2005), higher incarceration rates of marginalized populations (Keen & Jacobs, 2009; Myers, 1990), disproportionate sentencing outcomes for people of Color (Crawford et al., 1998; Crow & Johnson, 2008), more racial stereotyping and higher fear of crime (Chiricos et al., 2004; Welch et al., 2011), as well as increased perceptions of ethnic and immigrant "threat" (Feldmeyer et al., 2015; Wang & Mears, 2010). Other research finds that the perceived economic, political, and social advantages of being a racial minority leads white Americans to identify with conservative movements and to support discriminatory policies (Morrison et al., 2009; Willer et al., 2016). Even more, these feelings of status threat increase a sense of solidarity among the dominant group (i.e., whites), thus hardening hostile feelings toward the "threatening" group (Umphress et al., 2007) and even potentially leading to violence and crime (Isom* & Andersen, 2020; Isom* & Grosholz, 2019). Furthermore, modern day political media only reinforces these polarities and perceived threats to whites, increasing the perceived divide (Garimella et al., 2018; Klein, 2020).

"Threat" as "Reverse" Discrimination and "Victimhood"

Literature has long established that threats to status and loss of power and privilege are a distinctly white strains rooted in their dominant social position in

American society. While white people's privileged position in society disallows their *true* oppression, many *still feel* discriminated against (Anderson, 2016; Hammon, 2013), and these feelings have real consequences, including potential violence and offending. One of the most common manifestations of whites' perceived status threat is their assessments of supposed "reverse" discrimination or anti-white bias (e.g., Craig & Richeson, 2017; Dover et al., 2016; Major et al., 2018; Scheepers & Ellemers, 2019). The limited research on whites who perceive experiencing anti-white bias finds that those who perceive the most discrimination tend to be the most downwardly mobile – lower income, less education (Borrell et al., 2007; Hausmann et al., 2008; Watson et al., 2002), and unemployed (Mayrl & Saperstein, 2013).* Yet, men with high levels of education also perceive substantial levels of anti-white bias (Lynch, 1989; Mayrl & Saperstein, 2013; Pincus, 2000). Other research finds white men are significantly more likely than their white female counterparts to report personally experiencing anti-white bias as well as believing such biases exists in society at large (Isom*, 2018). Increased perceptions of anti-white bias for whites are also associated with negative racial attitudes (Krysan, 2000; Rabinowitz et al., 2009; Tuch & Hughes, 2011), more conservative political and religious beliefs, as well as region of the country, particularly the South (Mayrl & Saperstein, 2013). Overall, men and those with the most orthodox views of social order tend to perceive the most anti-white bias.

Several qualitative scholars have linked whites' perceptions of anti-white bias with negative emotionality and potentially extremist beliefs and violence. For instance, through an examination of extremist discourse over a 20-year period, Berbrier (2000) uncovered how white supremacists have constructed themselves and all whites as victims of a changing society. He found perceptions of "reverse discrimination" are driven by the ideas that policies intended to level the playing field for marginalized groups, such as affirmative action, only benefit those populations at the expense of whites. Furthermore, the media is seen as an enemy spreading propaganda that degrades and devalues white people (Berbrier, 2000; also see Chapter 1). Another common belief is that there is a "double standard" in that "Other" groups have the right to preserve and celebrate their culture and heritage, but such is denied white Americans. Moreover, white supremacists often claim whites "built this great country" (David Duke as quoted by Berbrier, 2000, p. 181), thus whites' supposed distinct history, culture, and contributions are forgotten. Additionally, white supremacist groups claim having racial pride in being white is deemed unacceptable by society, and those that openly demonstrate such are scorned (Berbrier, 2000).

Around the same time as Berbrier (2000), Ferber (1998) engaged in a qualitative critical assessment of white supremacist ideological narratives and revealed how "throughout white supremacist discourse, whites are depicted as the victims of racial oppression" (p. 3). Ferber (1998), however, also assessed the intersections of gender and race revealing the myth of white superiority is not solely about the dominance of white people over non-white people, but white men over all others. And, when this preeminence is deemed to be under attack, some white men feel "anger, fear, confusion, and dedication" to defending their position in society (Ferber, 1998, p. 14). Notably, these victimhood sentiments are not limited to extremist groups but appear to be increasingly shared among more traditionally Republican and moderate whites who feel they have become politically and economically displaced (e.g., Kaufman, 2022; Kaufmann, 2019; Parker, 2021; Winlow et al., 2019; also see Chapter 1).* Thus, there is an existential "threat" to the status quo from "Others" due to perceptions of alienation on account of liberal policies and social progress (Wimberly, 2021).

"Threats" to White America and the Growing Far-Right

Recent racial and political tensions have sparked an upsurge in research on right-leaning political ideologies, particularly in rural[2] (white) America. For instance, in a qualitative examination of rural, small town USA, Wuthnow (2018) found such towns tend to establish "moral communities," in which morals are largely influenced by Christian values. Members of these moral communities feel a comfort within and obligation to their community and way of life. Fear and anger emerge as members of the community believe that their way of life is threatened by the government's inability to protect their economic and social interests. Furthermore, Wuthnow (2018) exposes an "us vs. them" culture in which misogyny and racism are firmly entrenched in the community. Overall, Wuthnow (2018) identifies how rural (white) America perceives social and economic shifts as problems rooted in the government's "failures" to preserve the "good ole days."

In a similar vein, Hochschild (2016) spent time in a rural city in Louisiana. She revealed that the cultural fabric nested within this community greatly influenced the community members' political ideologies. Hochschild (2016) notes that in a town consisting of mostly whites, its citizens believe that the government is willing to go out of its way to support women, immigrants, and people of Color in obtaining the American Dream, but not themselves. Thus, the town yearned for the "old days" that conservative groups, such as the Tea Party movement – and more recently Trump and the Alt-Right – promised to bring back.

Wuthnow (2018) and Hochschild's (2016) findings, along with others (e.g., Ferber, 1998; Isom*, 2018; Outten et al., 2012; Willer et al., 2016),* align with the emerging literature attempting to understand the recent far-right conservative movement, particularly among white Americans, and the election of Donald Trump. For instance, scholars find that Donald Trump's campaign promise to return America to the Christian and conservative values it (supposedly) once held significantly aided in his election and particularly appealed to white America (Gorski, 2019; Mutz, 2018). Moreover, many of the messages brandished from now former President Trump and the far-right parallel the ideologies of white supremacy (Eddington, 2018; Pettigrew, 2017; also see Chapter 1). Some scholars suggest that the spread of multiculturalism throughout society has led whites to perceive they are being "attacked" (Maskovsky, 2017; Sanchez, 2018). A key tactic of the white supremacist movement is to utilize victimhood rhetoric and discourse to attract followers (Ferber, 1998; Garland & Simi, 2011). A consensus of this research on such recruitment strategies has concluded that this victimhood rhetoric rests on the ideology that whites are facing "reverse racism" and are becoming the numerical and power minority in the American society (Ferber, 1998; Futrell & Simi, 2017; Lyons, 2017). Furthermore, as women continue to establish themselves in the workforce and in politics, many white men perceive a compounding threat of losing their rights and power to both people of Color and women (Blee & Creasap, 2010; DeKeseredy, 2022; Ferber, 2004). Additionally, adversarial trepidations around social issues such as pro-choice policies (Andaya, 2019), LGBTQ rights (Jones, 2018), immigration (Hooghe & Dassonneville, 2018), and healthcare (Sides et al., 2018) were (and still are) key concerns of Trumpers, the far-right, and a large portion of white America.

Yet, as Kaufmann points out, "in approaching populism, many have been seduced by stories of 'left-behind' working-class whites, the opioid crisis and rusting factories, so we've had numerous media 'safaris' into Trumpland which tend to simply confirm reporters' biases... Looking at fine-grained surveys of individual voters produces a different picture, in which values count for more than economics or geography" (2019, p. 6). Feeling discriminated against, devalued, and stigmatized are taken as attacks on one's identity, and thus impact one's self-esteem – and feeling of status dissonance (see Chapter 2). Furthermore, many believe the accumulation of all these "attacks" on whites will be the extinction of the white race, particularly among those with more far-right leanings. Thus, many whites believe steps must be taken to ensure the future and survival of white people (Berbrier, 2000). As Winlow and colleagues state, "...it's perfectly clear that anger, fear, and simmering resentment exist in abundance out there in the real world and people are looking for someone to blame" (2019, p. 28). Such narratives play off the fears and insecurities of people to construct a "victim" ideology (Boehme & Isom, 2020; Isom et al., 2022), as well as reinforce a white racial frame (Feagin, 2013) and threaten white habitus (Bonilla-Silva, 2018), thus creating habitus angst.

White Women Under "Threat"

Much of the extant research focuses on the "threats" felt by white men. This is reasonable given whites' perceptions and experiences of supposed threat are highly gendered. As America becomes a more equitable society, white privilege is not only under attack, but so is patriarchy. Hegemonic masculinity (i.e., white manhood) "... requires a double hierarchy: the power of men over women (as groups) and the power of some men over other men (by race, class, ethnicity, religion, and so on)" (2017*, p. 185; also see Ferber, 1998; Messerschmidt, 2014). Thus, men holding the most orthodox conservative beliefs about social order feel attacked from all sides when marginalized groups are granted the rights that they believe have been denied to them.

This is not to say, however, that white women do not also feel racially threatened. The white habitus is decidedly patriarchal, yet research suggests many white women tend to still internalize these orthodox normative referential structures and in turn perceive "threat" themselves for two distinct reasons: (1) while recognizing their subordination to white men, white women perceive their dominant status over people of Color as threatened; or (2) rather than seeking power, women desire the traditional patriarchal lifestyle valued within white normative ideology.

Sociological perspectives suggest that status hierarchies, such as those based on race, ethnicity, gender, and class, work in tandem; that is—one's overall status in the social hierarchy is based on the combined status value of one's characteristics (e.g., Collins, 2019; Crenshaw, 1990; Isom*, 2020a). Premised in Black feminist thought, some argue that white women do seek to maintain some semblance of power by asserting their status over men and women of Color (Collins, 2000). This is exemplified historically when examining white women's role in maintaining the system of slavery and asserting dominance over Black men and women—a role now believed to be far more prominent than previously suggested (e.g., Jones-Rogers, 2019)—as well as contemporarily when analyzing white women's egregious disrespect toward people of Color (e.g., using "Karen" to denote white women's racist behaviors [Romano, 2020]), attempts to control the Black population through calls to police (e.g., Amy Cooper [Bromwich, 2021]) or personal and instigated attacks, such as that on Emmet Till (Tyson, 2017). In essence, while white women may accept their subordination to white men, they may seek a sense of authority, superiority, and power over Black men and women, a desire that aligns well with the ideology of white habitus.

An alternative explanation is based on white women's strong commitment to patriarchy and traditional gender roles. Those who are most likely to support white habitus ideologies tend to endorse patriarchal gender normative beliefs, namely protecting women's roles as caregivers and men's roles as patriarchs (e.g., Blee, 1991, 1996, 2002, 2005; Blee & Creasap, 2010; Houts Picca & Feagin, 2007). Women, thus, may be driven by beliefs in traditional family norms and motherhood ideologies (Dow, 2016) whereby women are viewed as nonpolitical, mothers, wives, and nurturers (Lesselier, 2002). These women, who desire to live in a traditional, conservative household, may share in experiences of supposed threat and the sense of white victimhood because they want their men to be the traditional heads of household, the breadwinners, who support their families.* In other words, while white women may not seek to establish or maintain power, they may support white habitus notions when they perceive that their conservative orthodox lifestyle is under siege in a culturally evolving society.

Applying an intersectional lens may contextualize differences in the perspectives of white men and women. Specifically, understanding how statuses of race and gender are interrelated may shed light on women's alignment with far-right movements as well as explain differences in perceptions of threat and the resultant "victim" ideology between men and women. While intersectional approaches were developed as a framework for studying the experiences of historically marginalized people (Collins, 2019; Crenshaw, 1990), theorists have expanded the application of intersectionality to include those with both privileged and oppressed identities (Carbado, 2013; Frankenberg, 1993; Potter, 2015). This broadened application recognizes the multiplicity of identity and understands that social status is "simultaneously [influenced by] both oppression and privilege" (Burgess-Proctor, 2006, p. 36). Ultimately, white men and women likely perceive experiencing status threat and "victim" ideology, or habitus angst, differently as a result of their gendered lives, even while sharing a strong racial identity. I will return to this point in Chapter 7.

Status, Identity, Fragility, and the Resulting Angst

There is some debate in the literature if the "threat" felt in white America is rooted in power and status (e.g., Anderson, 2016)* or identity (e.g., Jardina, 2019; Kaufmann, 2019). Some of my recent work (Isom, Mikell, et al., 2021) lends credence to both arguments and the intricate relationships between them. While Kaufmann (2019) in particular outlines a general "whiteshift" across all the Western world, the unique racialized history of America (Anderson, 2016; Kendi, 2016; Wallis, 2016) must be central to understanding the distinct polarization in the United States. To be white in America means sitting atop the status hierarchy, holding most positions of power, setting the rules for social structure, and sharing an identity founded on *not* being a person of Color (Anderson, 2016; Rothstein, 2017; Wallis, 2016). Thus, to be pro-white in America is inherently anti-Black, and that racialized hierarchy cannot be ignored.[3] For America to overcome our polarized divides, we must first reconcile our racial past, including confronting our white supremacist underpinnings.

Such sentiments were reinforced in a recent qualitative investigation I conducted with colleagues (Isom, Mikell, et al., 2021) analyzing the relationships between perceptions of social concerns, feelings of status threat, perceptions of media and technology, and affiliation with the Alt-Right among white Americans. Overall, we found white Alt-Righters discussed feeling threatened and alienated by a changing society, a corrupt and too big government, and the liberal media. They blamed marginalized others, such as Blacks, women, immigrants, and the LGBTQ community for the shifting tides, and they yearned for a return to a time when their way of thinking and lifestyle went unquestioned. In other words, they felt habitus angst due to their fear of losing power, status, and sense of self tied to their whiteness. Yet, as mentioned prior, such feelings of habitus angst are not limited to those solely affiliated with extremist groups, but also overwhelmingly common in the (white) "Average Joe" (and Jane) (see Chapter 1). Furthermore, much of this habitus angst is tied to white fragility.

White fragility, as DiAngelo (2018) states, "is triggered by discomfort and anxiety, (and) is born of superiority and entitlement... is a powerful means of white racial control and the protection of white advantage" (p. 2). White fragility is associated with the range of negative emotions – anger, fear, guilt, shame – and behaviors – arguments, aggression, silence – that emerge when whites face some form of racial challenge. Though many whites do not consider themselves overtly racist, and particularly do not outwardly align with white supremacist extremism (Horowitz et al., 2019; Southern Poverty Law Center, n.d.), all people, and particularly whites, have been socialized into the norms of American society (i.e., orthodox referential structures) – informed by the white racial frame and myths of white superiority. Specifically, DiAngelo (2018) argues our white racial frame (Feagin, 2013) is upheld by three pillars of whiteness: (1) individualism; (2) that "racism" is only discrete, overt actions; and (3) the entitlement of white people. Therefore, we are socialized to believe only "bad" people are racist; one must engage in explicit, blatant bigoted behavior to be racist; racism is not systemic or a societal issue; and therefore (somehow), white people are meritoriously worthy of their status in society. Thus, any challenge to the orthodox racial (and other social) hierarch(ies) (i.e., normative referential structures, particularly the white racial frame) triggers a defense response in whites to one's sense of self and understanding of society (i.e., angst in response to their fragility). Even progressive whites are often triggered by a sense of superior morality to say, "but not me," but often still engage in behaviors that perpetuate inequities and do not challenge the status quo (DiAngelo, 2018; 2021; Hagerman, 2018).[4]

Therefore, all white people from across socioeconomic, political, sexuality, and gender identities, and all other status and identity spectrums, are susceptible to white fragility. In turn, they vary in their internalization of the white racial frame, and thus feelings of status dissonance, and therefore differ in their positional lens and embodiment of habitus angst – whether it manifest as shame or anger. Yet, underlying all the strife are feelings of fear – fear of change, fear of loss of sense of self, and fear of the unknown. Understanding the complexities of our history and resultant social structure and varied identities that are tied to differential internalized socialization (see Chapter 7), helps us better disentangle the experiences and expressions of habitus angst, as well as the varied coping strategies for it, within and between white people. Some of my research to date supports these associations.

For instance, some of my recent research found a lack of concern for discrimination toward Blacks, concern for illegal immigration, and concern about discrimination toward whites are significantly associated with stronger feelings of status threat (or habitus angst) for whites (Isom, Boehme, et al., 2021). A related study revealed holding a "victim" ideology was significantly associated with support for Donald Trump as well as anti-Black Lives Matter sentiments among white Americans. Moreover, holding patriarchal gender normative beliefs further amplified these associations (Isom et al., 2022). Additionally, a nationally representative survey revealed a sense of blame toward marginalized groups is significantly associated with feelings of anti-white bias for white Americans (Isom* & Andersen, 2018). My previous work has also found perceiving anti-white bias associated with anger and the likelihood of serious and violent offending, particularly for young white men (Isom* & Andersen, 2020), and these associations with deviant and criminal outcomes are stronger for whites than for Black or Latine youth (Isom*, 2020b; Isom* & Grosholz, 2019).[5]

From Angst to Entitlement

In this chapter, I argued what has long been labeled "threat" to white people is truly angst – or unspecified feelings of anxiety, fear, anger, frustration, or apprehension – and particularly habitus angst. The threat literature often highlights those in positions of power's fear of losing their status or challenges to the normative structure (e.g., Al-Kire et al., 2021), or white's fear of what may happen if they are no longer the numerical majority in society (Bai & Federico, 2020). Yet, these "threats" are unfounded and truly a folk devil[6] (Goode & Ben-Yehuda, 2009) as history, research, and cultural comparisons suggest societies thrive under more equitable circumstances and conditions (e.g., Bearfield et al., 2023; Blanchet et al., 2022; Bowdler & Harris, 2022; Schneider et al., 2021; Siripurapu, 2022). Far too many whites from across the board of other statuses and identities still hold on to (either explicitly or implicitly) notions of a white habitus that produces angst when opposed. This angst varies in scale and expression, but still requires some form of coping to return its host to equilibrium. In the following chapters, I present how one such coping strategy may be deviant and criminal behaviors, particularly violence, especially if one feels protected by their white privilege (see Chapter 5).

Such habitus angst is exemplified by two of the participants in one of my recent works[7] (Isom, Mikell, et al., 2021):

> Political correct individuals, feminist, the media, liberals, black lives matter are all able to voice their opinions and not receive backlash from all side but when people like me [white men] stand up and speak up for what's right we get slammed for it, it's bullshit.

> Somehow theres nothing wrong with gay pride, black power, or liking your own race but the second someone mentions white people being proud of being white, they act like someone was murdered.

These sentiments capture the feelings of many white Americans; a yearning for times of a more stable racial and social hierarchy and acceptance of the myth of white supremacy. Challenges to the status quo result in feelings of habitus angst for many whites. This habitus angst arises from fear of uncertainty, particularly about the uncertainty of the future and one's supposed entitlement to their position at the top of the racial strata. In Chapter 4, I explore whites' feelings of (aggrieved) entitlement, their ties to habitus angst, and their distinct, though not mutually exclusive, potential association with deviant and violent behavior.

Notes

1 Potions of this chapter appeared in or were revised from some of my earlier works, including Boehme and Isom (2020) https://www.tandfonline.com/doi/full/10.1080/15564886.2019.1679308; Isom*(2018); Isom* and Andersen (2020) Whitelash?'status threat, anger, and white America: A general strain theory approach. *Journal of Crime and Justice, copyright ©Midwestern Criminal Justice Association, reprinted by permission of Taylor & Francis Ltd*, https://www.tandfonline.com/doi/full/10.1080/0735648X.2019.1704835 on behalf of Midwestern Criminal Justice Association.; Isom et al. (2022), Isom, Boehme, et al. (2021), and Isom, Mikell, et al. (2021) https://www.tandfonline.com/doi/full/10.1080/02732173.2021.1885531. All used with permission.

2 Rural is defined as geographic areas consisting of low population numbers and an agriculturally driven economy that supplies much of America's food, water, energy, and other natural resource production (Goetz et al., 2018). "Rural" may be considered synonymous with white given most rural communities are majority white (typically upwards of 90%).

3 And the reverse – being pro-Black as fundamentally anti-white – is *not true* due to the racialized hierarchical social structure of America as well as the common history and culture that is often shared by Black people that is not the same for white people. Also see Note 1 of the Introduction.

4 These notions are similar to Messerschmidt's (2004) concept of complicit masculinity, or men who benefit from the normative ideals of hegemonic masculinity but are not necessarily engaged in direct forms of dominance and subordination of women. As well as Katz's (2006) macho paradox, where "not all men" are engaging in derogatory behaviors themselves or holding other men accountable, but still benefit from

being men. Thus, men such as this are complicitly reinforcing patriarchal power. So too are many liberal and progressive whites that fail to recognize their own white privilege nor do anything to counter it for the benefit of oppressed and marginalized others.

5 Isom* (2020b) and Isom* and Grosholz (2019) utilize the same data and measures making the resultant coefficients comparable. Blacks and whites are directly compared in Isom and Grosholz (2019): the incidence rate ratios (IRRs) for "microaggressions" or "perceived discrimination" on serious and violent offending = 1.25 and 3.62, respectively. The same measures in Isom* (2020b) assessing the same associations for Latine youth reveal an IRR = 2.99. Thus, within the Project on Human Development in Chicago Neighborhoods data (Earls et al., 2006), the associations between reported experiences of "discrimination" and criminal and deviant behaviors were strongest for white youth compared to Black and Latine youth.

6 A folk devil is the focus of a moral panic and the target of derogatory, stereotypical, and at times dangerous, scrutiny through the use of tactical imagery, framing, and rhetoric to justify the supposed "threat" from the demonized "Other" (Cohen, 1972; Goode & Ben-Yehuda, 2009).

7 Quotes are presented as they are in raw data form. Thus, any grammatical errors are the respondent's, not the author's. See Isom, Mikell, et al. (2021) for specific details about the data and study.

References

Al-Kire, R. L., Pasek, M. H., Tsang, J. A., & Rowatt, W. C. (2021). Christian no more: Christian Americans are threatened by their impending minority status. *Journal of Experimental Social Psychology, 97*, 104223.

Andaya, E. (2019). "I'm building a wall around my uterus": Abortion politics and the politics of othering in Trump's America. *Cultural Anthropology, 34*, 10–17.

Anderson, C. (2016). *White rage: The unspoken truth of our racial divide*. Bloomsbury.

Bai, H., & Federico, C. M. (2020). Collective existential threat mediates white population decline's effect on defensive reactions. *Group Processes and Intergroup Relations, 23*(3), 361–377.

Battalora, J. (2013). *Birth of a white nation: The invention of white people and its relevance today*. Strategic Book Publishing.

Bearfield, D., Humphrey, N., Portillo, S., & Riccucci, N. (2023). Dismantling institutional and structural racism: Implementation strategies across the United States. *Journal of Social Equity and Public Administration, 1*(1), 75–92.

Berbrier, M. (2000). The victim ideology of white supremacists and white separatists in the United States. *Sociological Focus, 33*(2), 175–191.

Berger, J., & Conner, T. L. (1974). Performance expectations and behavior in small groups: A revised formulation. In J. Berger, T. L. Conner, & M. H. Fisek (Eds.), *Expectation states theory: A theoretical program* (pp. 85–109). Wintrhrop.

Blalock, H. M. (1967). *Toward a theory of minority-group relations*. Macmillan.

Blanchet, T., Chancel, L., & Gethin, A. (2022). Why is Europe more equal than the United States? *American Economic Journal, 14*(4), 480–518.

Blau, P. M. (1977). A macrosociological theory of social structure. *The American Journal of Sociology, 83*(1), 26–54.

Blee, K. M. (1991). *Women and the Klan: Racism and gender in the 1920's*. University of California Press.

Blee, K. M. (1996). Becoming a racist: Women in contemporary Ku Klux Klan and neo-Nazi groups. *Gender & Society, 10*(6), 680–702.

Blee, K. M. (2002). *Inside organized racism: Women in the hate movement.* University of California Press.

Blee, K. M. (2005). Women and organized racial terrorism in the United States. *Studies in Conflict & Terrorism, 28*(5), 421–433.

Blee, K. M., & Creasap, K. A. (2010). Conservative and right-wing movements. *Annual Review of Sociology, 36*, 269–286.

Blumer, H. (1958). Race prejudice as a sense of group position. *The Pacific Sociological Review, 1*(1), 3–7.

Bobo, L. D. (1983). Whites' opposition to busing: Symbolic racism or realistic group conflict? *Journal of Personality and Social Psychology, 45*(6), 1196–1210.

Bobo, L. D. (1999). Prejudice as group position: Microfoundations of a sociological approach to racism and race relations. *Journal of Social Issues, 55*(3), 445–472.

Bobo, L., & Hutchings, V. L. (1996). Perceptions of racial group competition: Extending Blumer's theory of group position to a multiracial social context. *American Sociological Review, 61*(6), 951–972.

Boehme, H. M., & Isom, D. A. (2020). Alt-white? A gendered look at "victim" ideology and the alt-right. *Victims and Offenders, 15*(2), 174–196.

Bonilla-Silva, E. (2018). *Racism without racists: Color-blind racism and the persistence of racial inequality in America* (5th ed.). Rowman & Littlefield.

Borrell, L. N., Jacobs, D. R., Williams, D. R., Pletcher, M. J., Houston, T. K., & Kiefe, C. I. (2007). Self-reported racial discrimination and substance use in the coronary artery risk development in adults study. *American Journal of Epidemiology, 166*(9), 1068–1079.

Bourdieu, P. (1977). *Outline of a theory of practice.* Translated by Richard Nice. Cambridge University Press.

Bourdieu, P. (1990). *The logic of practice.* Polity Press.

Bowdler, J., & Harris, B. (2022, July 21). *Racial inequality in the United States.* U.S. Department of the Treasury. https://home.treasury.gov/news/featured-stories/racial-inequality-in-the-united-states

Bromwich, J. E. (2021, February 16). Amy Cooper, who falsely accused black birdwatcher, has charge dismissed. *The New York Times.* https://www.nytimes.com/2021/02/16/nyregion/amy-cooper-charges-dismissed.html

Burgess-Proctor, A. (2006). Intersections of race, class, gender, and crime: Future directions for feminist criminology. *Feminist Criminology, 1*(1), 27–47.

Carbado, D. W. (2013). Colorblind intersectionality. *Signs, 38*(4), 811–845.

Chiricos, T., Welch, K., & Gertz, M. (2004). Racial typification of crime and support for punitive measures. *Criminology, 42*(2), 358–390.

Cohen, S. (1972). *Folk devils and moral panics: The creation of the mods and the rockers.* MacGibbon and Kee Ltd.

Collins, P. H. (2000). *Black feminist thought: Knowledge, consciousness, and the politics of empowerment.* Routledge.

Collins, P. H. (2019). *Intersectionality as critical social theory.* Duke University Press.

Craig, M. A., & Richeson, J. A. (2014). On the precipice of a "majority-minority" America: Perceived status threat from the racial demographic shift affects white Americans' political ideology. *Psychological Science, 25*(6), 1189–1197.

Craig, M. A., & Richeson, J. A. (2017). Information about the U.S. racial demographic shifts triggers concerns about anti-white discrimination among the prospective white "minority. *PLoS One*, *12*(9), e0185389.

Crawford, C., Chiricos, T., & Kleck, G. (1998). Race, racial threat, and sentencing of habitual offenders. *Criminology*, *36*(3), 481–512.

Crenshaw, K. (1990). Mapping the margins: Intersectionality, identity politics, and violence against women of color. *Stanford Law Review*, *43*(6), 1241–1299.

Crow, M. S., & Johnson, K. A. (2008). Race, ethnicity, and habitual-offender sentencing: A multilevel analysis of individual and contextual threat. *Criminal Justice Policy Review*, *19*(1), 63–83.

DeKeseredy, W. S. (2022). Men's rights, gun ownership, racism, and the assault on women's reproductive health rights: Hidden connections. *Dignity*, *7*(3), Article 5.

DiAngelo, R. (2018). *White fragility: Why it's so hard for white people to talk about racism*. Beacon Press.

DiAngelo, R. (2021). *Nice racism: How progressive white people perpetuate racial harm*. Beacon Press.

Dover, T. L., Major, B., & Kaiser, C. R. (2016). Members of high-status groups are threatened by pro-diversity organizational messages. *Journal of Experimental Social Psychology*, *62*, 58–67.

Dow, D. M. (2016). Integrated motherhood: Beyond hegemonic ideologies of motherhood. *Journal of Marriage and Family*, *78*(1), 180–196.

Dunbar-Ortiz, R. (2015). *An indigenous peoples' history in the United States*. Beacon Press.

Dunbar-Ortiz, R. (2021). *Not "a nation of immigrants": Settler colonialism, white supremacy, and a history or erasure and exclusion*. Beacon Press.

Earls, F. J., Brooks-Gunn, J., Raudenbush, S. W., & Sampson, R. J. (2006). *Project on human development in Chicago neighborhoods (PHDCN): Master file, wave 3, 2000-2002*. Inter-university Consortium for Political and Social Research [distributor].

Eddington, S. M. (2018). The communicative constitution of hate organizations online: A semantic network analysis of "make America great again. *Social Media + Society*, *4*(3), 2056305118790763.

Eitle, D., D'Alessio, S. J., & Stolzenberg, L. (2002). Racial threat and social control: A test of the political, economic, and threat of black crime hypotheses. *Social Forces*, *81*(2), 557–576.

Feagin, J. R. (2013). *The white racial frame* (2nd ed.). Routledge.

Feldman, S., & Stenner, K. (1997). Perceived threat and authoritarianism. *Political Psychology*, *18*(4), 741–770.

Feldmeyer, B., Warren, P. Y., Siennick, S. E., & Neptune, M. (2015). Racial, ethnic, and immigrant threat: Is there a new criminal threat on state sentencing? *Journal of Research in Crime and Delinquency*, *52*(1), 62–92.

Ferber, A. L. (1998). *White man falling: Race, gender, and white supremacy*. Rowman & Littlefield.

Ferber, A. L. (Ed.). (2004). *Home-grown hate: Gender and organized racism*. Psychology Press.

Fiske, S. T., & Taylor, S. E. (2017). *Social cognition: From brains to culture* (3rd ed.). Sage.

Frankenberg, R. (1993). *White women, race matters: The social construction of whiteness*. University of Minnesota Press.

Futrell, R., & Simi, P. (2017, August 18). The [un] surprising alt-right. *Contexts*. https://contexts.org/articles/the-unsurprising-alt-right/

Garimella, K., De Francisci Morales, G., Gionis, A., & Mathioudakis, M. (2018, April). Political discourse on social media: Echo chambers, gatekeepers, and the price of bipartisanship. In *Proceedings of the 2018 world wide web conference* (pp. 913–922). International World Wide Web Conferences Steering Committee.

Garland, B., & Simi, P. (2011). A critique of using civil litigation to suppress white supremacist violence. *Criminal Justice Review, 36*(4), 498–512.

Glaude, E. S. Jr. (2016). *Democracy in black: How race still enslaves the American soul*. Crown Publishers.

Goar, C., & Sell, J. (2005). Using task definition to modify racial inequality within task groups. *The Sociological Quarterly, 46*, 525–543.

Goetz, S. J., Partridge, M. D., & Stephens, H. M. (2018). The economic status of rural America in the President Trump era and beyond. *Applied Economic Perspectives and Policy, 40*, 97–118.

Goffman, E. (1959). *The presentation of self in everyday life*. Anchor Books.

Goode, E., & Ben-Yehuda, N. (2009). *Moral panics: The social construction of deviance* (2nd ed.). Wiley-Blackwell.

Gorski, P. (2019). Why evangelicals voted for Trump: A critical cultural sociology. In J. L. Mast & J. C. Alexander (Eds.), *Politics of meaning/meaning of politics* (pp. 165–183). Springer.

Hagerman, M. A. (2018). *White kids: Growing up with privilege in a racially divided America*. NYU Press.

Hammon, B. (2013). Playing the race card: White Americans' sense of victimization in response to affirmative action. *Texas Hispanic Journal of Law and Policy, 19*, 95–120.

Hannah-Jones, N., Roper, C., Silverman, I., & Silverstein, J. (2021). *The 1619 project: A new origin story*. One World.

Hausmann, L. R. M., Jeong, K., Bost, J. E., & Ibrahim, S. A. (2008). Perceived discrimination in health care and health status in a racially diverse sample. *Medical Care, 46*(9), 905–914.

Hewston, M., Rubin, M., & Willis, H. (2002). Intergroup bias. *Annual Review of Psychology, 53*(1), 575–604.

Hochschild, A. R. (2016). *Strangers in their own land: Anger and mourning on the American right*. The New Press.

Hooghe, M., & Dassonneville, R. (2018). Explaining the Trump vote: The effect of racist resentment and antiimmigrant sentiments. *PS: Political Science and Politics, 51*(3), 528–534.

Horowitz, J. M., Brown, A., & Cox, K. (2019). *Views on race in America 2019*. Pew Research Center. https://www.pewsocialtrends.org/2019/04/09/race-in-america-2019/

Houts Picca, L., & Feagin, J. R. (2007). *Two-faced racism: Whites in the backstage and frontstage*. Routledge.

Isom*, D. A. (2018). Understanding white Americans' perceptions of "reverse" discrimination: An application of a new theory of status dissonance. In E. J. Lawler (Ed.), *Advances in group processes* (pp. 129–157). Emerald Publishing Limited.

Isom*, D. A. (2020a). Status, socialization, and identities: Central factors to understanding disparities in crime. *Sociology Compass, 14*(9), e12825.

Isom*, D. A. (2020b). The new Juan Crow? Unpacking the links between discrimination and crime for Latinxs. *Race and Justice, 10*(1), 20–42.

Isom*, D. A., & Andersen, T. S. (2018). *Aggrieved entitlement and discrimination* [Unpublished data set]. University of South Carolina.

Isom*, D. A., & Andersen, T. S. (2020). 'Whitelash?'status threat, anger, and white America: A general strain theory approach. *Journal of Crime and Justice, copyright, 43*(4), 414–432.

Isom, D. A., Boehme, H. M., Cann, D., & Wilson, A. (2022). The white right: A gendered look at the links between 'victim' ideology and anti-black lives matter sentiments in the era of Trump. *Critical Sociology, 48*(3), 475–500.

Isom, D. A., Boehme, H. M., Mikell, T. C., Chicoine, S., & Renner, M. (2021). Status threat, social concerns, and conservative media: A look at white America and the alt-right. *Societies, 11*, 72. https://doi.org/10.3390/soc11030072

Isom*, D. A., & Grosholz, J. M. (2019). Unpacking the racial disparity in crime from a racialized general strain theory perspective. *Deviant Behavior, 40*(12), 1445–1463.

Isom, D. A., Mikell, T. C., & Boehme, H. M. (2021). White America, threat to the status quo, and affiliation with the alt-right: A qualitative approach. *Sociological Spectrum, 41*(3), 213–228.

Jardina, A. (2019). *White identity politics*. Cambridge University Press.

Jones, T. (2018). Trump, trans students and transnational progress. *Sex Education, 18*(4), 479–494.

Jones-Rogers, S. E. (2019). *They were her property: White women as slave owners in the American south*. Yale University Press.

Jost, J. T., Glaser, J., Kruglanski, A. W., & Sulloway, F. J. (2003). Political conservatism as motivated social cognition. *Psychological Bulletin, 129*(3), 339–375.

Katz, J. (2006). *Macho paradox: Why some men hurt women and how all men can help*. Sourcebooks, Inc.

Kaufman, S. J. (2022). Is the US heading for a civil war? Scenarios for 2024-2025. *Studies in Conflict & Terrorism*. Advance online publication. http://doi.org/10.1080/1057 610X.2022.2137892.

Kaufmann, E. (2019). *Whiteshift: Populism, immigration, and the future of white majorities*. Abrams Press.

Keen, B., & Jacobs, D. (2009). Racial threat, partisan politics, and racial disparities in prison admissions: A panel analysis. *Criminology, 47*(1), 209–238.

Kendi, I. X. (2016). *Stamped from the beginning*. Bold Type Books.

♠Kimmel, M. (2017). *Angry white men: American masculinity at the end of an era*. Nation Books.

♠^Kimmel, M. (2018). *Guyland: The perilous world where boys become men*. Harper Perennial.

Klein, E. (2020). *Why we're polarized*. Avid Reader Press.

Krysan, M. (2000). Prejudice, politics, and public opinion: Understanding the sources of racial policy attitudes. *Annual Review of Sociology, 26*, 135–168.

Lesselier, C. (2002). Far-right women in France: The case of the national front. In P. Bacchetta & M. Power (Eds.), *Right-wing women: From conservatives to extremists around the world* (pp. 127–140). Routledge.

Liska, A. E. (Ed.). 1992. *Social threat and social control*. Suny Press.

Lizardo, O. (2004). The cognitive origins of Bourdieu's habitus. *Journal for the Theory of Social Behavior, 34*(4), 375–401.

López, I. H. (2006). *White by law: The legal construction of race*. New York University Press.

Lynch, F. (1989). *Invisible victims: White males and the crisis of affirmative action*. Praeger.

Lyons, M. N. (2017, January 20). *Ctrl-alt-delete: The origins and ideology of the alternative right*. Political Research Associates. https://politicalresearch.org/2017/01/20/ctrl-alt-delete-report-on-the-alternative-right

Major, B., Blodorn, A., & Blascovich, G. M. (2018). The threat of increasing diversity: Why many white Americans support Trump in the 2016 presidential election. *Group Processes & Intergroup Relations, 21*(6), 931–940.

Maskovsky, J. (2017). Toward the anthropology of white nationalist postracialism: Comments inspired by Hall, Goldstein, and Ingram's "The hands of Donald Trump. *HAU: Journal of Ethnographic Theory, 7*(1), 433–440.

Mayrl, D., & Saperstein, A. (2013). When white people report racial discrimination: The role of region, religion, and politics. *Social Science Research, 42*(3), 742–754.

McGhee, H. (2021). *The sum of us: What racism cost everyone and how we can prosper together*. One World.

Mead, G. H. (1934[1967]). *Mind, self, and society from the standpoint of a social behaviorist*. The University of Chicago Press.

Messerschmidt, J. W. (2000). *Nine lives: Adolescent masculinities, the body, and violence*. Routledge.

Messerschmidt, J. W. (2004). *Flesh & blood*. Rowman & Littlefield.

Messerschmidt, J. W. (2014). *Crime as structured action: Doing masculinities, race, class, sexuality, and crime* (2nd ed.). Rowman & Littlefield.

Mills, C. (1997). *The racial contract*. Cornell University Press.

Morrison, K. R., Fast, N. J., & Ybarra, O. (2009). Group status, perceptions of threat, and support for social inequality. *Journal of Experimental Social Psychology, 45*(1), 204–210.

Mutz, D. C. (2018). Status threat, not economic hardship, explains the 2016 presidential vote. *Proceedings of the National Academy of Sciences, 115*(19), E4330–E4339.

Myers, M. A. (1990). Black threat and incarceration in postbellum Georgia. *Social Forces, 69*(2), 373–393.

Nagi, S. Z. (1963). Status profile and reactions to status threats. *American Sociological Review, 28*, 440–443.

Outten, H. R., Schmitt, M. T., Miller, D. A., & Garcia, A. L. (2012). Feeling threatened about the future: Whites' emotional reactions to anticipated ethnic demographic changes. *Personality & Social Psychology Bulletin, 38*(1), 14–25.

Parker, C. S. (2021). Status threat: Moving the right further to the right? *Dædalus, 150*(2), 56–75.

Parker, K. F., Stults, B. J., & Rice, S. K. (2005). Racial threat, concentrated disadvantage and social control: Considering the macro-level sources of variation in arrests. *Criminology, 43*(4), 1111–1134.

Pettigrew, T. F. (2017). Social psychological perspectives on Trump supporters. *Journal of Social and Political Psychology, 5*(1), 107–116.

Pincus, F. L. (2000). Reverse discrimination vs. white privilege: An empirical study of alleged victims of affirmative action. *Race & Society, 3*, 1–22.

Potter, H. (2015). *Intersectionality and criminology: Disrupting and revolutionizing studies of crime*. Routledge.

Rabinowitz, J. L., Sears, D. O., Sidanius, J., & Krosnik, J. A. (2009). Why do white Americans oppose race-targeted policies? Clarifying the impact of symbolic racism. *Political Psychology, 30*(5), 805–828.

Reiman, J., & Leighton, P. (2020). *The rich get richer and the poor get prison: Thinking critically about class and criminal justice* (12th ed.). Routledge.

Ridgeway, C. (1991). The social construction of status value: Gender and other nominal characteristics. *Social Forces, 70*, 367–386.

Ridgeway, C. (1997). Interaction and the conservation of gender inequality: Considering employment. *American Sociological Review, 62*, 218–235.

Ridgeway, C. L. (2011). *Framed by gender: How gender inequality persists in the modern world.* Oxford University Press.

Ridgeway, C. L., Backor, K., Li, Y. E., Tinkler, J. E., & Erickson, K. G. (2009). How easily does a social difference become a status distinction? Gender matters. *American Sociological Review, 74*, 44–62.

Ridgeway, C., & Correll, S. J. (2006). Consensus and the creation of status beliefs. *Social Forces, 85*(1), 431–453.

Ridgeway, C., & Erickson, K. G. (2000). Creating and spreading status beliefs. *American Journal of Sociology, 106*, 579–615.

Romano, A. (2020, July 21). How "Karen" became a symbol of racism. *Vox.* https://www.vox.com/21317728/karen-meaning-meme-racist-coronavirus

Rothstein, R. (2017). *The color of law.* Liveright Publishing Company/W.W. Norton & Company.

Russell-Brown, K. K. (2009). *The color of crime: Racial hoaxes, white fear, Black Protectionism, police harassment, and other microaggressions* (2nd ed.). New York University Press.

Sanchez, J. C. (2018). Trump, the KKK, and the versatility of white supremacy rhetoric. *Journal of Contemporary Rhetoric, 8*, 44–56.

Scheepers, D., & Ellemers, N. (2019). Status stress: Explaining defensiveness to the resolution of social inequality in members of dominant groups. In J. Jetten & K. Peters (Eds.), *The social psychology of inequality* (pp. 267–287). Springer Nature Switzerland AG.

Schneider, E. C., Shah, A., Doty, M. M., Tikkanen, R., Fields, K., & Williams, R. D. II (2021, August 4). *Mirror, mirror 2021 - Reflecting poorly: Health care in the U.S. compared to other high-income countries.* Commonwealth Fund. https://doi.org/10.26099/01dv-h208

Sides, J., Tesler, M., & Vavreck, L. (2018). Hunting where the ducks are: Activating support for Donald Trump in the 2016 republican primary. *Journal of Elections, Public Opinion and Parties, 28*(2), 135–156.

Siripurapu, A. (2022, April 20). *The U.S. inequality debate.* Council on Foreign Relations. https://www.cfr.org/backgrounder/us-inequality-debate

Smith, C. (2021). *How the word is passed: A reckoning with the history of slavery across America.* Little, Brown and Company.

Southern Poverty Law Center. (n.d.). *Extremist files.* https://www.splcenter.org/fighting-hate/extremist-files

Stults, B. J., & Baumer, E. P. (2007). Racial context and police force size: Evaluating the empirical validity of the minority threat perspective. *American Journal of Sociology, 113*(2), 507–546.

Tajfel, H., & Turner, J. (1979). An integrative theory of intergroup conflict. In M. J. Hatch & M. Schultz (Eds.), *Organizational identity: A reader* (pp. 56–65). Oxford University Press.

Tonry, M. (1995). *Malign neglect: Race, crime, and punishment in America.* Oxford University Press.

Tonry, M. (2004). *Thinking about crime: Sense and sensibility in American penal culture.* Oxford University Press.

Tonry, M. (2011). *Punishing race: A continuing American dilemma.* Oxford University Press.

Tuch, S. A., & Hughes, M. (2011). Whites' racial policy attitudes in the twenty-first century: The continuing significance of racial resentment. *The Annals of the American Academy of Political and Social Science, 634,* 134–152.

Tyson, T. B. (2017). *The blood of Emmett Till.* Simon and Schuster.

Umphress, E. E., Smith-Crowe, K., Brief, A. P., Dietz, J., & Watkins, M. B. (2007). When birds of a feather flock together and when they do not: Status composition, social dominance orientation, and organizational attractiveness. *The Journal of Applied Psychology, 92*(2), 396–409.

Wade, L., & Ferree, M. M. (2015). *Gender: Ideas, interactions, institutions.* W. W. Norton & Company, Inc.

Wallis, J. (2016). *America's original sin: Racism, white privilege, and the bridge to a new America.* Brazos Press.

Wang, X., & Mears, D. P. (2010). A multilevel test of minority threat effects on sentencing. *Journal of Quantitative Criminology, 26*(2), 191–215.

Watson, J. M., Scarinci, I. C., Klesges, R. C., Slawson, D., & Beech, B. (2002). Race, socioeconomic status, and perceived discrimination among healthy women. *Journal of Women's Health and Gender-Based Medicine, 11*(5), 441–451.

Welch, K., Payne, A. A., Chiricos, T., & Gertz, M. (2011). The typification of Hispanics as criminals and support for punitive crime control policies. *Social Science Research, 40*(3), 822–840.

Willer, R., Feinberg, M., & Watts, R. (2016). Threats to racial status promote tea party support among white Americans. http://dx.doi.org/10.2139/ssrn.2770186

Wimberly, C. (2021). Propaganda and the nihilism of the alt-right. *Radical Philosophy Review, 24*(1), 21–46.

Winlow, S., Hall, S., & Treadwell, J. (2019). Why the left must change: Right-wing populism in context. In W. S. DeKeseredy & E. Currie (Eds.), *Progressive justice in an age of repression* (pp. 26–41). Routledge.

Wuthnow, R. (2018). *The left behind: Decline and rage in small-town America.* Princeton University Press.

4

AGGRIEVED ENTITLEMENT AND WHITE AMERICAN OFFENDING

Yearning for the "Good Ole Days"

Oh, America and its "dream" – the land of opportunity; where anyone can do or be anything if you just "work" hard enough... However, a true meritocratic nation is far from the American reality and in fact meritocracy is just that, a dream.[1] Though, the American ideal of owning a home on a one-person income, having kids you can afford to take to Disney World and send to college, and having enough savings to retire at age 65 (or earlier) – things almost always out of reach for most Americans of Color (Derenoncourt et al., 2022; Hoffman et al., 2022; Wilson & Darity, 2022) – used to be much more attainable, especially if you were white. Millennials, in fact, are the first (white) generation to not exceed their parents' earnings and wealth (Cramer et al., 2019), and actually carry more debt than any generation prior (DeMatteo, 2023; Dickler, 2022; Perry et al., 2021), and many are angry about it.

Whites, and especially men, are the most likely to believe in the "American Dream," notions of individual merit, and ideologies of the just world (Isom*, 2018),* as well as to oppose policies that promote social equity and the leveling of the playing field for people of Color, women, the LGBTQ community, immigrants, and others that are marginalized and oppressed (Hochschild, 2016; Isom, Boehme et al., 2021; Isom, Mikell et al., 2021; Jardina, 2019; Wuthnow, 2018).* What the majority of those most adamant conservative, white believers in "the dream" do not acknowledge (or even realize) is that *their ancestors* more than likely *didn't* do it on their own – they were provided social supports and opportunities that allowed them to get an education, earn a living wage, buy a home, and build a pension or retirement savings that weren't accessible to

DOI: 10.4324/9781003167877-5

Black, Brown, and other oppressed people (e.g., GI Bill [Humes, 2006]; redlining [Rothstein, 2017]; equalization schools [Dobrasko, 2008; Moffson, 2010]; banking and credit [Baradaran, 2019]). Many social welfare policies and insurances were cut following the Civil Rights era of the 1960s as most whites did not want Blacks to sit next to them in a restaurant, much less be their classmates, colleagues, or neighbors (Marx, 2011).

Changes in technology, shifts from a majority manufacturing to a service economy, and rising costs of living without comparable changes in income (especially minimum wages) over the last several decades have left many, but particularly the Millennial and younger generations, one emergency away from financial ruin (Cramer et al., 2019; Horowitz et al., 2020), and a global pandemic just added fuel to the fire. Paralleling these changes in the labor market and economy also came great advances for those that have been historically marginalized, oppressed, and excluded (e.g., increasing numbers of postsecondary degrees being conferred to students of Color [National Center for Education Statistics, n.d.]; a "record number" of Black Fortune 500 CEOs [Giacomazzo, 2022]; and, having the most diverse US Congress to date [Schaeffer, 2023]), adding to the pool of contenders and making the competition that much harder, especially in the eyes of the white, "Average Joe" that just wants to follow in his father's footsteps.

As Wuthnow (2018), Hochschild (2016), and others (e.g., Clark et al., 2022; Desmond & Western, 2018; Fitchen, 1991; Tickamyer & Duncan, 1990)[*] highlight, due to the loss of antiquated industries without modern advancements to replace them (e.g., coal [Mayer, 2021], oil, and gas [Naquin, 2022]; also see Hochschild, 2016); climate change, technological innovations, and trade pushing farmers out of business (e.g., Johnson & Lichter, 2019; Porter, 2018); and lack of access to skills training for or jobs in the contemporary labor market (e.g., Douglas et al., 2022; Slack et al., 2020), many whites feel "left behind" and wonder what they did "wrong" and why they are now "losing." For instance, "(i)f one believes this story of whites losing the presidency, losing cultural icons, losing college admission opportunities, and losing jobs [...] (then they) feel like they have lost more than they actually have lost, because of the immense power and resources (whites) had to begin with" (Hammon, 2013, p. 119). Therefore, "efforts to level the playing field may feel like water is rushing uphill, like it's reverse discrimination against (whites). Meritocracy sucks when you are suddenly one of the losers and not the winners" (2017[*], p. xiii). Whites feel this sense of loss and anger because they believe they are entitled – due to their effort, their birthright, their white (male) skin – to the job, the house, the family, "the American Dream" – it is all *theirs*. And, they are looking for someone to blame – people of Color, women, immigrants, liberals – when things don't go according to their plan.[*] They long for the "good ole days" they heard about from their parents and grandparents (and nostalgic movies and television) – when it was easier for white men to achieve that American Dream, their way of thinking and lifestyle went unquestioned, and the myth of white supremacy was unchallenged. In other words, when they were "entitled" to all the rewards of being a white (man) in America.

Aggrieved Entitlement... A Distinctly White Man Problem?

A sociologist* recently investigated the sense of "aggrieved entitlement" felt by many white Americans, particularly men. They define aggrieved entitlement as the "sense that those benefits to which you believed yourself entitled have been snatched away from you by unseen forces larger and more powerful. You feel yourself to be the heir to a great promise, the American Dream, which has turned into an impossible fantasy for the very people who were supposed to inherit it" (2017*, p. 18). This zero-sum belief system leaves many whites, and especially men, resentful and angry.* These feelings are amplified for the rural, working-class, undereducated who have witnessed industries decimated and opportunities for a comfortable life vanish over the past several decades. Such upheaval to the status quo "invariably distorts one's vision and leads to misdirected anger" (2017*, p. 24), typically toward marginalized groups.

While similar to habitus angst (see Chapter 3), aggrieved entitlement is a distinct form of racialized strain that reflects whites' perceptions of a failure to achieve a highly valued goal (i.e., the American Dream)[2] (Agnew, 2006). Such strain is associated with negative emotional states, such as feelings of anger and resentment, which spark corrective action – sometimes political (like the election of Donald Trump to the presidency) and sometimes criminal (such as hate speech or violence) – to retaliate against an alleged wrong and to restore the status quo.* These associations are further amplified by negative emotionality, such as an angry disposition (Agnew, 2006), which is fueled by consuming information and conversing with like-minded others that reinforce such sentiments (e.g., Martin & Yurukoglu, 2017; also see Chapters 1 and 2).

As the world around white men continues to move away from the life their parents and grandparents had, their aggrieved entitlement may surface in a form of victimhood. White men hold tightest to the American Dream; the idea that with diligence and hard work, anyone (like them particularly) can succeed. But, when the American Dream slips through their fingers, many internalize a victim ideology and potentially lash out in anger. Their attachment to the American Dream is grounded in a (white) masculine ideology, one that places self-worth on being a stoic, unemotional provider, the "company man," and a "guy's guy." But, with more people in the playing field, white men now feel disadvantaged and the victims of social progress. They blame people of Color, immigrants, women, the LGBTQ community, and policies surrounding the protection of marginalized groups. "A lot of men seem to believe … that a reassertion of traditional ideologies of masculinity – and a return to the exclusion of 'others' from the competitive marketplace – will somehow resolve this present malice" (2017*, p. 10). Thus, fear of change, competition, and failure fuel a sense of loss and victimhood, and blame is wrongly placed on marginalized others instead of social shifts (i.e., habitus angst), and it is all rooted in this sense of entitlement that comes from the internalized notions of patriarchy, the myths of white supremacy, and the white racial frame (see previous chapters, particularly the Introduction, Chapter 1, and Chapter 3). Thus, habitus angst and aggrieved entitlement reciprocally reinforce and amplify each other, fueling a need to cope with the educed strains.

Scholars further propose that class, like gender and race, also contributes to white men's aggrieved entitlement. Because class in today's America is more "racially and gender equal than ever before … it is the growing chasm between rich and poor that is the engine of that rage [of the angry white American]" (2017*, p. 25). Thus, it is the intersections of status and identities that facilitate one's sense of entitlement and in turn their angst at unmet expectations, and as status dissonance theory (Isom*, 2018; see Chapter 2) would posit, this is felt most by white men.

Entitled Patriarchy

While the ideologies of white supremacy, patriarchy, and capitalism that are the pillars of American society cannot be disentangled (hooks, 1984/2000), the argument that white men feel more aggrieved entitlement is not to say that white women do not feel entitled. Just as discussed in Chapter 3, white women may also internalize the normative referential structures that impact how they perceive and respond to social shifts. In particular, whites are more likely to internalize gender normative beliefs (e.g., Bjork-James, 2020a, 2020b; Blee & Tickamyer, 1995; DuRocher, 2011; Isom*, 2018; Nelson, 1998)*, thus notions about hegemonic masculinity and emphasized femininity (Connell, 1987; Katz, 2016; Messerschmidt, 2000, 2004, 2014, 2019), and in turn "do" and "redo" gender according to these frameworks (West & Zimmerman, 1987, 2009). Yet, numerous forms of masculinity and femininity exist depending on how consistent or inconsistent one's gender enactment is with the culturally normed ideals. "(H)egemonic masculinity emphasizes practices toward authority, control, competitive individualism, independence, aggressiveness, and the capacity for violence" (Messerschmidt, 1993, p. 385), or the ideologies that legitimize male domination over women and subordinate men (Connell & Messerschmidt, 2005; DeKeseredy, 2017; Katz, 2016). Such values are seen throughout American culture from the street to the boardroom, particularly for white men, and especially in those who many (white) Americans desire for a leader (Dragiewicz, 2018; Katz, 2016).

All other gender formulations, whether masculine or feminine, are defined in relation to this masculine ideal due to the patriarchal nature of Western society (Messerschmidt, 1993, 2014). Emphasized femininity is the cultural standard for women and the polar opposite of hegemonic masculinity. It is centered on serving the interests of men and can therefore be classified as a subordinated form of gender (Messerschmidt, 2004, 2014). Emphasized femininity reinforces notions of patriarchy and gender inequality by reiterating women's need to be compliant to men, nurturing to children, and empathic to others (Connell, 1987; Schippers, 2007). Thus, internalizing referential structures of emphasized femininity means women often long to be a mother and housewife and her husband to be the breadwinner, as well as being idolized over women of Color (see Chapter 3).

Furthermore, emphasized femininity informs our cultural standards of venerated beauty – particularly the glorification of youth, fair skin, light hair and eyes, and thinness, even if they are unrealistic and manufactured (e.g., Bar-Tal & Saxe, 1976; Cash & Henry, 1995; Deliovsky, 2008; Frankenberg, 1993; Henriques & Patnaik, 2020; Koontz Anthony et al., 2016; Ridgeway, 2011). These along with the reverence of female purity and chastity, have conventionally been used to frame white women as an entity to be protected and cherished (and Black women as objects to be used for men's pleasure or other gains [Collins, 2000; Stanton et al., 2022; Watson et al., 2019]). The internalization of these notions by (all) men justifies the abuse, mistreatment, oppression, and objectification of (all) women who fail to live up to such standards (e.g., De Coster & Heimer, 2021; DeKeseredy, 2021; Lateef et al., 2023; Lelaurain et al., 2021; McKinley et al., 2021; Ritchie, 2017). And the belief in such referential structures for women creates body image issues, harms social relationships, and causes emotional distress (e.g., Bryant, 2019; Martz et al., 1995; Poran, 2002), along with other negative outcomes. Furthermore, for white women, adopting the patriarchal norms of emphasized femininity not only influences feelings of habitus angst (see Chapter 3), but creates distinct perceptions of entitlement. White women may feel entitled to the *choice* of working or being a stay-at-home mother, men's adoration, or the protections of the police. While these too may lead to negative behaviors and disparate outcomes, they are less likely to result in direct harm or violence (except in the case of the police). Hegemonic masculinity, on the other hand, emphasizes anger and violence as ideal masculine resources to demonstrate control and power, and in turn one's "manliness" (Messerschmidt, 2000, 2004, 2014, 2019). Therefore, some of the most directly harmful outcomes of aggrieved entitlement are tied to the myths of white supremacist patriarchy and their influence on white men. Below I outline some of the more egregious examples and how they are associated with crime and violence.

Entitled to Power

As discussed at the beginning of this book (see Introduction), America was created *by* white men *for* white men. For centuries, women and people of Color were seen as property – *not* people – not allowed to get an education, to vote, to have wealth or property themselves, or to be recognized as equal human beings with inalienable rights that deserved dignity and respect (Anderson, 2016; Kendi, 2016; McGhee, 2021; Smith, 2021; Wallis, 2016). Despite the historically utilized rationales, white men's touted "superiority" is *not* innate or biological *nor* imposed by some higher being, but socially constructed to serve a purpose that has been absorbed into the fabric of America's structure, institutions, and norms (Battalora, 2013; Feagin, 2013; López, 2006; Mills, 1997). And while those that are oppressed and marginalized have fought for centuries for America to live up to its imagined claims of "for all," in reality, the system works just as it was intended by the Founding Fathers – "…to ensure that white men hoard power" (Oluo, 2021, p. 4).

There is a reason the United States has yet to have a woman president and only one male president of Color. There is a reason the top ten of the Forbes 400 richest people in America are white men (LaFranco & Peterson-Withorn, 2023). Beyond the historical barriers to wealth, education, and access that overwhelming advantaged white men, there are also our cultural norms informed by the myths of white supremacy and patriarchy that define who is entitled to such positions of power. As Katz (2016) states, "the desire for a strong virile man in the White House runs deep in the American DNA" (p. ix). The myths of white male superiority have tainted American culture's notions about the qualities of good leadership and who embodies them. Therefore, we often elect people that are not the best for the country, or our own personal interests (Hochschild, 2016; Katz, 2016; Nance, 2022; Oluo, 2021), but instead folks that reflect the orthodox referential structural norms of (white) masculinity.

Entangled in these (racialized) gendered notions of worth are also our false beliefs in American meritocracy, meaning the idea that people get what they deserve based on their merit in terms of intellect, talent, effort, and achievement, not wealth or social status. Thus, when for centuries white men have held all the power and influence, this mythical notion reinforced the idea that this was something white men were worthy of and entitled to. As Homans (1950) would put it, what *is* became what *ought* to be. Yet, instead of those holding positions of power and influence attaining such because of legitimate qualifications, the myths of white male supremacy spawned a culture of mediocrity, or more specifically, a mediocre-white-man-industrial complex (Oluo, 2021).

As Oluo (2021) explains, the deep roots of the myth of white male supremacy have led to white men assuming superiority is their birthright, or in other words, their entitlement. "All you need to be successful as a white man is to be better off than women and people of Color. And all you need to do to distract white men from how they are actually fairing is to task them with the responsibility of ensuring that people of Color and women don't take what little might be theirs" (Oluo, 2021, p. 11). So, the wealthy white men that truly hold the power maintain their positions at the top by convincing the white "Average Joe" that he is "better than" simply by existing, and that he is entitled to those sentiments. Therefore, perceived entitlement to status (in the workplace, in public, or the home) is an assumed inheritance removed from any legitimate effort, achievements, worth, or excellence, and instead sparks mediocrity (Oluo, 2021). "Our culture has shaped the expectation of greatness exclusively around white men by erasing the achievements of women and people of Color from our histories, by excluding women and people of Color as heroes in our films and books, by ensuring that the qualified applicant pool is restricted to white male social networks... It is a mediocrity that maintains a violent, sexist, racist status quo... all because it would challenge the idea of white men as the center of our country" (Oluo, 2021, pp. 6–7). Perceptions of entitlement to positions of power and influence do not only lead to white men behaving badly but also limits the possibilities of greatness for our society. More inclusive and complete education, more diverse social networks, more equitable boardrooms, and a more representative government facilitate creativity and innovation (and justice) more so than from any homogeneous perspective (e.g., Cunningham & Nite, 2020; Hunt et al., 2020; Miller Cole, 2020; Stanford, 2020). Thus, America's touted "greatness" is hindered, not amplified, by its own internalization of the myth of white men's entitlement to power. And even more so, far too many of its citizens are not only held back but also harmed by oppressive (and violent) institutional and political policies and actions.

Entitled to Individualism

White folks are also free from essentialism. Essentialism is the belief that those within a common culture or social status share inherent, universal qualities or essences (Popper, 1962). Such ideas often underlie stereotypes and tokenism frequently applied to people of Color and other marginalized groups (hooks, 1991). Yet, white people never have to speak on behalf of their entire race or answer for the actions of someone else because of their white skin; they are free from the burden of race, thus often claim to be "color-blind" (Bonilla-Silva, 2018; DiAngelo, 2018). White people, and especially white men, are allowed to be distinct and unique individuals when other folks are often not.

More broadly speaking, white people are allowed to be fully complete human beings navigating a society that was crafted *for them*. White people, particularly men, rarely enter a space and don't feel like they belong. And why shouldn't they? American society and institutions were built for them (Anderson, 2015).

They have always been reflected in our history books, on television and the big screen, in politics, as the heads of boardrooms, and even at the front of our class-rooms. Our heroes, fictional and otherwise, have historically been white. White children, again especially boys, have had zero problems finding reflections of themselves in positions of power, influence, and prominence; they truly could be anything they wanted to be (DiAngelo, 2018). (And so could white girls if they wanted to be a princess, a housewife, or a teacher.) It has only been recently that children of Color, LGBTQ folks, those with disabilities, and other marginalized people could see themselves reflected by the media or having great power and influence (Abbott, 2021; Bakkenes, 2022; Huang, 2021). Yet, this too has been met with opposition as state governments are attempting to ban and criminalize the teaching of others' lived experiences and limit what is available in public libraries (e.g., Friedman & Johnson, 2022; Schwartz, 2021; Young, 2023).

Furthermore, "being white" in the United States is an identity often left un-questioned. White people don't think about their race; they are "just people" (DiAngelo, 2018). Whiteness and Americanness have become so closely inter-twined that they are almost indistinguishable in public discourse. While other ethnic and racial groups (e.g., Black Americans or Asian Americans) must often use qualifiers to demonstrate their belonging to the nation, white Americans typically don't face such challenges. Whiteness therefore appears as a default, invisible identity, a norm against which people of Color are defined as "Oth-ers." Thus, whites are entitled to be individuals and assessed as such while our society does not give that same leeway to people of Color. Race is an unspoken mitigating factor to understanding white people's successes and strife, but an exacerbating factor that prohibits the consideration of individual abilities or cir-cumstances for others.

Even well-intentioned white people often cannot step outside of themselves to try to center the experiences of others and allow others' voices to be heard over themselves (DiAngelo, 2018; 2021), and often progressive whites do more harm in their attempts at allyship than good. In efforts to find commonality across racial lines, whites may (often unintentionally) patronize or belittle peo-ple of Color as they frequently try to step into the "white savior" role (DiAn-gelo, 2021; Hagerman, 2018; Wise, 2010). White people habitually feel entitled to the position of leader, helper, or even savior for those in marginalized posi-tions, especially when they see racism as an individual problem instead of a structural one. When whites cannot recognize that racism and myths of white supremacy are embedded within society and social structures, then they define racism solely as overtly, individual racist actions enacted by "racists," which they themselves cannot be (DiAngelo, 2018). Not being able to understand "whiteness" and the myth of white supremacy as ideologies that they too benefit from due to their white skin disallows them from seeing beyond their individual selves (DiAngelo, 2018, 2021; Wise, 2010). Thus, the entitlement of individualism protects them from being "racist" (by their definition) and blinds them from truly hearing marginalized others and seeing the inequities and injustices around them due to their positional lens (see Bonilla-Silva, 2018; DiAngelo, 2018, 2021; Wise, 2010).

Entitled to Women and Sex

A central aspect of hegemonic masculinity is one's sexual prowess and the objectification of women, thus it is fundamentally anti-feminist (Connell & Messerschmidt, 2005; DeKeseredy, 2017; Messerschmidt, 2019). The "decline of men" rhetoric and rise of men's rights groups as backlash to the second wave feminism in the 1970s (Carrigan et al., 1985; Messner, 2016) have evolved into the modern "manosphere," especially online (Ging, 2019; Nagle, 2017). The internet has allowed these groups to connect like never before, and the positive reinforcement of interacting with each other has made their discourse, ideologies, and behaviors even more extreme and dangerous (Nagle, 2017). While there are distinctions between varied "men's interests" groups that fall under the wide umbrella of the manosphere, there are also several commonalities: they are extremely misogynistic and advocate sexism, racism, and violence against women (Baele et al., 2021; Chang, 2022; Ging, 2019; Menzie, 2022; Nagle, 2017; O'Malley et al., 2022; Pelzer et al., 2021; Preston et al., 2021); they promote the philosophy of the Red Pill, taken from the film *The Matrix*, referring to men recognizing women's and feminism's purported brainwashing and bigotry and calls for men to reclaim their privileges and dominance over women (Ging, 2019; Glace et al., 2021; Halpin, 2022); and, they are associated with, support, and/or celebrate mass violence (Chemaly, 2015; Menzie, 2022; Nagle, 2017). While there is much debate about how these groups "do" masculinity (e.g., Bridges & Pascoe, 2014; Ging, 2019; Nagle, 2017; Witt, 2020), Halpin (2022) argues that overall, they utilize the perceptions of hegemonic masculinity to legitimize the subordination, degradation, and victimization of women. One such group that exemplifies this notion are "incels" (or "involuntary celibates").

Incels, largely a disjointed online network (see Ging, 2019; Witt, 2020; very similar to and entangled with the far-right [see Halpin, 2022; also earlier chapters, particularly Chapters 1 and 3]), generally believe women, and particularly feminism, is to blame for their celibacy; they blame gender equity policies for many of the world's problems; and, they yearn for a time when orthodox patriarchy ruled society and men had more control over women (Daly & Reed, 2022; Ging, 2019; Hoffman et al., 2020). Extensive qualitative research has examined incels' online discourse (e.g., Byerly, 2020; Farrell et al., 2019; Ging, 2019; Maxwell et al., 2020; O'Malley et al., 2022; van Valkenburgh, 2021; Zimmerman, 2022) finding repeatedly themes of perceived loss, injury, and entitlement.

"Incels have strong connections to other extreme right-wing movements like those promoting unbridled gun ownership, homophobia, racist discourses and practices, and policies and laws aimed at ending women's control over their reproductive health" (DeKeseredy, 2022, p. 3). Some have even argued incels are essentially domestic terrorists (Hoffman et al., 2020) and that such online misogyny should be considered a hate crime (Barker & Jurasz, 2019; also see Bates, 2020; Belew & Gutiérrez, 2021; DePrince, 2022). Daly and Reed (2022) conducted interviews with self-identified incels to better understand their situations, attitudes, and experiences. Participants described challenges finding an intimate partner and often emphasized their shortcomings or inadequacies based on cultural norms that they believed women find unappealing. Many also discussed being bullied as children for their looks or lack of athletic abilities. As a result, many reported "black pilling" or accepting their supposed fate as celibate, and thus in turn engaging in "shit-posting" (i.e., "commenting or posting intentionally shocking or disturbing content for reactions or popularity on forums or social media sites" [Daly & Reed, 2022, p. 15]) out of anger and retribution for their presumed destiny (also see Rowland (2022) for a discussion of the rhetoric around incels' "small dick problems"; as well as DeKeseredy (2023)). Daly and Reed's (2022) findings not only align with the assessments of incel and manosphere online discourse but also provide insight on how these men's understanding of manhood and masculinity fuels their perceptions of entitlement to sex and women and the resulting misogynistic, derogatory, and sometimes violent behaviors.

These feelings, however, are not limited to those whom self-identify with inceldom. Drawing upon the common themes tied to incels and the larger manosphere, Scaptura and Boyle (2020) found those reporting more strain related to living up to hegemonic masculine ideals and those reporting a more hateful disposition were significantly more likely to disclose having fantasies about rape as well as mass violence among their sample of young men. Furthermore, in a qualitative assessment of the open-ended supplementary questions of a college campus climate survey, DeKeseredy and colleagues (2019) found perceptions of aggrieved entitlement were prominent among college-aged, white men, regardless of socioeconomic class. And, similar to Scaptura and Boyle (2020), they found feelings of aggrieved entitlement were closely intertwined with promotion of rape myths and the denial of issues of sexual assault on campus (DeKeseredy et al., 2019). Thus, these sentiments and the resultant impacts, much like those aligning with far-right notions (Boehme & Isom*, 2020; Isom et al., 2022), are much more common among (white) men than many want to believe. While the incel community is not exclusively white (much like the Proud Boys [Campbell, 2022]), the vast majority are (Halpin & Richard, 2021), and the myth of white male supremacy is central to their habitus angst and aggrieved entitlement. Their alleged entitlement to sex and women because they are men underlies their frustration, anger, and resultant violence and terror – online and in reality – that they impose upon women and others. These associations also shed light on why so many white men abuse their intimate partners and significant others (Durose et al., 2005; US Department of Health & Human Services, 2022). Yet, perceived entitlement to sex is not white men's only trigger for violence – as many believe white men have an innate right to violence.

Entitled to Violence

White men have always used violence to maintain their positions of power and social control, from the whips, shackles, and muskets used to terrorize and control enslaved people (Hadden, 2001) to the tasers, pepper spray, billy clubs, semi-automatic handguns, and assault rifles of modern policing (Balko, 2021; also see Box 4.1). The Second Amendment to the US Constitution was ratified on December 15, 1791, and states, "A well regulated Militia, being necessary to the security of a free State, the right of the people to keep and bear Arms, shall not be infringed." Yet, just as with the Constitution and other amendments of the Bill of Rights, the Founding Fathers did not intend such rights be extended to people of Color when they stated, "the right of the people." In fact, slave codes throughout the South during the time prohibited enslaved people from carrying or using a firearm unless under the supervision of a white person (Anderson, 2021; Ekwell, n.d.). Furthermore, "the militia" were not meant to protect citizens against a tyrannical government as orthodoxically advertised, but to bolster slave patrols (the original police force [Hadden, 2001]) to maintain control of the enslaved population (Anderson, 2021). Therefore, firearms as a means of control through violence was intended for white men – to control Black people – and white men only.

Having a firearm, and thus the easily accessible ability to readily violently harm or kill someone, is the epitome of white hegemonic masculinity. Thus, it follows that this "right" is a foundational pillar of this country that was built on the backs of enslaved Black labor. It is also, therefore, unsurprising that the United States has the second highest firearm-related deaths in the world (World Population Review, 2023), with the highest rates of death being in the Southern and Midwest regions of the country (Centers of Disease Control and Prevention, 2022) which are also home to the most gun-friendly states (Wood, 2022). Over 40,000 people in the United States died due to gun related injuries in 2020, more than any year prior; and for the first time in history, guns are the leading cause of death for those under the age of 20 (National Institute of Health Care Management, 2022). Gun violence, in fact, is now considered a major public health problem by the American Public Health Association (n.d.). There are more firearms than people in the United States (Azrael et al., 2017; Karp, 2018), and most of those weapons are owned by white, rural people, particularly men

(Schaeffer, 2021). We are also a country plagued by mass violence, as we have seen an ever-growing rise in mass shootings and hate crimes in recent years (The Violence Project, n.d.; Southern Poverty Law Center, 2022); and, at the time of authorship in early 2023, the United States has had more mass shooting incidents than days this year (Gun Violence Archive, 2023). Perpetrators of mass violence are most commonly white men, and many are motivated by sexist, racist, homophobic, and xenophobic beliefs (Peterson & Densley, 2021).

In the wake of such perpetual violence, most in this country want stricter gun control policies (Schaeffer, 2021). Yet, groups such as the National Rifle Association (NRA) and Gun Owners of America (GOA), along with the far-right, use their political clout to ease gun restrictions instead of promoting policies that would lessen the likelihood of gun violence (Giffords, 2023).[3] There are limited regulations on who may purchase a firearm; there are loopholes in place to bypass waiting periods and background checks; there are no standards for training on use of or safety around firearms; there are no databases of gun owners or the types and number of guns one may possess, nor limits on such; and, there are no regulations or oversights on how guns are to be locked up and maintained (see Smart et al. (2023) for a more detailed discussion of the limitations on gun control policies in the United States). Yet, the NRA, GOA, and others promote the myths of the "good guy with a gun" who will save us all (Cutilletta, 2020) despite the vast majority of the guns used in crimes being legally obtained, and nearly 46% of firearms utilized in crimes being purchased within three years prior to the criminal offense (Bureau of Alcohol, Tobacco, Firearms and Explosives, 2023). Thus, in reality, there seems to be fewer "good guys with guns" than (white) America wants to believe.

Beyond actually engaging in violence, white men often use guns as a symbolic threat of their willingness to partake in violence, and they feel strongly about their entitlement to do so. For instance, in opposition to the COVID-19 restrictions in Michigan, armed protestors – many of whom who were members of extremist groups (Nance, 2022) – gathered inside the state capitol building multiple times shouting threatening remarks, wielding signs with nooses and Confederate flags, and pushing aggressively against a line of Michigan state police (Censkey, 2020). Groups of armed white men – including Oath Keepers, Three-Percent Militia, Boogaloo Bois, and Proud Boys – repeatedly showed up at racial justice and Black Lives Matters protests and events, as well as held their own rallies, in the wake of the death of George Floyd in 2020 and enticed extensive violence (Campbell, 2022; Nance, 2022). And arguably one of the most egregious displays, was the Insurrection of the US Capitol on January 6, 2021, as thousands of armed Trump supporters stormed the Capitol looking to harm law makers and chanting "this is our house" (Royer, 2022).

These examples – and there are many more just from recent years – are only the modern iterations of such entitled displays of white violence. From the terror and violence used to undermine Reconstruction (Equal Justice Initiative, 2020), to the cross burnings and lynchings across the South during the era of Jim Crow (Equal Justice Initiative, 2017), the Tulsa massacre and burning of Black Wall Street (Messer, 2021), the bombing of churches (Jones, 2019), not to mention the historically repeated state sanctioned terror employed by the police (e.g., Bloody Sunday [Equal Justice Initiative, n.d.; Hinton, 2021], the Orangeburg Massacre [Bass & Nelson, 1996], Rodney King's murder [Lasley, 1994], the BLM movement [Garza, 2020; Ritchie, 2017]), whites have always felt entitled to – and have utilized – violence in response to Black excellence, social progress, or changes in the status quo.

Underlying all these actions are a sense of entitlement to their "rights" – rights as men, rights as whites, rights as Americans. What the events of the past few years, particularly in the Trump-era uncovered, is that these white men "…revealed themselves as a much larger armed militant force determined to use the Second Amendment as both a shield and a potential cudgel to bully the nation" (Nance, 2022, p. 5). A majority of white men are willing to use violence to protect what they believe is "rightfully" theirs (Isom, 2022; Nance, 2022) – their believed "honor," "manhood," "family" or "independence." This "fight for what's mine" mentality comes from the internalization of the myth of white male supremacy and the perceived entitlements it bestows. Yet, as society moves away from accepting these antiquated notions, white men's entitlement to violence makes them a danger to all.

Entitled to Privileged Protections

As Nance writes, "Many of (Trump's) most devoted followers harbor the fantasy of being a billionaire, having a fashion-model wife, and saying whatever they want, whenever they want, and not giving a damn about how people feel about it. This myth, though, is only for white men and their white families. These same devotees yearn to undo the diversity of the nation because it threatens their privilege, passed down from centuries of killing or enslaving all people of Color" (2022, p. 34). These sentiments are not solely found in Trumpers, but more broadly in white America, and always have been. Furthermore, such fantasies are perceived entitlements, and when they are aggrieved, many white men become increasingly aggressive, dangerous, and violent, particularly toward the oppressed, the marginalized, and those that oppose them. Yet, many do not face punishment or repercussions for their actions. For example, an all-white jury acquitted Roy Bryant and John Milam of the murder of Emmett Till (WGBH Educational Foundation, 2023). More recently, Kyle Rittenhouse was acquitted after he shot and killed two people at a racial justice protest in Kenosha, Washington (The New York Times, n.d.). And more broadly speaking, a federal appeals court just ruled the government cannot prohibit those with a record of domestic violence from owning a firearm (Beam, 2023); hence failing to safeguard people, and particularly women, from those with a known violent past, many of whom are white men. This is especially dangerous given a woman is 5 times more likely to be murdered when her abuser has access to a gun, and that nearly half of all women killed in the United States die at the hands of a current or former partner (The Educational Fund to Stop Gun Violence, 2020).

Thus, just as our Founding Fathers established a land that bestowed status, and in turn entitlements, to white men solely due to the body they were born in, so too do our institutions and legal system provide them with protections from its most severe punishments. In the next chapter I'll discuss the concept of white privilege and specifically how it protects whites, especially men, from the harshest punishments of our criminal legal system.

BOX 4.1   POLICING AS THE "AVERAGE JOE'S" MANIFESTATION OF WHITE MALE ENTITLEMENTS?

Again, as Nance states, "Many [white men] harbor the fantasy of being a billionaire, having a fashion-model wife, and saying whatever they want, whenever they want, and not giving a damn about how people feel about it. This myth, though, is only for white men and their white families. These same [white men] yearn to undo the diversity of the nation because it threatens their privilege, passed down from centuries of killing or enslaving all people of Color" (2022, p. 34). While most white "Average Joes" will not nor cannot obtain true positions of power, influence, and wealth, many believe their race and gender entitle them to it. And actually, there is a profession that allows them to (potentially) acquire all their patriarchal white male desires to some degree: *policing*. The central elements of white (male) entitlement – power, individualism, women and sex, violence, and privileged protections – are attainable to police officers. Police officers are the enforcers of the law; they are the agents of social control through coercive power (e.g., Marx, 1981; Passavant, 2021; Tyler et al., 2007). Police officers have individualism as they are allotted discretion to decide what, where, how, and who to police, contributing to the disparities seen in crime statistics (Tonry, 2004, 2011). Police are the "guardians" of white habitus, the status quo, and white femininity, and the "warriors" against "threats" from "dangerous" others, especially men of Color (Carlson, 2020b). Police are also granted abilities to enact their entitlement to women and sex in very racialized and gendered ways. Many police often see it as their duty to enforce gender norms, particularly for women who are deemed "out of control." As Ritchie states, "...controlling images developed in the service of colonialism and white supremacy transform women of color into a caricature, an implicit threat justifying violent responses" (2017, p. 236). And far too often, the police are the one's assessing and responding to that supposed "threat," so much so that many women of Color feel excluded from "protections" from the state and instead fear police brutality (Ritchie, 2017). Likewise, those in the LGBTQ community, particularly those of Color, are acutely vulnerable to predatory policing (Gaynor & Blessett, 2022; Goldberg et al., 2019). And, many officers take those believed rights home, as partners and families of police officers are two to four times more likely to experience violence and abuse than the general population (National Center for Women & Policing, 2013; also see Goodmark, 2015). Violence is also embedded in policing, not only because of the tools of the trade (i.e., access to firearms), but due to its white supremacist and misogynist roots (e.g., Go, 2020; Hadden, 2001; McGinley, 2015; Silvestri, 2017), and has increased with the modern militarization of law enforcement (Balko, 2021; Koslicki et al., 2019; Masera, 2021). And finally, police are granted privileged protections by the "blue code of silence" and the "thin blue line" (Chammah & Aspinwall, 2020; Westmarland, 2005). Hence, policing may be a very attractive profession to white men who subscribe to the values outlined in this book. Research does suggest white men in law enforcement tend to lean politically right, many affiliating with far-right extremist groups (Campbell, 2022; Kaufman, 2022; Nance, 2022). I readily admit this is a gross overgeneralization of policing and does not address all the complexities and nuances of it as an institution or culture. Yet, this conjectural overview suggests there are deeper connections to be explored, and that an examination of policing through an intersectional critical whiteness lens, such as the theory of whiteness and crime, is a worthwhile endeavor. This is particularly true as progressive scholars aim to provide not just suggestions for police reform, but a re-imagining of policing within society, to better serve and truly protect all people.

Notes

1 Portions of this chapter appeared in or are revisions of some of my earlier works, including Boehme and Isom* (2020) https://www.tandfonline.com/doi/full/10.10 80/15564886.2019.1679308; Isom* & Andersen (2020) Whitelash?'status threat, anger, and white America: A general strain theory approach. *Journal of Crime and Justice, copyright ©Midwestern Criminal Justice Association, reprinted by permission of Taylor & Francis Ltd*, https://www.tandfonline.com/doi/full/10.1080/ 0735648X.2019.1704835 on behalf of Midwestern Criminal Justice Association;

and Isom, Mikell, et al. (2021) https://www.tandfonline.com/doi/full/10.1080/02732173.2021.1885531. All used by permission.

2 Habitus angst, on the other hand, aligns with Agnew's (2006) other two strain classifications of either loss of something valued or anticipation of something negative.

3 The debates around gun control have shifted over time but have always been related to race. For example, the NRA and conservatives supported California's Mulford Act in 1967 that was a direct response to the Black Panther Party. For more discussion on the racialized gun debate at this time see Winkler (2013) and Manson (2019). And for more discussion on race and the Second Amendment in general see Carlson (2020a) and Dunbar-Ortiz (2018).

References

Abbott, J. (2021). *Representation in media matters*. WGBH Educational Foundation. https://www.wgbh.org/foundation/representation-in-media-matters

Agnew, R. (2006). *Pressured into crime: An overview of general strain theory*. Roxbury.

American Public Health Association. (n.d.). *Gun violence is a public health crisis*. https://www.apha.org/-/media/files/pdf/factsheets/200221_gun_violence_fact_sheet.ashx

Anderson, C. (2016). *White rage: The unspoken truth of our racial divide*. Bloomsbury.

Anderson, C. (2021). *The second: Race and guns in a fatally unequal America*. Bloomsbury.

Anderson, E. (2015). "The white space". *Sociology of Race and Ethnicity*, *1*(1), 10–21.

Azrael, D., Hepburn, L., Hemenway, D., & Miller, M. (2017). The stock and flow of U.S. firearms: Results from the 2015 national firearms survey. *The Russell Sage Foundation Journal of Social Sciences*, *3*(5), 38–57.

Baele, S. J., Brace, L., & Coan, T. G. (2021). From "incel" to "saint": Analyzing the violent worldview behind the 2018 Toronto attack. *Terrorism and Political Violence*, *33*(8), 1667–1691.

Bakkenes, F. (2022). Diversity and representation in TV and movies and why it matters. *Diggit Magazine*. https://www.diggitmagazine.com/papers/diversity-and-representation-tv-and-movies-and-why-it-matters

Balko, R. (2021). *Rise of the warrior cop: The militarization of America's police forces*. Public Affairs.

Baradaran, M. (2019). *The color of money: Black banks and the racial wealth gap*. Belknap Press.

Barker, K., & Jurasz, O. (2019). *Online misogyny as a hate crime*. Routledge.

Bar-Tal, D., & Saxe, L. (1976). Physical attractiveness and it's relationship to sex-role stereotyping. *Sex Roles*, *2*, 123–133.

Bass, J., & Nelson, J. (1996). *The Orangeburg massacre*. Mercer University Press.

Bates, L. (2020). *Men who hate women: The extremism body nobody is talking about*. Simon & Schuster.

Battalora, J. (2013). *Birth of a white nation: The invention of white people and its relevance today*. Strategic Book Publishing.

Beam, A. (2023, February 2). Federal appeals court strikes down domestic violence gun law. *AP News*. https://apnews.com/article/us-supreme-court-politics-crime-texas-violence-6d2af127ca14c65ca9a925645a5ee546

Belew, K., & Gutiérrez, R. A. (Eds.). (2021). *A field guide to white supremacy*. University of California Press.

Bjork-James, S. (2020a). Racializing misogyny: Sexuality and gender in the new online white nationalism. *Feminist Anthropology, 1*(2), 176–183.

Bjork-James, S. (2020b). White sexual politics: The patriarchal family in white nationalism and the religious right. *Transforming Anthropology, 28*(1), 58–73.

Blee, K. M., & Tickamyer, A. R. (1995). Racial differences in men's attitudes about women's gender roles. *Journal of Marriage and Family, 57*(1), 21–30.

Boehme, H. M., & Isom, D. A. (2020). Alt-white? A gendered look at "victim" ideology and the alt-right. *Victims and Offenders, 15*(2), 174–196.

Bonilla-Silva, E. (2018). *Racism without racists: Color-blind racism and the persistence of racial inequality in America* (5th ed.). Rowman & Littlefield.

Bridges, T., & Pascoe, C. J. (2014). Hybrid masculinities: New directions in the sociology of men and masculinities. *Sociology Compass, 8*(3), 246–258.

Bryant, S. L. (2019). The beauty ideal: The effects of European standards of beauty on Black women. *Columbia Social Work Review, 11*(1), 80–91.

Bureau of Alcohol, Tobacco, Firearms and Explosives. (2023). *National firearms commerce and trafficking assessment (NFCTA): Crime guns – volume two*. U.S. Department of Justice. https://www.atf.gov/firearms/national-firearms-commerce-and-trafficking-assessment-nfcta-crime-guns-volume-two

Byerly, C. M. (2020). Incels online reframing sexual violence. *The Communication Review, 23*(4), 290–308.

Campbell, A. (2022). *We are proud boys: How a right-wing street gang ushered in a new era of American extremism*. Hachette Books.

Carlson, J. (2020a). *Policing the second amendment: Guns, law enforcement, and the politics of race*. Princeton University Press.

Carlson, J. (2020b). Police warriors and police guardians: Race, masculinity, and the construction of gun violence. *Social Problems, 67*(3), 399–417.

Carrigan, T., Connell, B., & Lee, J. (1985). Toward a new sociology of masculinity. *Theory and Society, 14*, 551–604.

Cash, T. F., & Henry, P. E. (1995). Women's body images: The results of a national survey in the U.S.A. *Sex Roles, 33*, 19–28.

Censkey, A. (2020, May 14). Heavily armed protestors gather again at Michigan capitol to decry stay-at-home order. *NPR*. https://www.npr.org/2020/05/14/855918852/heavily-armed-protesters-gather-again-at-michigans-capitol-denouncing-home-order

Centers for Disease Control and Prevention. (2022). *Firearm mortality by state*. https://www.cdc.gov/nchs/pressroom/sosmap/firearm_mortality/firearm.htm

Chammah, M., & Aspinwall, C. (2020, June 9). The short, fraught history of the 'thin blue line' American flag. *Politico*. https://www.politico.com/news/magazine/2020/06/09/the-short-fraught-history-of-the-thin-blue-line-american-flag-309767

Chang, W. (2022). The monstrous-feminine in the incel imagination: Investigating the representation of women as "femoids" on/r/Braincels. *Feminist Media Studies, 22*(2), 254–270.

Chemaly, S. (2015, October 5). Mass killings in the US: Masculinity, masculinity, masculinity. *Huff Post*. http://www.huffingtonpost.com/soraya-chemaly/mass-killings-in-the-us-w_b_8234322.html

Clark, S., Harper, S., & Weber, B. (2022). Growing up in rural America. *The Russell Sage Foundation Journal of the Social Sciences, 8*(4), 1–47.

Collins, P. H. (2000). *Black feminist thought: Knowledge, consciousness, and the politics of empowerment.* Routledge.

Connell, R. W. (1987). *Gender and power: Society, the person and sexual politics.* Stanford University Press.

Connell, R. W., & Messerschmidt, J. W. (2005). Hegemonic masculinity: Rethinking the concept. *Gender & Society, 19,* 829–859.

Cramer, R., Addo, F. R., Campbell, C., Choi, J., Cohen, B. J., & Zhang, Y. (2019, October). *The emerging millennial wealth gap.* New America. Washington, DC. https://www.newamerica.org/millennials/reports/emerging-millennial-wealth-gap/

Cunningham, G. B., & Nite, C. (2020). LGBT diversity and inclusion, community characteristics, and success. *Journal of Sport Management, 34,* 533–541.

Cutilletta, L. (2020, October 1). *The "good guy with a gun" myth.* Giffords. https://giffords.org/blog/2020/10/the-good-guy-with-a-gun-myth/

Daly, S. E., & Reed, S. M. (2022). "I think most of society hates us": A qualitative thematic analysis of interview of incels. *Sex Roles, 86,* 14–33.

De Coster, S., & Heimer, K. (2021). Unifying theory and research on intimate partner violence: A feminist perspective. *Feminist Criminology, 16*(3), 286–303.

DeKeseredy, W. S. (2017). Masculinities, aggression, and violence. In P. Sturmey (Ed.), *The Wiley handbook of violence and aggression.* John Wiley & Sons. http://doi.org/10.1002/9781119057574.whbva024

DeKeseredy, W. S. (2021). Bringing feminist sociological analyses of patriarchy back to the forefront of the study of woman abuse. *Violence Against Women, 27*(5), 621–638.

DeKeseredy, W. S. (2022). Men's rights, gun ownership, racism, and the assault on women's reproductive health rights: Hidden connections. *Dignity, 7*(3), Article 5. https://doi.org/10.23860/dignity.2022.07.03.05

DeKeseredy, W. S. (2023). *Misogyny and woman abuse in the manosphere: The role of incel male peer support* [Paper presentation]. *Conference on the social processes of online hate,* University of California Santa Barbara.

DeKeseredy, W. S., Burnham, K., Nicewarner, R., Nolan, J., & Hall-Sanchez, A. K. (2019). Aggrieved entitlement in the ivory tower: Exploratory qualitative results from a large-scale campus climate survey. *Journal of Qualitative Criminal Justice & Criminology, 8*(1), 3–20.

Deliovsky, K. (2008). Normative white femininity: Race, gender, and the politics of beauty. *Atlantis, 33*(1), 49–59.

DeMatteo, M. (2023, January 31). The average millennial has $27,251 in non-mortgage consumer debt – here's how they compare to other generations. *CNBC.* https://www.cnbc.com/select/how-much-debt-do-millennials-have/

DePrince, A. P. (2022). *Every 90 seconds: Our common cause ending violence against women.* Oxford University Press.

Derenoncourt, E., Kim, C. H., Kuhn, M., & Schularick, M. (2022, June). *Wealth of two nations: The U.S. racial wealth gap, 1860-2020.* National Bureau of Economic Research, working paper 30101. https://www.nber.org/system/files/working_papers/w30101/w30101.pdf

Desmond, M., & Western, B. (2018). Poverty in America: New directions and debates. *Annual Review of Sociology, 44,* 305–318.

DiAngelo, R. (2018). *White fragility: Why it's so hard for white people to talk about racism*. Beacon Press.

DiAngelo, R. (2021). *Nice racism: How progressive white people perpetuate racial harm*. Beacon Press.

Dickler, J. (2022, December 9). Boomers have more wealth 'than any other generation,' but millennials many not inherit as much as they hope. *CNBC*. https://www.cnbc.com/2022/12/09/great-wealth-transfer-why-millennials-may-inherit-less-than-expected.html

Dobrasko, R. (2008, February). Equalization schools in South Carolina, 1951-1959. [online report.] https://static1.squarespace.com/static/520061e1e4b0929e453c5305/t/57289ea93c44d8d1105cfbc7/1462279854952/Equalization+Schools+in+South+Carolina%E2%80%9D.pdf

Douglas, D., Lichter, A., & Rembert, M. (2022). *Rural America's tech employment landscape: How to increase tech talent and tech employment*. Center for Rural Innovation. http://ruralinnovation.us/wp-content/uploads/2022/06/CORI_Rural_Tech_Landscape.pdf

Dragiewicz, M. (2018). Antifeminism and backlash: A critical criminological imperative. In W. S. DeKeseredy & M. Dragiewicz (Eds.), *Routledge handbook of critical criminology* (2nd ed.) (pp. 334–347). Routledge.

Dunbar-Ortiz, R. (2018). *Loaded: A disarming history of the second amendment*. City Light Books.

DuRocher, K. (2011). *Raising racists: The socialization of white children in the Jim Crow south*. The University of Kentucky Press.

Durose, M. R., Harlow, C. W., Langan, P. A., Motivans, M., Rantala, R. R., & Smith, E. L. (2005). *Family violence statistics*. Bureau of Justice Statistics, Department of Justice. https://bjs.ojp.gov/content/pub/pdf/fvs.pdf

Ekwell, S. (n.d.). *The racist origins of US gun controls: Laws designed to disarm slaves, freedmen, and African-Americans*. [online document]. https://www.sedgwickcounty.org/media/29093/the-racist-origins-of-us-gun-control.pdf

Equal Justice Initiative. (2017). *Lynching in America: Confronting the legacy of racial terror* (3rd ed.). https://eji.org/reports/lynching-in-america/

Equal Justice Initiative. (2020). *Reconstruction in America: Racial violence after the Civil War, 1865-1876*. https://eji.org/report/reconstruction-in-america/a-truth-that-needs-telling/

Equal Justice Initiative. (n.d.). *Bloody Sunday: Civil rights activists brutally attacked in Selma*. https://calendar.eji.org/racial-injustice/mar/7

Farrell, T., Fernandez, M., Novotny, J., & Alani, H. (2019). Exploring misogyny across the manosphere in reddit. *WebSci '19: Proceedings of the 10th ACM conference on web science* (pp. 87–96). https://oro.open.ac.uk/61128/1/WebScience139.pdf

Feagin, J. R. (2013). *The white racial frame* (2nd ed.). Routledge.

Fitchen, J. M. (1991). *Endangered spaces, enduring places: Change, identity, and survival in rural America*. Routledge.

Frankenberg, R. (1993). *White women, race matters: The social construction of whiteness*. University of Minnesota Press.

Friedman, J., & Johnson, N. F. (2022, September 19). *Banned in the USA: The growing movement to censor books in schools*. PEN America. https://pen.org/report/banned-usa-growing-movement-to-censor-books-in-schools/

Garza, A. (2020). *The purpose of power: How we come together when we fall apart*. One World.

Gaynor, T. S., & Blessett, B. (2022). Predatory policing, intersectional subjection, and the experiences of LGBTQ people of color in New Orleans. *Urban Affairs Review*, *58*(5), 1305–1339.

Giacomazzo, B. (2022, May 30). *The Fortune 500 list has 'record number' of black CEOs – but there's still only 6 of them*. AfroTech. https://afrotech.com/fortune-500-black-ceos

Giffords. (2023). *The gun lobby*. https://giffords.org/issues/the-gun-lobby/

Ging, D. (2019). Alphas, betas, and incels: Theorizing the masculinities of the manosphere. *Men and Masculinities*, *22*(4), 638–657.

Glace, A. M., Dover, T. L., & Zatkin, J. G. (2021). Taking the black pill: An empirical analysis of the "incel". *Psychology of Men & Masculinities*, *22*(2), 288–297.

Go, J. (2020). The imperial origins of American policing: Militarization and imperial feedback in the early 20th century. *American Journal of Sociology*, *125*(5), 1193–1254.

Goldberg, N. G., Mallory, C., Hasenbush, A., Stemple, L., & Meyer, I. H. (2019). Police and the criminalization of LGBT people. In T. Rice Lave & E. J. Miller (Eds.), *The Cambridge handbook of policing in the United States* (pp. 374–391). Cambridge University Press.

Goodmark, L. (2015). Hands up at home: Militarized masculinity and police officers who commit intimate partner abuse. *Brigham Young Law Review*, *2015*(5), 1183–1246.

Gun Violence Archive. (2023). *Mass shootings in 2023*. (Visited February 3, 2023). https://www.gunviolencearchive.org/reports/mass-shooting?page=1

Hadden, S. (2001). *Slave patrols: Law and violence in Virginia and the Carolinas*. Harvard University Press.

Hagerman, M. A. (2018). *White kids: Growing up with privilege in a racially divided America*. NYU Press.

Halpin, M. (2022). Weaponized subordination: How incels discredit themselves to degrade women. *Gender & Society*, *36*(6), 813–837.

Halpin, M., & Richard, N. (2021). An invitation to analytic abduction. *Methods in Psychology*, *5*, 100052.

Hammon, B. (2013). Playing the race card: White Americans' sense of victimization in response to affirmative action. *Texas Hispanic Journal of Law and Policy*, *19*, 95–120.

Henriques, M., & Patnaik, D. (2020). Social media and its effects on beauty. In M. P. Levine & J. S. Santos (Eds.), *Beauty: Cosmetic science, cultural issues, and creative developments*. http://doi.org/10.5772/intechopen.93322

Hinton, E. (2021). *America on fire: The untold history of police violence and black rebellion since the 1960s*. Liveright Publishing Corporation.

Hochschild, A. R. (2016). *Strangers in their own land: Anger and mourning on the American right*. The New Press.

Hoffman, B., Ware, J., & Shapiro, E. (2020). Assessing the threat of incel violence. *Studies in Conflict and Terrorism*, *43*(7), 565–585.

Hoffman, M. G., Klee, M. A., & Sullivan, B. (2022, August 31). *Who has retirement accounts? New data reveal inequality in retirement account ownership*. U.S. Census Bureau. https://www.census.gov/library/stories/2022/08/who-has-retirement-accounts.html

Homans, G. C. (1950). *The human group*. Harcourt, Brace and Company.

hooks, b. (1984/2000). *Feminist theory: From margin to center*. Pluto Press.

hooks, b. (1991). Essentialism and experience. *American Literary History*, *3*(1), 172–183.

Horowitz, J., Igielnik, R., & Kochhar, R. (2020, January 9). *Trends in income and wealth inequality*. Pew Research Center. https://www.pewresearch.org/social-trends/2020/01/09/trends-in-income-and-wealth-inequality/

Huang, V. (2021, June 12). *The importance of representation in media*. Race to a Cure. https://www.racetoacure.org/post/the-importance-of-representation-in-media

Humes, E. (2006). How the GI bill shunted blacks into vocational training. *The Journal of Blacks in Higher Education*, *53*, 92–104.

Hunt, V., Prince, S., Dixon-Fyle, S., & Dolan, K. (2020). *Diversity wins: How inclusion matters*. McKinsey & Company. https://www.mckinsey.com/featured-insights/diversity-and-inclusion/diversity-wins-how-inclusion-matters#/

Isom*, D. A. (2018). Understanding white Americans' perceptions of "reverse" discrimination: An application of a new theory of status dissonance. In E. J. Lawler (Ed.), *Advances in group processes* (pp. 129–157). Emerald Publishing Limited.

Isom, D. A. (2022). *Whiteness and crime* [Unpublished data set]. University of South Carolina.

Isom*, D. A., & Andersen, T. S. (2020). 'Whitelash?'status threat, anger, and white America: A general strain theory approach. *Journal of Crime and Justice*, *43*(4), 414–432.

Isom, D. A., Boehme, H. M., Cann, D., & Wilson, A. (2022). The white right: A gendered look at the links between 'victim' ideology and anti-black lives matter sentiments in the era of Trump. *Critical Sociology*, *48*(3), 475–500.

Isom, D. A., Boehme, H. M., Mikell, T. C., Chicoine, S., & Renner, M. (2021). Status threat, social concerns, and conservative media: A look at white America and the alt-right. *Societies*, *11*, 72. https://doi.org/10.3390/soc11030072

Isom, D. A., Mikell, T. C., & Boehme, H. M. (2021). White America, threat to the status quo, and affiliation with the alt-right: A qualitative approach. *Sociological Spectrum*, *41*(3), 213–228.

Jardina, A. (2019). *White identity politics*. Cambridge University Press.

Johnson, K. M., & Lichter, D. T. (2019). Rural depopulation: Growth and decline processes over the past century. *Rural Sociology*, *84*(1), 3–27.

Jones, D. (2019). *Bending toward justice: The Birmingham church bombing that changed the course of civil rights*. All Points Books.

Katz, J. (2006). *The macho paradox: Why some men hurt women and how all men can help*. Sourcebooks.

Katz, J. (2016). *Man enough? Donald Trump, Hillary Clinton and the politics of presidential masculinity*. Interlink Books.

Karp, A. (2018, June). *Estimating global civilian-held firearms numbers*. Small Arms Survey. https://www.smallarmssurvey.org/sites/default/files/resources/SAS-BP-Civilian-Firearms-Numbers.pdf

Kaufman, S. J. (2022). Is the US heading for a civil war? Scenarios for 2024-2025. *Studies in Conflict & Terrorism*, Advance online publication. http://doi.org/10.1080/1057610X.2022.2137892

Kendi, I. X. (2016). *Stamped from the beginning*. Bold Type Books.

♠Kimmel, M. (2017). *Angry white men: American masculinity at the end of an era*. Nation Books.

Koontz Anthony, A., Okorie, S., & Norman, L. (2016). When beauty brings out the beast: Female comparisons and the feminine rivalry. *Gender Issues, 33*, 311–334.

Koslicki, W. M., Willits, D. W., & Brooks, R. (2019). Fatal outcomes of militarization: Re-examining the relationship between the 1033 program and police deadly force. *Journal of Criminal Justice, 72*, 101781.

LaFranco, R., & Peterson-Withorn, C. (2023). *The Forbes 400: The definitive ranking of the wealthiest Americans in 2022*. Forbes. https://www.forbes.com/forbes-400/

Lasley, J. R. (1994). The impact of the Rodney King incident on citizen attitudes toward police. *Policing and Society, 3*(4), 245–255.

Lateef, H., Baldwin-White, A., Jellesma, F., Borgstrom, E., & Nartey, P. (2023). Afrocentric cultural norms, mental health functioning, and the perception of intimate partner violence among young black men. *Journal of Racial and Ethnic Health Disparities*. Advance online publication. https://doi.org/10.1007/s40615-023-01536-2

Lelaurain, S., Fonte, D., Giger, J.-C., Guignard, S., & Lo Monaco, G. (2021). Legitimizing intimate partner violence: The role of romantic love and the mediating effect of patriarchal ideologies. *Journal of Interpersonal Violence, 36*(13–14), 6351–6368.

López, I. H. (2006). *White by law: The legal construction of race*. New York University Press.

Manson, J. (2019, August 9). When Black Panthers carried guns, conservatives supported gun control. *BuzzFeed*. https://www.buzzfeednews.com/article/joshuamanson/gun-control-history-race-black-panther-party-conservatives

Martin, G. J., & Yurukoglu, A. (2017). Bias in cable news: Persuasion and polarization. *American Economic Review, 107*(9), 2565–2599.

Martz, D. M., Handley, K. B., & Eisler, R. M. (1995). The relationship between feminine gender role stress, body image, and eating disorders. *Psychology of Women Quarterly, 19*, 493–508.

Marx, G. T. (1981). Ironies of social control: Authorities as contributors to deviance through escalation, nonenforcement and covert facilitation. *Social Problems, 28*(3), 221–246.

Marx, J. D. (2011). *The conservative transition in American social policy*. Social Welfare History Project. https://socialwelfare.library.vcu.edu/eras/the-conservative-transition-in-american-social-policy/

Masera, F. (2021). Police safety, killings by police, and the militarization of US law enforcement. *Journal of Urban Economics, 124*, 103365.

Maxwell, D., Robinson, S. R., Williams, J. R., & Keaton, C. (2020). A short story of a lonely guy: A qualitative thematic analysis of involuntary celibacy using reddit. *Sexuality & Culture, 24*(6), 1852–1874.

Mayer, A. (2021). Economic change, the death of the coal industry, and migration intentions in rural Colorado, USA. *Journal of Rural Social Sciences, 36*(1): Article 4. https://egrove.olemiss.edu/jrss/vol36/iss1/4

McGhee, H. (2021). *The sum of us: What racism cost everyone and how we can prosper together*. One World.

McGinley, A. (2015). Policing and the clashes of masculinities. *Howard Law Journal, 59*(1), 221–270.

McKinley, C. E., Lilly, J. M., Knipp, H., & Liddell, J. L. (2021). "A dad can get the money and the mom stays at home": Patriarchal gender role attitudes, intimate partner violence, historical oppression, and resilience among indigenous peoples. *Sex Roles*, *85*, 499–514.

Menzie, L. (2022). Stacys, Beckys, and Chads: The construction of femininity and hegemonic masculinity within incel rhetoric. *Psychology & Sexuality*, *13*(1), 69–85.

Messer, C. M. (2021). *The 1921 Tulsa race massacre: Crafting a legacy*. Palgrave MacMillan.

Messerschmidt, J. W. (1993). Masculinities and crime. In F. T. Cullen & R. Agnew (Eds.), *Criminological theory past to the present* (pp. 383–293). Roxbury Publishing Company.

Messerschmidt, J. W. (2000). *Nine lives: Adolescent masculinities, the body, and violence*. Westview Press.

Messerschmidt, J. W. (2004). *Flesh & blood: Adolescent gender diversity and violence*. Rowman & Littlefield.

Messerschmidt, J. W. (2014). *Crime as structured action: Gender, race, class and crime in the making* (2nd ed.). Sage.

Messerschmidt, J. W. (2019). *Nine lives: Adolescent masculinities, the body, and violence*. Routledge.

Messner, M. A. (2016). Forks in the road of men's gender politics: Men's rights vs feminist allies. *International Journal for Crime, Justice and Social Democracy*, *5*, 6–20.

Miller Cole, B. (2020, September 15). 8 reasons why diversity and inclusion are essential to business success. *Forbes*. https://www.forbes.com/sites/biancamillercole/2020/09/15/8-reasons-why-diversity-and-inclusion-are-essential-to-business-success/?sh=696c58071824

Mills, C. (1997). *The racial contract*. Cornell University Press.

Moffson, S. (2010, September 20). *Equalization schools in Georgia's African-American communities, 1951-1970*. Georgia Department of Natural Resources, Historic Preservation Division. https://www.dca.ga.gov/sites/default/files/equalization_schools_in_georgia_0.pdf

Nagle, A. (2017). *Kill all normies: The online culture wars from Tumblr and 4Chan to the Alt-right and Trump*. Zero Books.

Nance, M. (2022). *They want to kill Americans: The militias, terrorists, and deranged ideology of the Trump insurgency*. St. Martin's Press.

Naquin, C. (2022, December 10). Oil companies have plundered Louisiana's coast. They owe us reparations. *InTheseTimes*. https://inthesetimes.com/article/louisiana-land-loss-fossil-fuels-reparations

National Center for Education Statistics. (n.d.). *Degrees conferred by race/ethnicity and sex*. Institute for Education Science, U.S. Department of Education. https://nces.ed.gov/fastfacts/display.asp?id=72

National Center for Women & Policing. (2013). *Police family violence fact sheet*. Feminist Majority Foundation. https://olis.oregonlegislature.gov/liz/2017R1/Downloads/CommitteeMeetingDocument/132808

National Institute of Health Care Management. (2022, July 12). *Gun violence: The impact on public health*. https://nihcm.org/publications/gun-violence-the-impact-on-public-health

Nelson, D. D. (1998). *National manhood: Capitalist citizenship and the imagined fraternity of white men*. Duke University Press.

The New York Times. (n.d.). *The Kyle Rittenhouse Trial*. https://www.nytimes.com/news-event/kyle-rittenhouse-trial

Oluo, I. (2021). *Mediocre: The dangerous legacy of white male America*. Seal Press.

O'Malley, R. L., Holt, K., & Holt, T. J. (2022). An exploration of the involuntary celibate (incel) subculture online. *Journal of Interpersonal Violence*, *37*(7–8), NP4981–NP5008.

Passavant, P. (2021). *Policing protests: The post-democratic state and the figure of black insurrection*. Duke University Press.

Pelzer, B., Kaati, L., Cohen, K., & Fernquist, J. (2021). Toxic language in online incel communities. *SN Social Sciences*, *1*(8), 1–22.

Perry, A. M., Steinbaum, M., & Romer, C. (2021, June 23). *Student loans, the racial wealth divide, and why we need full student debt cancellation*. Brookings. https://www.brookings.edu/research/student-loans-the-racial-wealth-divide-and-why-we-need-full-student-debt-cancellation/

Peterson, J., & Densley, J. (2021). *The violence project: How to stop a mass shooting epidemic*. Abrams Press.

Popper, K. R. (1962). *Conjectures and refutations: The growth of scientific knowledge*. Basic Books.

Poran, M. A. (2002). Denying diversity: Perceptions of beauty and social comparison processes among Latina, Black, and White women. *Sex Roles: A Journal of Research*, *47*(1–2), 65–81.

Porter, E. (2018, December 14). The hard truths about trying to 'save' the rural economy. *The New York Times*. https://www.nytimes.com/interactive/2018/12/14/opinion/rural-america-trump-decline.html

Preston, K., Halpin, M., & Maguire, F. (2021). The black pill: New technology and the male supremacy of involuntarily celibate men. *Men and Masculinities*, *24*(5), 823–841.

Ridgeway, C. L. (2011). *Framed by gender: How gender inequality persists in the modern world*. Oxford University Press.

Ritchie, A. J. (2017). *Invisible no more: Police violence against black women and women of color*. Beacon Press.

Rowland, A. L. (2022). Small dick problems: Masculine entitlement as rhetorical strategy. *Quarterly Journal of Speech*, *109*(1), 26–47.

Rothstein, R. (2017). *The color of law*. Liveright Publishing Company/W.W. Norton & Company.

Royer, D. (2022, July 21). Capitol rioter who declared 'This is our house' is convicted of Jan. 6 crimes. *The Hill*. https://thehill.com/homenews/wire/3569552-capitol-rioter-who-declared-this-is-our-house-is-convicted-of-jan-6-crimes/

Scaptura, M. N., & Boyle, K. M. (2020). Masculinity threat, "incel" traits, and violent fantasies among heterosexual men in the United States. *Feminist Criminology*, *15*(3), 278–298.

Schaeffer, K. (2021, September 13). *Key facts about Americans and guns*. Pew Research Center. https://www.pewresearch.org/fact-tank/2021/09/13/key-facts-about-americans-and-guns/

Schaeffer, K. (2023, January 9). *U.S. Congress continues to grow in racial, ethnic diversity*. Pew Research Center. https://www.pewresearch.org/fact-tank/2023/01/09/u-s-congress-continues-to-grow-in-racial-ethnic-diversity/

Schippers, M. (2007). Recovering the feminine other: Masculinity, femininity, and gender hegemony. *Theory and Society*, *36*, 85–102.

Schwartz, S. (2021, May 17). Four states have placed legal limits on how teachers can discuss race. More may follow. *Education Week*. https://www.edweek.org/policy-politics/four-states-have-placed-legal-limits-on-how-teachers-can-discuss-race-more-may-follow/2021/05

Silvestri, M. (2017). Police culture and gender: Revisiting the 'cult of masculinity. *Policing: A Journal of Policy and Practice*, *11*(3), 289–300.

Slack, T., Thiede, B. C., & Jensen, L. (2020). Race, residence, and underemployment: Fifty years in comparative perspective, 1968-2017. *Rural Sociology*, *85*(2), 275–315.

Smart, R., Morral, A. R., Ranchand, R., Charbonneau, A., Williams, J., Smucker, S., Cherney, S., & Xenakis, L. (2023). *The science of gun policy: A critical synthesis of research evidence on the effects of gun policies in the United States*. Rand Corporation. https://www.rand.org/pubs/research_reports/RR2088.html

Smith, C. (2021). *How the word is passed: A reckoning with the history of slavery across America*. Little, Brown and Company.

Southern Poverty Law Center. (2022). *The Year in Hate & Extremism 2021*. https://www.splcenter.org/sites/default/files/splc-2021-year-in-hate-extremism-report.pdf

Stanford, F. C. (2020). The importance of diversity and inclusion in the healthcare workforce. *Journal of the National Medical Association*, *112*(3), 247–249.

Stanton, A. G., Avery, L. R., Matsuzaka, S., & Espinel, S. (2022). Black women's experiences of gendered racial sexual objectification, body image, and depressive symptoms. *Body Image*, *41*, 443–452.

The Educational Fund to Stop Gun Violence. (2020). *Domestic violence and firearms*. https://efsgv.org/learn/type-of-gun-violence/domestic-violence-and-firearms/

Tickamyer, A. R., & Duncan, C. M. (1990). Poverty and opportunity structures in rural America. *Annual Review of Sociology*, *16*, 67–86.

Tonry, M. (2004). *Thinking about crime: Sense and sensibility in American penal culture*. Oxford University Press.

Tonry, M. (2011). *Punishing race: A continuing American dilemma*. Oxford University Press.

Tyler, T. R., Callahan, P. E., & Frost, J. (2007). Armed, and dangerous(?): Motivating rule adherence among agents of social control. *Law & Society Review*, *41*(2), 457–492.

The Violence Project. (n.d.). *Mass public shootings in the United States, 1966-present*. https://www.theviolenceproject.org/mass-shooter-database/

U.S. Department of Health & Human Services. (2022, April). *National snapshot of trends in the national domestic violence hotline's contact data before and during the covid-19 pandemic*. Office of Inspector General. https://oig.hhs.gov/oas/reports/region9/92106000.pdf

van Valkenburgh, S. P. (2021). Digesting the red pill: Masculinity and neoliberalism in the manosphere. *Men and Masculinities*, *24*(1), 84–103.

Wallis, J. (2016). *America's original sin: Racism, white privilege, and the bridge to a new America*. Brazos Press.

Watson, L. B., Lewis, J. A., & Moody, A. T. (2019). A sociocultural examination of body image among Black women. *Body Image*, *31*, 280–287.

West, C., & Zimmerman, D. H. (1987). Doing gender. *Gender & Society*, *1*(2), 125–151.

West, C., & Zimmerman, D. H. (2009). Accounting for doing gender. *Gender & Society*, *23*(1), 112–122.

Westmarland, L. (2005). Police ethics and integrity: Breaking the blue code of silence. *Policing and Society*, *15*(2), 145–165.

WGBH Educational Foundation. (2023). The murder of Emmett Till: The Trial of J.W. Milam and Roy Bryant. *PBS*. https://www.pbs.org/wgbh/americanexperience/features/emmett-trial-jw-milam-and-roy-bryant/

Wilson, V., & Darity, W. Jr. (2022, March 25). *Understanding black-white dispari-ties in labor market outcomes requires models that account for persistent dis-crimination and unequal bargaining power*. Economic Policy Institute. https://www.epi.org/unequalpower/publications/understanding-black-white-disparities-in-labor-market-outcomes/

Winkler, A. (2013). *Gun fight: The battle over the right to bear arms in America*. W. W. Norton & Company.

Wise, T. (2010). *Color-blind: The rise of post-racial politics and the retreat from racial equity*. City Light Books.

Witt, T. (2020). "If i cannot have it, i will do everything i can to destroy it." The canoni-zation of Elliot Rodger: "Incel" masculinities, secular sainthood, and justifications of ideological violence. *Social Identities*, *26*(5), 675–689.

Wood, K. (2022, August 18). 2022 best states for gun owners. *Guns & Ammo*. https://www.gunsandammo.com/editorial/best-states-for-gun-owners-2022/463592

World Population Review. (2023). *Gun deaths by country 2023*. https://worldpopulationreview.com/country-rankings/gun-deaths-by-country

Wuthnow, R. (2018). *The left behind: Decline and rage in small-town America*. Princeton University Press.

Young, J. C. (2023, January 19). Florida's ban on an AP African American studies class is authoritarian. *The Daily Beast*. https://www.thedailybeast.com/floridas-ban-on-an-ap-african-american-studies-class-is-authoritarian

Zimmerman, S. (2022). The ideology of incels: Misogyny and victimhood as justification for political violence. *Terrorism and Political Violence*. Advance online publication. http://doi.org/10.1080/09546553.2022.2129014

5

THE PROTECTION OF PRIVILEGE AND WHITE AMERICANS' CRIMINAL LEGAL ENTANGLEMENT

What Exactly *Is* White Privilege and Who Has It?

A common rebuttal from white people, particularly those on the lower realms of the socioeconomic ladder, is to claim that they are *not* privileged, and certainly do not benefit from white privilege.[1] For instance, two white male participants of Forscher and Kteily (2017)[2] stated:

> "I am a white male who is sick of being accused of being a sexist, homo-phobe and racist. I am sick of hearing about white privilege."

> "I believe in limited government, freedom of speech and that whites shouldn't be neglected based on some incorrect left field theory based on mythical 'privilege'. I tend to notice the majority of the left wingers who cry the most about 'privilege' are ironically privileged themselves and also reside in all white, upper class communities and cities."

Many white folks, particularly those in the lower class, use shifts in society as justification for these sentiments – over the past few decades, they've lost their jobs, they've lost their homes, they can't afford to pay bills or put food on the table, much less send their children to college (just as people of Color have also struggled to do for generations) – yet, they are purportedly "privileged." They tend not to question how political and economic shifts have led to this, and instead look around and see people who don't look like them supposedly "succeeding." Thus, "those people" must be to blame for taking "our" jobs and threatening our (the white) way of life (e.g., Hochschild, 2016; Tenold, 2018;

DOI: 10.4324/9781003167877-6

Wuthnow, 2018).* What they fail to see is that as hard as life is for them, it is exponentially that much harder for their equal counterparts in Black or Brown skin. Because of the lies of white supremacy and the resultant American Dream myth – particularly the notions of individualism and meritocracy – white people rarely can see beyond themselves and imagine life in someone else's shoes. White people, nor their ancestors, rarely can understand what it is like to be treated like an outsider in their own country, to be dehumanized and disallowed common decency and human dignity, to be blocked from all legitimate means of providing for one's self and family, much less accumulate wealth, and more so to be met with violence, terror, and even death, when you did persevere and overcome such obstacles (see Anderson, 2016; Crump, 2019; Hannah-Jones et al., 2021; Kendi, 2016; Kendi & Blain, 2021; McGhee, 2021; Smith, 2021; Wallis, 2016; Wilkerson, 2020). None of this is to say that some white individuals don't have a hard life. What it does acknowledge is that white people, due to the white supremacist capitalist patriarchal structure of America (hooks, 1984/2000), have more avenues out of hard times than people of Color. In other words, for equally situated poor white and Black boys, more things *must go wrong* for the young white man *not* to move up the status ladder than *must go right* for the Black young man, many of which are beyond his control, *to move up* the social hierarchy. Social networks; access to information, resources, and opportunities; positive assumptions made by creditors, lenders, and others in positions of influence and power; and most over, entry into and acceptance within auspicious spaces – are all examples of privileges granted to *all white* people in varied degrees that are *often denied* their marginalized and oppressed counterparts. That is, even without what whites perceive to be innate "privilege," their hardships are *not caused by their white skin*; whereas, for Black folks, *it is their Black skin* that quite literally causes hardship through de jure or de facto policies and norms. This is white privilege, and it cloaks all white people's lives.

White privilege is the unnoticed, heedless advantages granted to those in white skin (McIntosh, 1988). But it is also more than that; it's the ability to influence and manipulate institutions, systems, and structures. And, most importantly, it's a primary enduring legacy of the myth of white supremacy and leading cause of all forms of racism (Collins, 2018) – from systemic racism, and overt hatred and prejudices, to microaggressions. White privilege influences all the aspects already discussed in this book – status dissonance (see Chapter 2), habitus angst (see Chapter 3), and aggrieved entitlement (see Chapter 4). However, it also plays a distinct role in the theory of whiteness and crime (TWC) – it grants privileged protections from entanglements in the criminal legal system. Up until this point, I've discussed the elements that increase whites', and particularly white men's, likelihood for violence, crime, and other negative and harmful behaviors. Yet, as Andersen (2015) has demonstrated, despite engaging in substantial amounts of crime, white (men) are significantly less likely to face the ramifications of a conviction and incarceration. I argue here, that due to white privilege, whites tend to be granted more leniency from and/or have access to resources that protect them from the harshest elements of the criminal legal system. Beyond individuals, whites are privileged by the laws themselves, which far too often have disproportionate impacts on the poor, marginalized, and communities of Color. In what follows, I outline some of the most explicit exemplars of whites' privileged protections from criminal legal entanglements.

Privileged from the System's Wrath

To fully grasp the privileges granted to white folks by the criminal legal system, we must first understand the typical "crime" data. There are three primary sources of crime data: official data from law enforcement and corrections that captures crimes known to police, arrest rates, clearance rates, as well as information on who is incarcerated (e.g., Federal Bureau of Investigation's Uniform Crime Report and the Federal Bureau of Prisons' Statistics); victimization surveys that directly capture the experiences of (alleged) victims of various offenses (e.g., Bureau of Justice Statistic's National Crime Victimization Survey); and self-report surveys, which ask individuals about their own deviant and criminal behaviors, as well as various potential correlates of crime, including perceptions, circumstances, background information, and other factors (e.g., Krohn et al., 2010; Miech et al., n.d.).[3] None of these, however, capture the true "dark figure of crime" – or the real number of deviant and criminal behaviors that actually occur (Hansell et al., 2016); but, all of them tell a different (and incomplete) story about the deviance and crime happening in society and the legal system's response to it.

To demonstrate this disparity, look at Figure 5.1,[4] which shows the percentage of the white and Black US population, arrests, and incarceration from 1995 to 2021. The population numbers come from the US Census,[5] the arrests from the FBI's Uniform Crime Report,[6] and the incarceration numbers from the Bureau of Justice Statistics' Prisoners Series.[7] What this depicts are the vast disparities across these numbers. In particular, Blacks are disproportionately arrested (i.e., bar graph) compared to their percentage of the population (approximately 13% and represented by the shaded background), and that they are drastically over-incarcerated following those arrests (i.e., line graph). What is more telling is the drastic drop between the white arrest and incarceration percentages (i.e., the bar graph compared to the line graph). Moreover, is that self-report data consistently indicates nearly everyone – of all races, genders, and socioeconomic statuses – engage in some type of arrestable or deviant behaviors (e.g., Henry & Lanier, 2001; Maxfield et al., 2000; McNulty & Bellair, 2003; Piquero & Brame, 2008; Reiman & Leighton, 2020; Sampson et al., 2005; Tonry, 1995; Walker

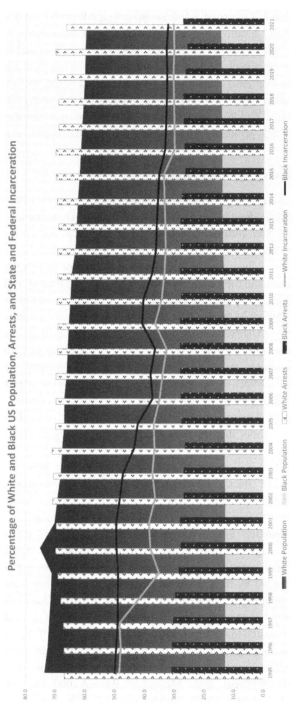

FIGURE 5.1 Percentage of white and Black population, arrests, and state and federal incarceration

et al., 2003). Thus, why do we see such vast racial disparities if we all engage in criminal and deviant actions? It is because whites are considerably more likely to fall out of the crime funnel.[8]

As noted in the Introduction, the crime funnel is a common metaphor for the narrowing of crime statistics as individuals move through the criminal legal system – from criminal and deviant actions (the true dark figure of crime), to known incidents, arrests, convictions, and incarcerations (see Hansell et al., 2016). People are freed from the entanglements of the system at all stages of the process due to conscious and unconscious decisions of people in positions of power as well as due to disparities in access to resources (Tonry, 2004, 2005, 2011). There are several places throughout the process where people may or may not stay in the crime data – from initial arrests to sentencing decisions – all determined by people in positions of power and influence using their discretion (Reiman & Leighton, 2020) – most of whom are white (Van Cleve, 2016). And far too often, those decisions benefit those with white skin over those with skin of color. Yet, these discriminatory decisions begin long before one's journey down (or escape from) the crime funnel – it begins with the creation of the law and our definitions of "crime."

Privileged Protections from the Law

The vast majority of orthodox criminologists take a consensus view of crime and the law. In other words, they utilize the legal definition of criminal behavior, or acts prohibited, prosecuted, and punished by law. Furthermore, most such scholars adhere to the belief that the law and legal system reflect a social contract of what will and will not be tolerated in society; therefore, the primary function of the law is to protect citizens and their rights (see Henry & Lanier, 2001; Tonry, 2004). Yet, as already discussed in this book (see Introduction and Chapter 1), the law was never intended for all and the legal system has been deliberately used to control oppressed and marginalized populations, particularly people of Color, throughout history. As 17th century author, Anatole France, famously wrote in his novel *The Red Lily* (1894), "The law, in its majestic equality, forbids the rich as well as the poor to sleep under bridges, to beg in the streets, and to steal bread." What this quote timelessly captures is the progressive criminological perspective that while all laws may be equal in their applicability, they are far from equal, equitable, or just in their impact, with the marginalized and oppressed, particularly the poor and people of Color, facing the brunt of the consequences.

Beyond the use of the law to control Blacks historically (e.g., slave codes, Black codes, and Jim Crow laws; see Introduction and Chapter 1), the law is still used today to control people of Color and privilege the white population. The United States imprisons people for lesser offenses for longer times than comparable nations (Tonry, 2004, 2005, 2011), leading America to have the highest incarceration rate in the world, despite not having the highest rates of violent crime (Widra & Herring, 2021). And, the majority of those left behind bars are poor and people of Color (Sawyer & Wagner, 2022; Wang et al., 2022), despite not being the one's to engage in the most (or most harmful) crime (Reiman & Leighton, 2020). These disparities are the result of conscious and unconscious policy decisions – zero tolerance policies, three strikes you're out mandates, disproportionate mandatory minimum sentences, career criminal statuses, life without parole sentences, cash bail systems, and others – that put people away for longer times for more minor offenses, especially those without the resources and knowledge to navigate their way out of the system – those that are poor and of Color (Tonry, 2004, 2005, 2011). Michelle Alexander (2010) has labeled such systemic and institutional discrimination the "New Jim Crow."

Alexander (2010) argues with the rise of the "colorblind" society following the 1960s Civil Rights Movement, America shifted away from openly discriminating against people of Color to discriminating against those labeled "criminal." Paralleling the massive rise in incarceration starting in the 1970s, we saw a net-widening not only of those locked away by the system – through new laws and increased policing tied to the "war on drugs" and other discriminatory policies (Anderson, 2016) that lead to 2.3 million people being incarcerated in the United States (about one-fifth of the world's imprisoned populations) (Wagner & Bertram, 2020) – but also of those unable to escape the entanglements of the system after their release. Policies were put in place that increased the collateral consequences of a felony conviction post-release; many of which aligned with the restrictions once placed on people simply for being Black. For instance, in most states, those with a felony conviction cannot register to vote, are excluded from juries, are often denied employment or housing, face barriers to obtaining education, and are denied public assistance or benefits (Alexander, 2010). Thus, a felony label – which is more likely obtained by the poor and people of Color – further disadvantages folks from living a full and complete life, or the American Dream. Hence, that law is not only sexist, male-oriented, and gendered (Smart, 1992), it's racist, white, and racialized (Daly, 1994). The law, therefore, works counter to social equity, and instead serves the status quo of white (male) privilege. And, this privilege is most often directly experienced in encounters with the police.

Privileged Relationships with the Police

The past decade has seen a proliferation of deaths of people of Color at the hands of police, further straining the relationships between law enforcement and communities of Color. While most white Americans view the police favorably, the same is not true in many Black communities (DeSilver et al., 2020;

Peck, 2015). Black Americans are more likely to be stopped by the police, have more overall contact with law enforcement, and more likely to encounter greater police use of force than their white counterparts (Davis et al., 2018), lending support to the notion that Black and Brown people are targeted, harassed, and over-policed in the United States (Butler, 2017; Evans et al., 2014; Rios, 2011; Weisburd et al., 2015). It is well-documented aggressive policing strategies such as stop-and-frisk are excessively used on people of Color (Ayres & Borowsky, 2008; Unger, 2014). Likewise, enforcement of minor "incivility" crimes, such as public intoxication, loitering, and panhandling, are significantly higher against people of Color (Cunneen, 1999), further increasing the likelihood of getting entangled and trapped with the legal system. Moreover, according to the Mapping Police Violence project, Blacks are nearly three times more likely to be killed by police than whites (https://mappingpoliceviolence. org/). Using this data, DeAngelis (2021) found the threshold of being perceived as dangerous, and thus encountering lethal force, was significantly higher for whites than their counterparts of Color. And, much of these negative encounters stem from law enforcement's "disproportionate attention to real or perceived or potential criminal activity suspects of racial minorities" (Perry, 2006, p. 416). Thus, while everyone's heart likely begins to race when the blue lights go on behind you while you're driving, whites generally fear a ticket, points on their insurance, or being late to an appointment, while their Black and Brown counterparts just hope to make it out of the encounter alive.

While police are often seen as enforcers for the state by people of Color, whites are more likely to take the police slogan "to protect and serve" to heart (Morin et al., 2017). Whites, and particularly women, tend to trust the police to come when called and to defend them when in need (Dukes & Hughes, 2004; Hurst et al., 2005; Visher, 1983; Wu & Miethe, 2022). White women often call the cops to their aid when they feel "threatened," and some have gone as far as to call the police their "protection service" (Gruber, 2020). Thus, whites often feel safe, protected, and validated by police, and most perceive law enforcement as just and legitimate (Cao, 2022; Tyler & Wakslak, 2004). Women of Color, however, have vastly different experiences. According to Ritchie (2017), "Black women, and their responses to white male authority, have been policed in brutal and deadly ways ever since the formation of slave patrols in the mid-eighteenth century…" (p. 11); leading many to feel that "…the police are not here to protect me. They are just as likely as anyone else to commit violence against me" (p. 4). Thus, the majority of people of Color are not privileged to positive encounters with law enforcement, and in effect cannot trust the police in their times of need.

In fact, research suggests that police may overlook communities of Color due to their beliefs that the citizens of these areas are responsible for the disorder and crime that happens in their neighborhoods (Gau et al., 2012; Klinger,

1997). Moreover, Black communities often criticize law enforcement for their lack of adequate response when they are in need of assistance or are victimized (Ben-Porat, 2008; Rios, 2011). Thus, this sense of being underserved by police often strains community-police relations as individuals feel as though they cannot trust police to help them when they need service or protection (Carr et al., 2007; Durose et al., 2005; Kearns, 2017). Research suggests that under-policing has been linked to increased vulnerability to violence (Crowther, 2013), decreased willingness to call on the police when in need (Carr et al., 2007; Kane, 2005), and tendencies to handle crime problems on one's own (Kubrin & Weitzer, 2003a, 2003b; also see Torres, 2017). Boehme et al. (2022), utilizing the Project on Human Development in Chicago Neighborhoods data, found Black and Latine people perceived both under- and over-policing more so than their white counterparts (also see Daly, 1994). Thus, police neglect – as well as harassment – serves to further marginalize the most vulnerable communities, leaving them to find ways to fend for themselves, many of which are criminalized.

Privileged to Resources to Escape Entanglement

As noted previously and shown in Figure 5.1, white people *do* get arrested and some are incarcerated, but they are still grossly underrepresented compared to the overall population and even arrest rates. Thus, despite engaging in similar behaviors at similar rates (according to self-report data), whites escape the entanglements of the criminal legal system much more frequently than their counterparts of Color, even if they are poor (though the odds are lower). This is because white privilege opens avenues to evade entrapment that are often blocked for others, particularly in the form of capital.

Financial Capital

As Bryan Stevenson (2012) has said, "We have a system of justice in this country that treats you much better if you are rich and guilty than if you are poor and innocent. Wealth, not culpability, shapes outcomes." And he's right – having access to money – to pay for bond or bail, to pay for legal representation, to pay court fines and fees – greatly increases your likelihood of staying out of jail or prison (Price, 2022; Reiman & Leighton, 2020; Tonry, 2004; Zaw et al., 2016). And, given white people hold the majority of wealth in this country, a system that uses finances as a means of punishment, deterrence, and retribution privileges whites. According to the US Census, the median white household wealth is US$187,300, compared to US$14,100 for Blacks and US$31,700 for Latines (Bennett et al., 2022). There are also significant differences in income, with whites having a mean household income of nearly

US$100,000 compared to households' of Color US$78,000 annual income (Peiffer, 2022). In addition to not having as much accessible financial capital, people of Color also carry more financial debt, with 35% of communities of Color, compared to 22% of white communities, having debts in collections (Peiffer, 2022). Thus, it is unsurprising how people of Color spend years behind bars awaiting trial (Sawyer, 2019) or die behind bars because they cannot afford bail (Ferkenhoff, 2023).

Social Capital

But privilege and capital come in more forms than wealth. Whites are also more likely to have financially richer and boarder social networks than people of Color (e.g., Munn, 2018), or in other words, social capital. Social capital refers to the advantages and opportunities people receive due to their social networks (Lin, 2001). Such connections and relationships are often segregated by race and gender, thus benefits are frequently greatest for white men. White men habitually advance in their careers or get financial advice due to unsolicited leads through such networks (e.g., McDonald, 2011; McDonald et al., 2009). It also means they have more people to lean on if they come in contact with the legal system. Because of historical barriers faced by marginalized groups, it is highly more likely white people will know a lawyer to call if one is needed or have someone to ask for financial assistance if they cannot cover legal costs themselves. For instance, in a recent national survey of white Americans, 68% reported having access to money or credit to pay for a major (over US$1,000) expense, and over 71% reported having access to a lawyer if necessary (Isom, 2022).

Additionally, it is likely these networks reach other positions of influence and power. For instance, more whites than people of Color are police officers (Brooks, 2022; Pew Research Center, 2018; also see Box 4.1). Given most communities are intra-racial, particularly in more rural areas, it seems likely people have stronger connections and larger social networks within their race than between. Thus, if a white person gets arrested, they likely have higher odds of having connections that increase their likelihood of leniency. Whites also hold more judgeships and district attorney positions than people of Color (Center for American Progress, 2020; Reflective Democracy Campaign, 2015). Thus, the same logic follows that whites are more likely to have a social network that spans the people in these positions of power that may use their influence for an individual's benefit. Such assertions are indirectly supported by the data shown in Figure 5.1 as well as the known disparities in criminal sentencing (The Sentencing Project, 2018), particularly for the death penalty (American Civil Liberties Union, n.d.). Yet, it is still more than just *who* one may know, but also *what* they know.

Cultural Capital

Cultural capital refers to the knowledge and appreciation of the dominant orthodox culture (Bourdieu, 1984), in other words knowledge of the white racial frame (Feagin, 2013). Beyond how we are socialized into the myths of white supremacy, patriarchy, and capitalism (see Chapters 1 and 2), cultural capital refers to educational attainment, exposure to and appreciation for art and music, opportunities to travel, and a taste for fine cuisine. In other words, access to and ability to fit in and maneuver in places of privilege and power (i.e., white spaces [Anderson, 2015]). Bourdieu (1984) describes three types of cultural capital: embodied, meaning how one presents themselves – from clothes, speech, manners, and personality; objectified, referring to what things are valued – such as music, literature, and fine art; and institutionalized, meaning credentials and qualifications that signify one's cultural competence – thus, an Ivy League education or Fortune 500 internship. Such knowledge is utilized as a resource for people to gain status, influence, and power (Bourdieu, 1984; Lamont & Lareau, 1988). And, as already discussed, access to cultural capital has been historically blocked to marginalized and oppressed groups. Many business and political deals have been made on golf courses, particularly those that until recently were not accessible to women or people of Color (e.g., Augusta National Golf Club [Associated Press, 1990]). Thus, while wealth has always opened doors to gaining cultural capital, it is much more easily obtained by whites (and particularly men) who are more readily accepted within those spaces than others (e.g., Anderson, 2015; Wildhagen, 2010).

Access to such knowledge not only likely expands one's social network, and therefore their social capital, but cultural capital also grants one knowledge to better navigate the legal system. The American legal and political systems are intentionally convoluted and exclusive as means to maintain the status quo (of a white supremacist patriarchal capitalist system [hooks, 1984/2000]) and control the masses (see Glaude, 2016; Goldstone, 2005; Lively, 1992; López, 2006; Mills, 1997; Wallis, 2016). It takes a level of finesse that comes through exposure and experience to understand legalese and to successfully navigate our legal system. The average person, even one with a college education, does not typically understand all their rights and the workings of a legal courtroom. But, such defendants, particularly if they are white, usually have the cultural capital to follow the proceedings and know they need a competent expert on their side, one they will likely have to pay for. While many public defenders are hardworking and well-intentioned, they are also grossly overburdened with indigent cases (National Partnership for Pretrial Justice, 2020; Pace et al., 2019). Many that face charges represented by a public defender don't understand what is happening and converse little with their attorney about their case (American Civil Liberties Union, 2013), thus are often disadvantaged not only by their indigent status but by their lack of all forms of capital.

Additionally, cultural capital may also grant many whites the shadow of a doubt by prosecutors, judges, and juries. The bar of guilt is much higher for a well-spoken, neatly dressed, white man than for a poor, young, Black man because the former doesn't fit the stereotype of a "typical criminal" like the latter (Reiman & Leighton, 2020; Russell-Brown, 2009). Common culture – through official crime statistics, the news media, and fictional portrayals – tell us who is supposedly "dangerous," and who we need to fear (e.g., Andersen et al., 2018; Dixon & Maddox, 2005; Entman & Gross, 2008; Intravia & Pickett, 2019). Such notions further reinforce the white racial frame, and in turn perceptions of cultural capital, about who and what are valued in society and deserve forgiveness and a chance at retribution – white people, especially those coming closest to fitting our referential structures of value and worth (also see earlier chapters, particularly Chapter 2). Thus, access to capital – whether in the form of finances, social networks, and/or cultural knowledge and value – privileges *all* white people, though to various degrees, with access to pathways away from criminal legal entanglements.

Thus, Privilege Prevails for Most (But Not All)

Again, not all white people who engage in crime escape the criminal legal system, as Figure 5.1 demonstrates. There is great variation within the white race in terms of access to capital that definitely impact outcomes; yet, *all* white people – even the poorest – *still benefit* from white privilege, even if only systemically or institutionally. And sometimes, even if white people do have all the advantages, the legal system does still prevail (e.g., George Floyd's murderer, Derek Chauvin; Ahmaud Arbery's murderers, Gregory McMichael, Travis McMichael, and William Bryan, Jr.; and the former renowned South Carolina attorney Alex Murdaugh who was recently convicted of murdering his wife and son). The legal and political systems informed by the myth of white supremacy and patriarchy, however, were never intended to protect all white people, just most, and particularly those in power. As the 1901 Alabama Constitutional Convention made clear, white political leaders were more than willing to sacrifice "their Confederate sons" through disfranchisement if it meant Black people were not allowed to vote (Alabama Department of Archives and History, n.d.; Feldman, 2004). More recently, many poor whites have gotten entangled in the system due to spillover effects of the "war on drugs" (e.g., Keller & Pearce, 2016),[9] but they too seem like a sacrifice many are willing to make to keep one in three Black men behind bars at some point in their lifetimes (Brame et al., 2014; Nellis, 2023). Yet, overall, the laws, policies, and the criminal legal system serve the purpose they are supposed to – to allow white men, particularly the rich, to do as they please, and granting them privileged protections from prosecution and punishment.

Notes

1 Portions of this chapter, particularly in reference to law enforcement, are inspired by and contain revisions of my earlier work (Boehme et al., 2022). Used by permission.
2 Quotes are presented as they are in raw data form. Thus, any grammatical errors are the respondent's, not the author's. See Forscher and Kteily (2017) for specific details on the dataset and methodology.
3 See Mosher et al. (2002) for a detailed discussion on the strengths, weaknesses, and limitations between official data, victimization surveys, and self-report data in measuring "crime."
4 The data complied by the author to create this graph are available upon request.
5 Population data were compiled from a variety of resources from the U.S. Census Bureau. Most racial distribution numbers come from the "Annual Selected Social Characteristics of the Population by Sex, Region, and Race" tables and report "White, non-Hispanic" and "Black alone or in combination" percentages of the US population. However, these tables were not created for all years and racial distributions of the population were unavailable for 2001, 2005, and 2006. For the missing years, the mean percentage was taken between the years prior and after the missing data to fill in the present data. Data can be found at https://www.census.gov/data.html and the specific data compiled by the author is available upon request.
6 Arrest data come from the FBI's Uniform Crime Report Arrest Table 43: Arrests by Race and Ethnicity. Years 1996–2019 may be found at https://ucr.fbi.gov/crime-in-the-u.s and 2020 through the present may be found using the FBI's Crime Data Explorer https://cde.ucr.cjis.gov/
7 Prisoner data come from the annual reports between 1995 and 2021 in the Prisoners Series available at https://bjs.ojp.gov/data-collection/national-prisoner-statistics-nps-program#publications-0
8 It is worth noting that for the most severe forms of violence, homicides in particular, some argue Black men do offend at higher rates than white men. Yet, research also finds theses disparities essentially disappear when structural and contextual factors are considered (see, for example, Peterson & Krivo (2010), Sampson et al. (2005) and Vélez et al. (2003)).
9 In addition to the spillover effects of the war on drugs impacting many poor whites, it is also worth noting the disparaging racial differences in the response to the (white) opioid epidemic as a health crisis compared to the (manufactured) crack cocaine problems in disadvantaged communities of Color. For further discussion, see Hansen and Netherland (2016), Netherland and Hansen (2017), Om (2018), and Shachar et al. (2020), among others.

References

Alabama Department of Archives and History. (n.d.). *Official proceedings of the constitutional convention of the State of Alabama May 21ˢᵗ, 1901 to September 3ʳᵈ, 1901.* https://digital.archives.alabama.gov/digital/collection/constitutions/id/120/

Alexander, M. (2010). *The new Jim Crow: Mass incarceration in the age of colorblindness.* The New Press.

American Civil Liberties Union. (n.d.). *Race and the death penalty.* https://www.aclu.org/other/race-and-death-penalty

American Civil Liberties Union. (2013, December 5). *Federal court finds public defense system violates constitutional rights of indigent defenders.* https://www.aclu.org/press-releases/federal-court-finds-public-defense-system-violates-constitutional-rights-indigent

Andersen, T. S. (2015). Race, ethnicity, and structural variations in youth risk of arrest: Evidence from a national longitudinal sample. *Criminal Justice and Behavior, 42*(9), 900–916.

Andersen, T. S., Isom*, D., & Collins, K. (2018). Constructing the "bad girls" hype: An intersectional analysis of news media's depictions of violent girls. In K. McQueeney, & A. Girgenti-Malone (Eds.), *Girls, aggression, and intersectionality: Transforming the discourse of "Mean girls" in the United States* (pp. 24–44). Routledge.

Anderson, C. (2016). *White rage: The unspoken truth of our racial divide.* Bloomsbury.

Anderson, E. (2015). The white space. *Sociology of Race and Ethnicity, 1*(1), 10–21.

Associated Press. (1990, September 11). *Augusta National accepts first black: Golf: The home of the Masters desegregates. The move follows the uproar elsewhere over exclusion of minorities and women.* Los Angeles Times. https://www.latimes.com/archives/la-xpm-1990-09-11-sp-437-story.html

Ayres, I., & Borowsky, J. (2008). *A study of racially disparate outcomes in the Los Angeles Police Department.* ACLU of Southern California.

Ben-Porat, G. (2008). Policing multicultural states: Lessons from the Canadian model. *Policing & Society, 18*(4), 411–425.

Bennett, N., Hays, D., & Sullivan, B. (2022, August 1). *Wealth inequality in the U.S. by Household Type: 2019 data show Baby Boomers nearly 9 times wealthier than millennials.* https://www.census.gov/library/stories/2022/08/wealth-inequality-by-household-type.html

Boehme, H. M., Cann, D., & Isom, D. A. (2022). Citizens' perceptions of over- and under-policing: A look at race, ethnicity, and community characteristics. *Crime & Delinquency, 68*(1), 123–154.

Bourdieu, P. (1984). *Distinction: A social critique of the judgement of taste* (Richard Nice, Trans.). Harvard Press.

Brame, R., Bushway, S. D., Paternoster, R., & Turner, M. G. (2014). Demographic patterns of cumulative arrest prevalence by ages 18 and 23. *Crime & Delinquency, 60*(3), 471–486.

Brooks, C. (2022, September). *Federal law enforcement officers, 2020 – statistical tables.* Bureau of Justice Statistics, U.S. Department of Justice. https://bjs.ojp.gov/sites/g/files/xyckuh236/files/media/document/fleo20st.pdf

Butler, P. (2017). *Chokehold: Policing Black men.* The New Press.

Cao, L. (2022). Police legitimacy in ethnic-racially and economically stratified democracies. *Canadian Journal of Criminology and Criminal Justice, 64*(3), 6–25.

Carr, P. J., Napolitano, L., & Keating, J. (2007). We never call the cops and here is why: A qualitative examination of legal cynicism in three Philadelphia neighborhoods. *Criminology, 45*(2), 445–480.

Center for American Progress. (2020, February 13). *Examining the demographic compositions of U.S. circuit and district courts.* https://www.americanprogress.org/article/examining-demographic-compositions-u-s-circuit-district-courts/

Collins, C. (2018). *What is white privilege, really? Recognizing white privilege begins with truly understanding the term itself.* Learning for Justice. https://www.learningforjustice.org/magazine/fall-2018/what-is-white-privilege-really

Crowther, C. (2013). Over-policing and under-policing social exclusion. In R. H. Burke (Ed.), *Hard cop, soft cop* (pp. 63–77). Willan.

Crump, B. (2019). *Open season: Legalized genocide of colored people.* Amistad/HarperCollins Publishers.

Cunneen, C. (1999). Zero tolerance policing and the experience of New York City. *Current Issues in Criminal Justice*, *10*(3), 299–313.

Daly, K. (1994). Criminal law as justice system practices as racist, white, and racialized. *Washington and Lee Law Review*, *51*(2), 431–464.

Davis, E., Whyde, A., & Langton, L. (2018). *Contacts between police and the public, 2015*. Bureau of Justice Statistics. https://bjs.ojp.gov/content/pub/pdf/cpp15.pdf

DeAngelis, R. T. (2021). Systemic racism in Police killings: New evidence from the Mapping Police Violence database, 2013–2021. *Race and Justice*. Advance online publication. https://doi.org/10.1177/21533687211047943

DeSilver, D., Lipka, M., & Fahmy, D. (2020). *10 things we know about race and policing in the U.S.* Pew Research Center. https://www.pewresearch.org/fact-tank/2020/06/03/10-things-we-know-about-race-and-policing-in-the-u-s/

Dixon, T. L., & Maddox, K. B. (2005). Skin tone, crime news, and social reality judgements: Priming the stereotype of the dark and dangerous black criminal. *Journal of Applied Social Psychology*, *35*(8), 1555–1570.

Dukes, R. L., & Hughes, R. H. (2004). Victimization, citizen fear, and attitudes toward police. *Free Inquiry in Creative Sociology*, *32*(1), 51–58.

Durose, M. R., Schmitt, E. L., & Langan, P. A. (2005). *Contacts between police and the public: Findings from the 2002 national survey*. US Department of Justice, Office of Justice Programs, Bureau of Justice Statistics. https://bjs.ojp.gov/library/publications/contacts-between-police-and-public-findings-2002-national-survey

Entman, R. M., & Gross, K. A. (2008). Race to judgement: Stereotyping media and criminal defendants. *Law and Contemporary Problems*, *71*(4), 93–133.

Evans, D. N., Maragh, C. L., & Porter, J. R. (2014). What do we know about NYC's stop and frisk program?: A spatial and statistical analysis. *Advances in Social Sciences Research Journal*, *1*(2), 130–144.

Feagin, J. R. (2013). *The white racial frame* (2nd ed.). Routledge.

Feldman, G. (2004). *The disfranchisement myth: Poor whites and the suffrage restriction in Alabama*. University of Georgia Press.

Ferkenhoff, E. (2023, January 13). Starved to death in an American jail, the man who couldn't pay $100 bail. *Newsweek*. https://www.newsweek.com/2023/01/20/starved-death-american-jail-man-who-couldnt-pay-100-bail-1773459.html

Forscher, P. S., & Kteily, N. S. (2017). *A psychological profile of the Alt-Right*. https://osf.io/xge8q/

France, A. (1894). *The red lily*. Borgo Press. (2002 English Reprint).

Gau, J. M., Corsaro, N., Stewart, E. A., & Brunson, R. K. (2012). Examining macrolevel impacts on procedural justice and police legitimacy. *Journal of Criminal Justice*, *40*(4), 333–343.

Glaude, E. S., Jr. (2016). *Democracy in black: How race still enslaves the American soul*. Crown Publishers.

Goldstone, L. (2005). *Slavery, profits, and the struggle for the constitution*. Walker and Company.

Gruber, A. (2020, May 27). Why Amy Cooper felt the police were her personal "protection agency". *Slate*. https://slate.com/news-and-politics/2020/05/amy-cooper-white-women-policing.html

Hannah-Jones, N., Roper, C., Silverman, I., & Silverstein, J. (2021). *The 1619 project: A new origin story*. One World.

Hansell, E., Bailey, C., Kamath, N., Corrigan, L., & Bessette, J. M. (2016). *The crime funnel*. Rose Institute of State and Local Government, Claremont McKenna College, Claremont, CA. https://s10294.pcdn.co/wp-content/uploads/2016/05/28-April-Crime-Funnel-Natl-Report.pdf

Hansen, H., & Netherland, J. (2016). Is the prescription opioid epidemic a white problem? *American Journal of Public Health, 106*, 2127–2129.

Henry, S., & Lanier, M. M. (Eds.). (2001). *What is crime?* Rowman & Littlefield.

Hochschild, A. R. (2016). *Strangers in their own land: Anger and mourning on the American right*. The New Press.

Hooks, B. (1984/2000). *Feminist theory: From margin to center*. Pluto Press.

Hurst, Y. G., McDermott, M. J., & Thomas, D. L. (2005). The attitudes of girls toward the police: Differences by race. *Policing: An International Journal of Police Strategies and Management, 28*(4), 578–593.

Intravia, J., & Pickett, J. T. (2019). Stereotyping online? Internet news, social media, and the racial typification of crime. *Sociological Forum, 34*(3), 616–642.

Isom, D. A. (2022). *Whiteness and crime* [unpublished data set]. University of South Carolina.

Kane, R. J. (2005). Compromised police legitimacy as a predictor of violent crime in structurally disadvantaged communities. *Criminology, 43*(2), 469–498.

Kearns, E. M. (2017). Why are some officers more supportive of community policing with minorities than others? *Justice Quarterly, 34*(7), 1213–1245.

Keller, J., & Pearce, A. (2016, September 2). A small Indiana county send more people to prison than San Francisco and Durham, N.C., combined. Why? *The New York Times.* https://www.nytimes.com/2016/09/02/upshot/new-geography-of-prisons.html?smid=pl-share

Kendi, I. X. (2016). *Stamped from the beginning*. Bold Type Books.

Kendi, I. X., & Blain, K. N. (Eds.). (2021). *Four hundred souls*. One World.

♠Kimmel, M. (2017). *Angry white men: American masculinity at the end of an era*. Nation Books.

Klinger, D. A. (1997). Negotiating order in patrol work: An ecological theory of police response to deviance. *Criminology, 35*(2), 277–306.

Krohn, M. D., Thornberry, T. P., Gibson, C. L., & Baldwin, J. M. (2010). The development and impact of self-report measures of crime and delinquency. *Journal of Quantitative Criminology, 26*, 509–525.

Kubrin, C. E., & Weitzer, R. (2003a). Retaliatory homicide: Concentrated disadvantage and neighborhood culture. *Social Problems, 50*(2), 157–180.

Kubrin, C. E., & Weitzer, R. (2003b). New directions in social disorganization theory. *Journal of Research in Crime and Delinquency, 40*(4), 374–402.

Lamont, M., & Lareau, A. (1988). Cultural capital: Allusions, gaps, and glissandos in recent theoretical developments. *Sociological Theory, 6*, 153–68.

Lin, N. (2001). *Social capital: A theory of social structure and action*. Cambridge University Press.

Lively, D. E. (1992). *The constitution and race*. Praeger.

López, I. H. (2006). *White by law: The legal construction of race*. New York University Press.

Maxfield, M. G., Luntz Weiler, B., & Spatz Widom, C. (2000). Comparing self-reports and official records of arrests. *Journal of Quantitative Criminology, 16*(1), 87–110.

McDonald, S. (2011). What's in the 'old boys' network? Accessing social capital in gendered and racialized networks. *Social Networks, 33*(4), 317–330.

McDonald, S., Lin, N., & Ao, D. (2009). Networks of opportunity: Gender, race, and job leads. *Social Problems, 56*, 385–402.

McGhee, H. (2021). *The sum of us: What racism cost everyone and how we can prosper together.* One World.

McIntosh, P. (1988). *White privilege and male privilege: A personal account of coming to see correspondences through work in Women's Studies.* https://www.collegeart.org/pdf/diversity/white-privilege-and-male-privilege.pdf

McNulty, T. L., & Bellair, P. E. (2003). Explaining racial and ethnic differences in serious adolescent violent behavior. *Criminology, 41*(3), 709–748.

Miech, R. A., Schulenberg, J. E., Johnston, L. D., Bachman, J. G., & O'Malley, P. M. (Principal Investigators). (n.d.). *Monitoring the future: A continuing study of American youth.* University of Michigan, Ann Arbor, MI. http://www.monitoringthefuture.org/

Mills, C. (1997). *The racial contract.* Cornell University Press.

Morin, R., Parker, K., Stepler, R., & Mercer, A. (2017, January 11). *Police views, public views.* Pew Research Center. https://www.pewresearch.org/social-trends/2017/01/11/police-views-public-views/

Mosher, C. J., Miethe, T. D., & Phillips, D. M. (2002). *The mismeasure of crime.* Sage.

Munn, C. W. (2018). The one friend rule: Race and social capital in an interracial network. *Social Problems, 65*(4), 473–490.

National Partnership for Pretrial Justice. (2020, November 30). *An unfair fight: Public defenders nationwide battle system with fewer resources, burdensome caseloads.* Arnold Ventures. https://www.arnoldventures.org/stories/an-unfair-fight-public-defenders-nationwide-battle-system-with-fewer-resources-burdensome-caseloads

Nellis, A. (2023, January 25). *Mass incarceration trends.* The Sentencing Project. https://www.sentencingproject.org/reports/mass-incarceration-trends/

Netherland, J., & Hansen, H. (2017). White opioids: Pharmaceutical race and the wart on drugs that wasn't. *BioSocieties, 12*, 217–238.

Om, A. (2018). The opioid crisis in black and white: The role of race in our nation's recent drug epidemic. *Journal of Public Health, 40*(4), e614–e615.

Pace, N. M., Woods, D., Anwar, S., Guevara, R., Pham, C., & Liu, K. (2019). *Caseload standards for Indigent defenders in Michigan: Final project report for the Michigan Indigent Defense Commission.* RAND Corporation. https://www.rand.org/pubs/research_reports/RR2988.html

Peck, J. H. (2015). Minority perceptions of the police: A state-of-the-art review. *Policing: An International Journal of Police Strategies & Management, 38*(1), 173–203.

Peiffer, E. (2022). *Debt in America: An interactive map.* Urban Institute. https://apps.urban.org/features/debt-interactive-map/?type=overall&variable=totcoll

Perry, B. (2006). Nobody trusts them! Under-and over-policing Native American communities. *Critical Criminology, 14*(4), 411–444.

Peterson, R. D., & Krivo, L. J. (2010). *Divergent social worlds: Neighborhood crime and the racial-spatial divide.* Russell Sage Foundation.

Pew Research Center. (2018, September 24). *In 2013, racial and ethnic minorities accounted for about a quarter of the police force and women made up about one-in-eight police officers.* https://www.pewresearch.org/social-trends/2017/01/11/police-culture/psdt_01-11-17-police-02-12-2/

Piquero, A. R., & Brame, R. W. (2008). Assessing the race–crime and ethnicity–crime relationship in a sample of serious adolescent delinquents. *Crime & Delinquency*, *54*(3), 390–422.

Price, G. N. (2022). Incarceration risk, asset pricing, and black-white wealth inequality. *Social Science Quarterly*, *103*, 1306–1319.

Reflective Democracy Campaign. (2015, July). *Justice for all: Who prosecutes in America?* https://wholeads.us/research/justice-for-all-report-elected-prosecutors/

Reiman, J., & Leighton, P. (2020). *The rich get richer and the poor get prison: Thinking critically about class and criminal justice* (12th ed.). Routledge.

Rios, V. M. (2011). *Punished: Policing the lives of Black and Latino boys*. New York University Press.

Ritchie, A. J. (2017). *Invisible no more: Police violence against Black women and women of color*. Beacon Press.

Russell-Brown, K. K. (2009). *The color of crime: Racial hoaxes, white fear, black protectionism, police harassment, and other microaggressions* (2nd ed.). New York University Press.

Sampson, R. J., Morenoff, J. D., & Raudenbush, S. W. (2005). Social anatomy of racial and ethnic disparities in violence. *American Journal of Public Health, 95*(2), 224–232.

Sawyer, W. (2019, October 9). *How race impacts who is detained pretrial*. Prison Policy Initiative. https://www.prisonpolicy.org/blog/2019/10/09/pretrial_race/

Sawyer, W., & Wagner, P. (2022, March 14). *Mass incarceration: The whole pie 2022*. Prison Policy Initiative. https://www.prisonpolicy.org/reports/pie2022.html

Shachar, C., Wise, T., Katznelson, G., & Campbell, A. L. (2020). Criminal justice or public health: A comparison of the representation of the crack cocaine and opioid epidemics in the media. *Journal of Health Politics, Policy and Law, 45*(2), 211–239.

Smart, C. (1992). The woman of legal discourse. *Social & Legal Studies, 1*(1), 29–44.

Smith, C. (2021). *How the word is passed: A reckoning with the history of slavery across America*. Little, Brown and Company.

Stevenson, B. (2012). *We need to talk about an injustice*. TED. https://www.ted.com/talks/bryan_stevenson_we_need_to_talk_about_an_injustice?language=en

The Sentencing Project. (2018, April 19). *Report to the United Nations on racial disparities in the U.S. criminal justice system*. https://www.sentencingproject.org/reports/report-to-the-united-nations-on-racial-disparities-in-the-u-s-criminal-justice-system/

Tenold, V. (2018). *Everything you love will burn: Inside the rebirth of white nationalism in America*. Nation Books.

Tonry, M. (1995). *Malign neglect: Race, crime, and punishment in America*. Oxford University Press.

Tonry, M. (2004). *Thinking about crime: Sense and sensibility in American penal culture*. Oxford University Press.

Tonry, M. (2005). *Malign neglect: Race, crime, and punishment in America*. Oxford University Press.

Tonry, M. (2011). *Punishing race: A continuing American dilemma*. Oxford University Press.

Torres, J. A. (2017). Predicting perceived police effectiveness in public housing: Police contact, police trust, and police responsiveness. *Policing and Society, 27*(4), 439–459.

Tyler, T. R., & Wakslak, C. J. (2004). Profiling and police legitimacy: Procedural justice, attributions of motive, and acceptance of police authority. *Criminology, 43*(2), 253–281.

Unger, J. (2014). Frisky business: Adapting New York City policing practices to ameliorate crime in modern day Chicago. *Suffolk University Law Review*, *47*, 659.

Van Cleve, N. G. (2016). *Crook county: Racism and injustice in America's largest criminal court*. Stanford University Press.

Vélez, M. A., Krivo, L. J., & Peterson, R. D. (2003). Structural inequality and homicide: An assessment of the black-white gap in killings. *Criminology*, *41*(3), 645–672.

Visher, C. A. (1983). Gender, police arrest decisions, and notions of chivalry. *Criminology*, *21*(1), 5–28.

Wagner, P., & Bertram, W. (2020, January 16). *"What percent of the U.S. is incarcerated?" (And other ways to measure mass incarceration)*. Prison Policy Initiative. https://www.prisonpolicy.org/blog/2020/01/16/percent-incarcerated/

Walker, S., Spohn, C., & DeLone, M. (2003). *The color of justice: Race and crime in America*. Wadsworth.

Wallis, J. (2016). *America's original sin: Racism, white privilege, and the bridge to a new America*. Brazos Press.

Wang, L., Sawyer, W., Herring, T., & Widra, E. (2022, April). *Beyond the count: A deep dive into state prison populations*. Prison Policy Initiative. https://www.prisonpolicy.org/reports/beyondthecount.html

Weisburd, D., Davis, M., & Gill, C. (2015). Increasing collective efficacy and social capital at crime hot spots: New crime control tools for police. *Policing: A Journal of Policy and Practice*, *9*(3), 265–274.

Widra, E., & Herring, T. (2021, September). *States of incarceration: The global context 2021*. The Prison Policy Initiative. https://www.prisonpolicy.org/global/2021.html

Wildhagen, T. (2010). Capitalizing on culture: How cultural capital shapes educational experiences and outcomes. *Sociology Compass*, *4*(7), 519–531.

Wilkerson, I. (2020). *Caste: The origins of our discontents*. Random House.

Wu, Y., & Miethe, T. D. (2022). Race/ethnicity, area and willingness to call police. *American Journal of Criminal Justice*. Advance online publication. https://doi.org/10.1007/s12103-022-09691-8

Wuthnow, R. (2018). *The left behind: Decline and rage in small-town America*. Princeton University Press.

Zaw, K., Hamilton, D., & Darity, W., Jr. (2016). Race, wealth and incarceration: Results from the National Longitudinal Survey of Youth. *Race and Social Problems*, *8*, 103–115.

6

A NEW RACIALIZED THEORY OF WHITENESS AND CRIME

In *The First Civil Right: How Liberals Built Prison America,* Naomi Murakawa (2014) states that the "United States (does not) face a crime problem that (is) racialized; it (faces) a race problem that (is) criminalized" (p. 3).[1] This sentiment is echoed by the numerous race, progressive, and critical race scholars that unpack the historical roots and intentions underlying the vast racial disparities in the American criminal legal system (as well as all of society) (e.g., Anderson, 2016; Davis, 2003; Gabbidon, 2015; Gabbidon et al., 2002; Greene & Gabbidon, 2000; Higgins, 2010; Peterson et al., 2006; Potter, 2015; Russell-Brown, 2009; Unnever et al., 2019; Walker et al., 2018; Wilson, 1987, just to name a few). Building on this rich tradition, I push this critique and analysis further and turn the microscope around on the powerful instead of the marginalized, on the oppressor instead of the oppressed. Within this book, I have applied a critical whiteness lens to our racialized investigations of crime to address two different questions: *How does being white impact one's likelihood of engaging in deviant, criminal, and/or violent behaviors?* And, *why are white people treated differently than other racial and ethnic groups by the criminal legal system*? Both are answered by the theory of whiteness and crime (TWC). Prior to this point, I have introduced the central components of this new progressive criminological theoretical framework. In the following sections, I synthesize how these factors are theorized to operate together to present a distinct racialized pathway to offending, yet privileged protection from prosecution, for white people.

DOI: 10.4324/9781003167877-7

The Theory of Whiteness and Crime

The TWC argues that white people, and especially men, are uniquely influenced by their internalization of the white habitus (Bonilla-Silva, 2018) through the socialization of the white racial frame (Feagin, 2013) that is informed by the white supremacist-patriarchal-capitalist systems that emerged from our imperialist, racist, sexist, and xenophobic roots (Collins, 2000; hooks, 1984/2000). Variations in the incorporation of these normative referential structures into our sense of self depends on the makeup of individual status characteristics and exposure to others and broadcast processes, which in turn provide a lens through which individuals perceive and interact with the social world (Isom*, 2018). Thus, this positional lens colors how individuals may experience feelings of habitus angst and aggrieved entitlement in regards to their perceived changing social position in society. In turn, these distinct racial strains may inspire acts of deviance, aggression, crime, or violence as means of coping with their felt anger and anxiety (Agnew, 2006; Isom* & Andersen, 2020). Yet, due to their inherent white privilege, especially regarding their relationships with the law and access to resources, they are also more likely to escape entanglements with the criminal legal system. Figure 6.1 depicts these theorized associations, and they are each discussed in more detail in what follows.

Status Dissonance

Status dissonance is the degree of disconnect between where one believes they *ought* to be in the social hierarchy compared to where they believe they *actually*

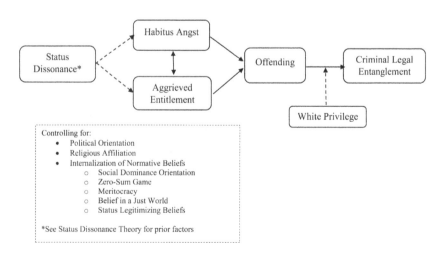

FIGURE 6.1   A theory of whiteness and crime

are. This disconnect comes from variations in the degree one accepts and internalizes normative referential structures about their perceived value and worth, particularly in terms of race, gender, socioeconomic status, and sexuality. Embodying more orthodoxically high-value traits, such as being white, male, and heterosexual, increases the likelihood one will accept and aim to adhere to the traditional standards of the white racial (patriarchal) frame. The incorporation of such beliefs into the self thus creates a lens that conditions how one perceives, interacts withs, and responds to the social world. Thus, status dissonance conditions one's experiences of habitus angst and aggrieved entitlement.

Habitus Angst

Habitus angst encompasses all the fears and negative feelings associated with perceived threats of change that white people have and often blame on "Others." Habitus angst is the anxiety, uncertainty, and anger whites feel in response to a changing culture; opposition to the status quo, orthodox beliefs, and social structure; and emerging viewpoints and lifestyles that counter how they believe things *should* be. Habitus angst is what happens when whites believe they are losing (or have lost) their advantaged position and influence in society. Habitus angst may lead to a range of negative behaviors – from drinking and drug use, to voting for racist and sexist political candidates and policies, to engaging with extremist ideologies and beliefs, to even violence and hate crimes. Habitus angst is also conditioned and reciprocally reinforced by another distinct, though not mutually exclusive, white-specific strain: aggrieved entitlement.

Aggrieved Entitlement

Habitus angst often arises from fear of uncertainty, particularly in relation to the future and one's supposed entitlement to their perch at the top of the social ladder. White people have an innate sense of entitlement – to respect, individuality, voice, space, time, access, opportunity – that is not granted to oppressed and marginalized others. And, when they feel those supposed entitlements are being infringed upon, they feel aggrieved. Thus, shifts in society not only lead to habitus angst, but a sense of aggrieved entitlement. Again, these sentiments fuel each other, and in turn inimitably and in conjunction potentially spark a range of negative behaviors. Yet, white privilege mitigates the likelihood one ends up entangled in the criminal legal system because of those actions.

White Privilege

While white privilege conditions all of the factors in TWC – status dissonance, habitus angst, and aggrieved entitlement – it specifically acts as a mitigating factor between deviant, criminal, and violent behaviors and criminal legal entanglement for white folks. In other words, embodying whiteness provides one with privileged protections from official (and unofficial) punishments for their negative behaviors. Moreover, the legacy of the myth of white supremacy embedded within American laws and legal structures advantages whites over their counterparts of Color. For example, police are significantly more likely to patrol Black communities and police Black behaviors than do the same to their white counterparts (Boehme et al., 2022; Daly, 1994; Rios, 2011; Stolper, 2019). Thus, whites are significantly less likely to come to the attention of the criminal legal system in the first place. Once they are, however, whites typically have access to more resources, either financially or socially, that allow them to circumvent the system. Furthermore, whites are also more likely to be granted the privilege of leniency by the agents of the court, greatly increasing their likelihood of escaping prosecution. Thus, white privilege provides means to avoid entrapment in the criminal legal system that are often elusive to others.

Unpacking Racialized Disparities Using the Theory of Whiteness and Crime

The TWC fills a vast cavern in our understanding of racial disparities in criminal and deviant behavior as well as entanglements in the system. In lieu of continuing to theorize and assess what is "different" about marginalized and oppressed groups, particularly Brown and Black people, that may explain why they disproportionately are represented in (some) crime data, TWC flips the focus away from people of Color and on to white folks. Instead of accepting white people's behaviors as individual deviations from "normal" behaviors, TWC questions the orthodox understandings of whiteness, white privilege, and the myth of white supremacy to understand the variations in deviant and criminal behaviors, particularly violence, and involvement with the legal system within the white population as well as between whites and other groups. TWC flips even progressive criminological theories upside down by questioning the role of whiteness in folks' deviant and criminal actions as well as the system's response to them.

Overall, TWC is a progressive, integrated, interactionist model of deviant and criminal behaviors. TWC aims to answer how being white distinctly impacts one's pathway to offending. To answer this question, the central framework of TWC draws heavily on a general strain theory (Agnew, 2006) tradition, applying a critical whiteness perspective to identify strains (i.e., habitus angst and aggrieved entitlement) that are distinctly and uniquely experienced by white people. Additionally, central orthodox concepts from control (e.g., in regards to internalized or applied constraints and access to positive coping strategies) and learning perspectives (e.g., socialization, reinforcement, referential structures, broadcast processes), and even elements of justice (e.g., positional lens, just world perspectives) are incorporated in TWC within focal concepts as well as in the acknowledgment of their impacts as exacerbating or mitigating factors. TWC is also grounded in the symbolic interactionist ideas of Cooley, Mead, and Goffman (see Chapters 2 and 7) and builds on the traditions of interactionalist theorists, such as Lemert (1951), Becker (1963), and Erikson (1962). As Ellis (1897) notes, "In most traditional perspectives (e.g., [classic] strain and control) social control is a reaction to deviance. In [an interactionalist] perspective, deviance... is a reaction to societal control" (p. 51). Thus, interactionalist perspectives suggest negative reactions to deviance cause further deviance. Yet, with TWC asking, "why are white folks treated differentially?," I propose *positive* societal reactions – in terms of white privilege (i.e., escape from the legal system) – provide protections from punishment and can lead to further negative outcomes, including aggression, deviance, and violence. Taken together and applying a socio-historical context to understanding the impact of power dynamics and social structures, this new model provides a theoretically integrated explanation for motives to and constraints from a range of negative, deviant, and dangerous behaviors (e.g., from voting for Donald Trump to committing mass murder). It explains social reactions (or lack thereof) that reinforce negative outcomes as social responses perpetuate "secret" (though not always so secret) negative behaviors and perpetrators are often awarded (at least perceived) power and influence, especially if you are a white, cisgender, heterosexual man.

Yet even this focus is incomplete if only the focus is on whiteness without an intersectional framework. As discussed throughout the book, there are distinct variations between genders, sexualities, and socioeconomic statuses in how TWC is proposed to work. In the next chapter, I introduce my recent contribution to intersectional perspectives and argue how it should be intwined with TWC.

Note

1 This chapter contains reference to my earlier work, Isom* and Andersen (2020) 'Whitelash?' status threat, anger, and white America: A general strain theory approach. *Journal of Crime and Justice, copyright ©Midwestern Criminal Justice Association, reprinted by permission of Taylor & Francis Ltd*, https://www.tandfonline.com/doi/full/10.1080/0735648X.2019.1704835 on behalf of Midwestern Criminal Justice Association.

References

Anderson, C. (2016). *White rage: The unspoken truth of our racial divide*. Bloomsbury.

Agnew, R. (2006). *Pressured into crime: An overview of general strain theory*. Roxbury Publishing Company.

Becker, H. (1963). *Outsiders*. Free Press.

Boehme, H. M., Cann, D., & Isom, D. A. (2022). Citizens' perceptions of over- and under- policing: A look at race, ethnicity, and community characteristics. *Crime & Delinquency, 68*(1), 123–154.

Bonilla-Silva, E. (2018). *Racism without racists: Color-blind racism and the persistence of racial inequality in America* (5th ed.). Rowman & Littlefield.

Collins, P. H. (2000). *Black feminist thought: Knowledge, consciousness, and the politics of empowerment*. Routledge.

Daly, K. (1994). Criminal law as justice system practices as racist, white, and racialized. *Washington and Lee Law Review, 51*(2), 431–464.

Davis, A. (2003). *Are prisons obsolete?* Seven Stories Press.

Ellis, D. (1987). *The wrong stuff*. Collier Macmillan.

Erikson, K. (1962). Notes on the sociology of deviance. *Social Problems, 9*, 307–314.

Feagin, J. R. (2013). *The white racial frame* (2nd ed.). Routledge.

Gabbidon, S. L. (2015). *Criminological perspectives on race and crime* (3rd ed.). Routledge.

Gabbidon, S. L., Greene, H. T., & Young, V. D. (Eds.). (2002). *African American classics in criminology & criminal justice*. Sage.

Greene, H. T., & Gabbidon, S. L. (2000). *African American Criminological thought*. State University of New York Press.

Higgins, G. E. (2010). *Race, crime, and delinquency: A criminological theory approach*. Prentice Hall.

hooks, b (1984/2000) *Feminist theory: From margin to center*. Pluto Press.

Isom*, D. A. (2018). Understanding white Americans' perceptions of "reverse" discrimination: An application of a new theory of status dissonance. In E. J. Lawler (Ed.), *Advances in group processes* (pp. 129–157). Emerald Publishing Limited.

Isom*, D. A., & Andersen, T. S. (2020). 'Whitelash?'status threat, anger, and white America: A general strain theory approach. *Journal of Crime and Justice, 43*(4), 414–432.

Lemert, E. (1951). *Social pathology*. McGraw-Hill.

Murakawa, N. (2014). *The first civil right: How liberals build prison America*. Oxford University Press.

Peterson, R. D., Krivo, L. J., & Hagan, J. (Eds.). (2006). *The many colors of crime: Inequalities of race, ethnicity, and crime in America*. New York University Press.

Potter, H. (2015). *Intersectionality and criminology: Disrupting and revolutionizing studies of crime*. Routledge.

Rios, V. M. (2011). *Punished: Policing the lives of Black and Latino boys*. New York University Press.

Russell-Brown, K. K. (2009). *The color of crime: Racial hoaxes, White fear, Black protectionism, police harassment, and other microaggressions* (2nd ed.). New York University Press.

Stolper, H. (2019, January 6). *New neighborhoods and the over-policing of communities of Color*. Community Service Society. https://www.cssny.org/news/entry/New-Neighbors

Unnever, J. D., Gabbidon, S. L., & Chouhy, C. (Eds.). (2019). *Building a Black criminology*. Routledge.

Walker, S., Spohn, C., & DeLone, M. (2018). *The color of justice: Race, ethnicity, and crime in America* (6th ed.). Cengage.

Wilson, W. J. (1987). *The truly disadvantaged: The inner city, the underclass, and public policy*. The University of Chicago Press.

7

UNEVEN INTERSECTIONS

While issues related to disparities and inequalities have long been assessed in criminological research (e.g., race, gender, and mental health – [Goddard, 1914; Lombroso, 1876/2007; Lombroso & Ferrero, 1893/2004; Murchison, 1926; Murchison & Nafe, 1925; Tulchin, 1939]), the orthodox approaches to understanding these differences have historically been largely rooted in cultural deficit or individual pathology perspectives.[1] Beyond inherent biological (e.g., Franz Joseph Gall [see Morin, 2014], William Sheldon [see Robertiello, 2014]) and overly simplistic essentialist (see Collins, 1993; Daly, 1994; Harris, 1990; Rock, 1973 for discussions) theories and explanations, the leading "general" theories of crime were not developed using an inclusive lens. Progressive scholars have long condemned these failings of orthodox criminology (e.g., Belknap & Holsinger, 2006; Buist & Lenning, 2016; Chesney-Lind, 1989; Chesney-Lind & Irwin, 2008; Daly & Chesney-Lind, 1988; Delgado Bernal, 2002; Delgado & Stefancic, 2017; Hawkins, 1995; Hurtado, 2003; Russell, 1992; Steffensmeier & Allan, 1996), calling for group-based theories of crime, with some scholars attempting to heed the call (e.g., Broidy & Agnew, 1997; Kaufman et al., 2008; Pérez et al., 2008). While such gendered, racialized, and ethnicity-based articulations are worthwhile endeavors, they still often overlook the intersectional, multileveled, and historically rooted lived experiences of diverse people. To best understand disparate pathways to and from criminal behavior and entanglements with the criminal legal system, variations in historically rooted social statuses, unique socialization experiences, and how these influence various intersecting emergent identities must be acknowledged and better accounted for in empirical work. Building on Potter's (2015) call for a disruption of criminology's theoretical footholds and taking an interdisciplinary approach, I present my integrative

DOI: 10.4324/9781003167877-8

structural identities model (ISIM) (Isom*, 2020) as a framework for achieving these aims, particularly around whiteness. Yet, before I present this integrative model, I begin with a review of the need for such a framework in criminology.

Crime as a White Man's Game

The leading orthodox theories of crime were developed by white, cisgender men based on (white) men's and boys' experiences. From Merton's (1938) focus on "normative" (white) goals and means, Burgess and Akers' (1966) emphasis on (white) children's interactions with "conventional" (white) others, Gottfredson and Hirschi's (1990) dismissiveness of racial and gendered variations in control, and even Shaw and McKay's (1942) exploration of (white) immigrant boys' arrests across communities that failed to acknowledge the previous work of Du Bois (1899), white and male experiences have been the foundation of the "general" theories of crime. Despite central aspects of strain, learning, control, and even social disorganization, theories finding empirical support with various demographics across different contexts (e.g., Broidy, 2001; Pratt & Cullen, 2000, 2005; Pratt et al., 2010), they all fail to fully explain the disparities in offending, particularly within-group differences. This is especially important given that despite marginalized people often facing risk factors that are more criminogenic, the vast majority *do not* offend.

As progressive scholars have proclaimed, such male- and white-oriented theories are insufficient for examining marginalized people's lived experiences (Daly & Chesney-Lind, 1988; Joseph, 2006; Lopez & Pasko, 2017; Messerschmidt, 2014; Peterson, 2012, 2017; Potter, 2006; Russell-Brown, 2009), with many calling for group-specific articulations or distinct theories of offending. The inadequacies of orthodox approaches are rooted in their lack of acknowledgment of the inherent racism, sexism, and marginalization embedded in American history that established the social structure and still encroaches on our institutions and everyday lives (Anderson, 2016; Gabbidon, 2015; Potter, 2015). Thus, they dismiss the disadvantages, inequities, and injustices faced to various degrees by non-white, non-male, non-cisgender, non-heterosexual, and other marginalized folks every day.

Of the leading orthodox theorists, Agnew is the only one to attempt to address this call with gendered (Broidy & Agnew, 1997) and racialized (Kaufman et al., 2008) articulations of general strain theory.[2] Group-specific theories of crime and paradigms have emerged over the years, such as the theory of African American offending (Unnever & Gabbidon, 2011), Black criminology (Russell, 1992; Unnever et al., 2018), feminist perspectives (e.g., Adler, 1975; Belknap, 1996; Chesney-Lind, 1989; Heimer & De Coster, 1999; Miller, 2001; Simpson, 1989), Black feminist criminology (Potter, 2006, 2015; Richie, 2012), and Queer criminology (Ball, 2016; Buist & Lenning, 2016; Mogul et al., 2011).

While these are valuable, empirically supported endeavors that move the field forward, they still often fall short of capturing the complexities of within-group variations. Group-based theories attempt to address the hierarchies of society by incorporating culturally specific aspects, such as a distinct shared worldview, socialization messages, and emergent identities. Yet, most fail to look at these processes fully intersectionally – either by only addressing intersectionality theoretically but failing to incorporate it empirically; treating varied experiences as an afterthought; or completely overlooking multiplicative identities. Thus, to truly achieve the aims of progressive scholarship, the full complexity of intersectionality must be acknowledged.

The Complexity of Intersectionality

Intersectionality has been described as a theory, method, paradigm, framework, praxis (Collins & Bilge, 2016), and even "buzzword" (Davis, 2008). Intersectionality is "the concept or conceptualization that each person has an assortment of coalesced socially constructed identities that are ordered into an inequitable social stratum" (Potter, 2015, p. 3). It "…is a term used to describe intersections between the social identities of an individual based on master statuses and the modes of their oppressions" (Hurtado, 2020, p. 144). It is also a paradigm that allows for the exploration of "…the ways in which race, class, gender, sexuality, nationality, disability, and other dimensions of difference and inequality shape the contours of social life and structures in the US and around the world" (Grzanka, 2019, p. 8). Intersectionality has a deep history in the discursive scholarship and activism of Black women (e.g., Collins, 2000; Davis, 1983; hooks, 1989; Lorde, 1984/2007), critical race theorists (see Crenshaw et al., 1995; Delgado & Stefancic, 2013), Chicana feminism (e.g., Anzaldúa, 1987; Baca Zinn & Dill, 1996; Baca Zinn & Zambrana, 2019; Hurtado, 2020), and other progressives, and has evolved rapidly since its coinage by Kimberlé Crenshaw (1991). In recent decades, numerous books (e.g., Bohrer, 2019; Collins, 2019; Collins & Bilge, 2016; Dill & Zambrana, 2009; Grzanka, 2019; Hancock, 2016; Hurtado, 2020; May, 2015; Nash, 2019), special issues (e.g., Cho et al., 2013; Else-Quest & Hyde, 2016a, 2016b; Misra, 2012; Phoenix & Pattynama, 2006), and editorials (e.g., Davis, 2020; Davis & Zarkov, 2017) have been produced debating and expounding on the concept, applications, and implications of intersectionality. As Patricia Hill Collins (2019, p. 3) states, "the scope of work that now exists under the umbrella term *intersectionality* provides a promising foundation for specifying intersectionality's distinctive questions, concerns, and analyses."

Despite the complexity of the historical roots and debates around semantics and applications, there are four central components to intersectional work: inclusion, multiplicity, stratification, and context. *Inclusion* refers to centering marginalized and oppressed experiences and providing voice to the often silenced. *Multiplicity* describes approaching identities and social locations in a nonadditive way by embracing the matrix of components that inform one's lived experiences. *Stratification* signifies the importance of recognizing the influence of social structure and institutions as well as history. And finally, *context* indicates the dynamic nature of the interplay between all these factors and how their salience may shift across time and space. While the verbiage may differ, these are the underlying aspects championed by all intersectional scholars and the defining aspects of intersectional best praxis (e.g., Baca Zinn & Zambrana, 2019; Bowleg, 2008; Choo & Ferree, 2010; Cole, 2009; Collins, 2015, 2019; Collins & Bilge, 2016; Cuadraz & Uttal, 1999; Davis & Zarkov, 2017; Else-Quest & Hyde, 2016a, 2016b; Grzanka, 2019; Hurtado, 2020; May, 2015; McCall, 2005; Potter, 2015; Sprague, 2016; Valdez & Golash-Boza, 2017).

Integrating all four components calls for a more intricate view and application of intersectionality that moves beyond solely granting voice to the marginalized, but investigates the complex, multilevel, and requited relationships between history, social structure, and power relationships that create and reinforce social positioning and identities. Hence, the centering of varied histories, pathways, and lives in any inquiry of disparities in behavior is needed to fully understand the causes and consequences of such differences. Therefore, "to better understand crime generally, we need to bring criminology "out of the closet" by supporting extensive historical and contemporary research on the relationship among sexualities, gender, race, class, and crime" (Messerschmidt, 2014, p. 124). Using intersectionality as a theoretical framework and methodological tool is the key to disrupting criminology and truly understanding within and between group disparities in offending (Potter, 2015). While this has long been the call of progressive scholars, how best to accomplish this empirically, especially quantitatively, remains a gap in the field. The following outlines one possible pathway to achieving this aim. Inclusion, multiplicity, stratification, and context are underscored by understanding the interconnected roles of statuses, socialization, and identities in the formation of intersectional beings.

Status: The Historical Root of Inequality

Despite the American ideals of freedom and justice for all, America has never been a land of equal access to resources or rights for all people. From the initial taking of land from Indigenous people to the enslavement of Africans, the United States was founded on a social hierarchy that assumed the myth of the superiority of whites and men to be true (Anderson, 2016; Feagin, 2013). Acknowledging these historical facts are essential to any authentic understanding of inequities and disparities in American society. Furthermore, understanding potential ways these hierarchies emerged and provided justification for the mistreatment of people solely due to their nominal differences from the white racial frame – the racialized normative standards of white superiority that has "long legitimated, rationalized, and shaped… oppression and inequality in this country" (Feagin, 2013, p. x) – provide insight into how we arrived at the current state as well as how to dismantle the status quo. Social psychology provides such a lens, as the values placed on nominal characteristics such as skin color and sex organs are social constructions whose creation, dissemination, and even dismantling, have long been theorized about and empirically examined in sociology (e.g., Berger & Conner, 1974; Blau, 1977; Ridgeway, 1991; Webster & Hysom, 1998).

As discussed in Chapter 2, status refers to the position one holds in society, particularly in regard to others; and status construction theory (Ridgeway, 1991; Ridgeway & Balkwell, 1997; Ridgeway & Correll, 2006; Ridgeway & Erickson, 2000; Ridgeway et al., 1998; with elaborations by Hysom, 2009; Webster & Hysom, 1998) describes how nominal characteristics gain value and become ingrained as culturally normative beliefs. Normative referential structures about status align with and reinforce a white racial frame (Feagin, 2013), assuming the value and worth of white, cisgender, heterosexual, men over others not (fully) embodying such characteristics. All those living in our society are exposed to normative referential structures by the cultural diffusion of ideals through means such as media messaging, interactions with institutions, observing people in public social interactions, as well as personal encounters with significant others (e.g., Berger & Webster, 2006; Ridgeway & Berger, 1986; Ridgeway, 1991; Ridgeway & Balkwell, 1997). Thus, we are all taught our supposed value in society based on the combination of nominal characteristics we possess (see Isom*, 2018b). In other words, normative referential structures and frames about self and others are learned and become ingrained due to socialization.

Socialization: Messages of Superiority and Marginalization

Socialization is the bridge between societal norms and individual selves. It is how people learn social norms, beliefs, and values. Through processes such as modeling, imitation, and differential reinforcement (see Bandura, 1977; Hernstein, 1961; Taylor et al., 2005), we all learn what are acceptable thoughts, actions, and behaviors in a given context. Furthermore, what is considered normatively acceptable varies based on the status characteristics one possesses. In other words, we learn the norms and ideals of society and how we compare to them. For instance, heteronormative gender socialization begins before birth with gender reveal parties, baby showers, and nursey decorations imposing normative ideals of femininity and masculinity upon new human beings solely based of the sex organs they possess (see Stockard, 2006). This continues throughout childhood as much of children's entertainment reinforces heteronormative standards of femininity and masculinity. Despite great shifts in media to counter these narratives (The White House, 2016) and many parents attempting to raise their children in gender-neutral ways, society still imposes the orthodox standards. Beyond media messages, advertising images, toys, teachers, institutions, and strangers all reinforce normative ideals and frames. In other words, we are all inundated with the socially constructed ideas of who we "should" be relative to society's standards from the time of conception.

Due to the inescapable barrage of messages and reinforcement, we are all socialized into the white racial frame (Feagin, 2013). Whether we can or choose to ascribe to them or not, most people know the socially constructed normative standards of beauty, what makes a man a "man," who is most suited to run a multi-billion dollar business or the country, as well as who is most likely to be a considered a criminal. Thus, all people know which statuses and social locations are valued and which are marginalized and reflect the normative (white) habitus of American society – the historically rooted understanding of how society "should be" that structures institutions, guides interactions, and provides a social lens that influences everyday life (Bonilla-Silva, 2018; Bourdieu & Wacquant, 1992; James, 1890/1950). Because these normative architypes are so ingrained within society, we are all judged by these standards, no matter our personal beliefs in them or our proximity to them; thus, they maintain and reinforce the status hierarchy.

In addition to being socialized by society, people are also shaped by their social networks, such as their family and peers as well as religious and civic organizations. Those holding marginalized statuses are often socialized to have pride in their group membership and taught how to cope with injustices in society. In other words, they learn counter-frames in contrast to white normative messaging (Feagin, 2013). For instance, racial socialization is the "specific verbal and nonverbal messages transmitted to younger generations for the development of values, attitudes, behaviors, and beliefs regarding the meaning and significance of race and racial stratification, intergroup and intragroup interactions, and personal and group identity" (Lesane-Brown, 2006, p. 400). Racial socialization for Black children is a complex and dynamic process of learning what it means to be Black in a racially stratified society and how to navigate an inequitable social world. Such culturally relevant and group specific counter-frames are crucial for marginalized groups to understand and resist oppression in an unjust society.

Thus, we are all taught various messages from society and others about normative ideals, where we are supposed to "fit" in society based on our embodied characteristics, as well as how to deal with obstacles and oppression if we hold marginalized statuses. Recognizing these processes further sensitizes our analyses "...of identities or social locations, by considering these as being constructed through, or co-constructed with, macro and meso categories and relations… (Thus, we can begin to examine) …racialization rather than races, economic exploitation rather than classes, gendering and gender performance rather than genders – and recognize the distinctiveness of how power operates across particular institutional fields" (Choo & Ferree, 2010, p. 134). In other words, understanding the historical social construction of status, how those orthodox ideals are perpetuated across time and space, and why different people adhere to such frames to various degrees provides insight into disparities between not only groups but also individuals. Individual differences primarily emerge due to variation in internalization of normative standards. We do not give all messages and frames the same weight to our sense of self. Those that are most significant shape our identities.

Identities: Internalization of the Narratives

One's identity is a key element of the self. Robinson and Smith-Lovin (1992, p. 13) suggest identities are created in social situations and allow "us to make choices, provide us with goals, and give us the strength and resilience to pursue them." Others posit identities emerge from one's social position, role requirements, or group memberships (e.g., Thoits, 1986, 1992; Turner, 1999). Additionally, Stryker (1980, p. 60) defines identities as "'parts' of self, internalized positional designations…which taken together comprise the self." One's identity is essentially the crystallization of socialization messages and experiences to form who one is. While symbolic interactionists have multiple conceptualizations of identity, they share the common assumptions that identity is meaningful and grounded in social interaction.

Symbolic interactionism suggests that an individual's identity, self-concept, cognitive processes, values, and attitudes exist only in the context of acting, reacting, and changing through social interaction with others (e.g., Blumer, 1969; Cooley, 1902; Felson, 1985; Mead, 1934; Stryker, 1980). One's self, therefore, is not innate, but a product of the social environment (Goffman, 1963). One has a social self that is negotiated with others in specific social interactions (Goffman, 1959; McCall & Simmons, 1978) as well as an internalized sense of self that is the culmination of all our (conflicting) internalized referential structures and frames (e.g., McCall, 2003; Turner, 1999). Thus, despite our focus on being distinct individuals, people do not have a concept of self or identity outside of their relationships and interactions with others and society. Therefore, one only knows their self within the context of our stratified society and their position within it. This is why we all have an internalized sense of who we are, but the social self that is shown to others varies based on context (e.g., Goffman, 1959, 1963).

Furthermore, our selves not only exist in our minds but also are embodied. "Indeed, it is only through our bodies that we experience the social world"

(Messerschmidt, 2004, p. 45; also see Messerschmidt, 2000). Our physical bodies house our selves and identities and in turn facilitate interactions with others and the environment. Our bodies provide agency (Giddens, 1991) and enable communication with others (Goffman, 1963). "Thus, the meaningfulness of our social action is based on the reaction of others to our embodiment – whether or not it is judged accountable is highly important to our sense of self" (Messerschmidt, 2004, p. 46). Our physical bodies, therefore, may facilitate, or hinder, the alignment between one's social selves and internalized selves as well as one's relationship to normative referential structures and the status quo.

An Integrative Structural Identities Model

To truly achieve an intersectional lens, one must acknowledge all levels of social interaction, varied lived experiences, and their dynamic multiplicative interactions. In other words, we must account for the social statuses, socialization, and identities of individuals within and between groups to understand disparities. A fully intersectional model encompasses inclusion, multiplicity, stratification, and context, which are all central to the ISIM. At the societal level, history defines power relations and determines the status value of nominally different people, establishing a hierarchical social structure that (currently) advantages white, heteronormative, cisgender men over all others and embedding such beliefs in all social institutions. The norms and ideals from the societal level are dispersed through social interaction. Through consumption of media, participation in orthodox educational systems, engagement in traditional religious and civic organizations, to interactions with family, peers, and even strangers, orthodox ideals are modeled, alignment is reinforced, and divergence is punished. Messages are internalized to various degrees and meld together to form our identities and sense of self and provide a lens through which we see and interact with the world. While the fundamental internalized self is fairly stable, our various identities have differing degrees of salience that vary within self as well as across social contexts impacting the social self that in turn is reflected to the world at a given moment. Some identities may align with orthodox standards, or even each other, more so than others, potentially creating conflict within one's self, sometimes providing advantages or resilience and other times creating obstacles to maneuver throughout society. Furthermore, these varying identities exist within a body that may either enable or restrain one's efforts to express their identities and/or achieve normative ideals. Thus, statuses inform socialization messages that influence identity formation which may reinforce, or counter, normative standards. Despite individuals having various degrees in which orthodox referential structures influence their sense of self, each person still must navigate a social world that is shaped by such orthodox beliefs and frames. Thus, these deeply embedded inequities impact all people and their lived experiences to different degrees.

Integrative Structural Identities Model

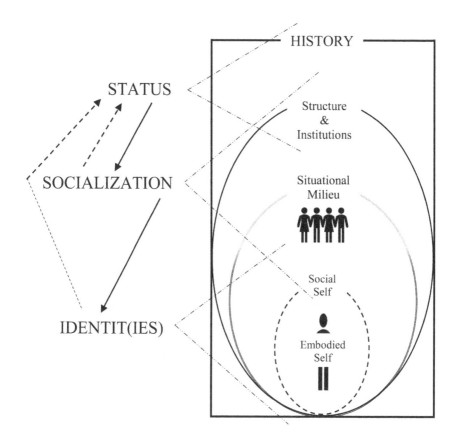

FIGURE 7.1   An integrative structural identities model

Therefore, a truly intersectional lens accounts for how status and socialization influence multiplicative identities. The ISIM is presented in Figure 7.1.

The ISIM is an example of "a complex intersectional approach that looks for such multilevel systems and situates them in local relations of power (that will) help to expose the processes that both create and transform inequalities over time" (Choo & Ferree, 2010, p. 145). It allows for the centering of marginalized experiences by not only including (and/or comparing between) various groups but also grounding their lived experiences in the socio-historical construction of stratified social locations (i.e., inclusion and stratification). Furthermore, it allows for the interplay of different messages and statuses to inform the creation of the internal self and expression of one's social selves in various locations (i.e., multiplicity and context). Thus, the ISIM provides a framework that not only encompasses the central components of intersectional best praxis but also more closely aligns with the true complexities of human life. Furthermore, beyond providing a more intricate model of disparities, the ISIM postulates a framework to problematize normative standards. By situating difference within a socio-historically constructed stratified society, the role of power in creating and perpetuating disparities is brought forefront. In doing so, hegemonic norms are questioned and the pathologizing and marginalization of difference is countered. In what follows, I outline some potential ways this framework may be achieved in practice, particularly for understanding the associations between whiteness and crime.

An Integrative Structural Identities Model in Practice: A Closer Look at Whiteness

The theory of whiteness and crime (TWC) puts the ISIM into practice through its central assumptions and propositions. First, it acknowledges the impact of our stratified history on our social structures, institutions, and selves in America. It then builds upon the theoretical assumptions of status dissonance theory (Isom*, 2018b) that acknowledges the various weight of differing status characteristics – such as race, gender, socioeconomic status, and sexuality – to assess one's assumed overall societal status value that in turn impacts one's likelihood of internalizing normative referential structures (i.e., acknowledging the "status" and "socialization" elements of ISIM). Yet, this perceived "value" of self is distinct, though not mutually exclusive, from one's intersectional identity. One's intersectional identity is conditioned by whiteness and greatly impacted by the physical body in which one resides. As discussed intermittently throughout this book, whiteness operates differently across gender identity, socioeconomic status, and sexuality – with heterosexual, cisgender, middle- and upper-class men holding the most privileges (i.e., the "identity" element of ISIM). Therefore, to fully understand the influence of whiteness requires applying an intersectional lens to unpacking the multiplicative ways it conditions, mitigates, and exacerbates varied experiences between individuals holding differing statuses and identities across the spectrum of whiteness in various contexts. And this means not just within white folks – but turning a microscope on how the ideologies of whiteness contribute to differences between other racial and ethnic groups as well.

What Does This Mean Empirically?

By far, intersectionality and the proposed ISIM are most easily achieved qualitatively. As Potter (2015) highlights, ethnographies and in-depth interviews allow the participants' voices to be heard, centralizing their lived experiences. Yet, strides are being made to quantitatively assess intersectionality, by moving beyond simplistic interaction terms of researcher-determined social categories to inclusion of participant-designated identities and use of measures of socialization messages and identity salience (e.g., Bell, 2013; Farrell et al., 2010; Isom*, 2018a; Isom* & Mikell, 2019; Parker & Hefner, 2015; Rodriguez-Seijas et al., 2019; Rogers et al., 2023). Incorporating an ISIM builds on these established efforts.

Quantitatively, survey instruments must be crafted to be inclusive and comprehensive (e.g., Bowleg, 2008; Else-Quest & Hyde, 2016b). Participants should be allowed to self-identify on all types of social categories. Providing categorical responses, allowing for multiple answers, as well as open-ended responses, gives participants control over their own narratives as well as provides multiple data points to compare and validate responses for researchers. Furthermore, indicators of how identities and social categories may vary by context provide insights into additional complexities (for instance see López et al., 2018). Beyond self-identification, inclusion of validated measures of identity salience for various social statuses is vital to understanding within-group differences.

Measures related to socialization messages and experiences are also important. Although such measures exist for some groups (e.g., Bem, 1974; Briggs et al., 2015; Phinney, 1992; Sellers et al., 1998), continued refinement as well as creation of measures for other groups are worthy empirical endeavors. Survey instruments should also aim to capture various experiences with institutions and structural barriers. Additionally, designing a sampling frame to capture a diversity of individuals as well as social context is ideal (Else-Quest & Hyde, 2016b). The influence of structures and institutions may also be gauged by linking institutional data (i.e., educational, healthcare, or criminal legal involvement) and structural data (e.g., city or neighborhood characteristics) to individual participants. Furthermore, to capture the enduring significance of history, shifts in demographics, political representation, laws and policies of a place (locally, state-level, as well as federally) over time are suitable markers. Although such data collection is timely, costly, and complicated, indicators from every level over time are needed to fully assess within and between group disparities.

Potter (2015) highlights several qualitative scholars that do intersectional criminology well (e.g., Anderson, 1999; Jones, 2010; McCorkel, 2013; Messerschmidt, 2000, 2004, 2014; Miller, 2008; Potter, 2008; Richie, 2012; Rios, 2011). And as noted throughout this book – there are several wonderful examples of qualitative work that examine the intersections of whiteness with gender (e.g., Blee, 2002; Ferber, 1998), masculinity*, as well as class and region (e.g., Hochschild, 2016; Wuthnow, 2018). Employing an ISIM would add further breadth and depth to such already rich analyses. For instance, researchers may interview multiple members of a family to gain intergenerational life histories to further investigate the impact of institutions and orthodox referential structures overtime and within families. Additionally, scholars should incorporate archival methods in addition to ethnographies to capture and contextualize how changes throughout history – from the demographics of a neighborhood, to shifts in political representation, changes in laws and policies, significant events and their media coverage, to shifts in industry – have impacted the people and phenomena of interest. Again, such integration of methods are lofty ideals, but worthwhile aims to move toward a more inclusive and complete understanding of variations in behavior and other outcomes. And, of course, taking a mixed-methods approach that optimizes quantitative and qualitative data and methodologies in tangent would not only triangulate information but also further deepen our understanding of causes and consequences of within and between group disparities.

Yet, most research is unlikely to be able to capture all the aspects of the ISIM methodologically. However, its employ would still bolster any investigation of disparities through its main contribution – the conceptual centrality of a socio-historically constructed stratified society. This conceptual cornerstone provides a lens that not only guides the design of one's study, but more importantly, the interpretation of the findings. The significance of contextualized interpretation is stressed repeatedly by intersectional scholars (e.g., Bowleg, 2008; Choo & Ferree, 2010; Cuadraz & Uttal, 1999; Else-Quest & Hyde, 2016a, 2016b; May, 2015). "A comprehensive intersectional approach makes the role of power and inequality explicit and requires interpretation of findings with the knowledge that groups exist within a context in which power and inequality are linked, rooted in, and perpetuated by social categories" (Else-Quest & Hyde, 2016b, p. 332). The ISIM provides a framework for such interpretations, which in turn will lead to new empirical questions, more nuanced investigations, and deeper understandings of disparities – and is a core underlying assumption of TWC.

Calling for an Inclusive Look at Crime

Intersectionality is central to progressive criminology, appearing frequently in scholarship featured in *Feminist Criminology*, *Race and Justice*, and *Critical Criminology*, but is often marginalized by mainstream criminology (Sharp & Hefley, 2007). Given that criminal behavior and entanglement with the criminal legal system present some of the largest social disparities, the lack of a nuanced understanding of difference is a gross negligence of orthodox scholarship. While ISIM is applicable to all forms of disparities in social behavior, such a framework is well overdue in criminology. Beyond the leading orthodox "general" theories of crime being far from general, there is much theoretical infighting within the field. Agnew (2011) argues these divisions only hinder the progress of scholarship and its ability to serve larger society through sound policy based on unified understandings of crime. Like Potter's (2015) call for intersectional approaches, the implementation of ISIM could unify the field as Agnew suggests.

ISIM does not necessarily introduce anything novel to the theoretical conversation of crime that has not already been presented by sociologists, criminologists, and progressive scholars. What is innovative is the unified approach to these concepts to bring deeper understanding to disparities, particularly in relation to crime. Such unification pushes against the walls of orthodox paradigmatic frameworks in regard to inequities and crime to "enable us to move beyond the limitations of conventional scientific approaches... (that) do not capture or explain the deep structural realities of this society's ... oppression in the past or present" (Feagin, 2013, p. 3).

Progressive scholars are often condemned for critiquing the lack of inclusion in criminological theory and the inherent injustices within our criminal legal system without offering viable solutions (see DeKeseredy & Dragiewicz, 2018 for discussion). Furthermore, Black feminist scholars have long said theory without action is essentially pointless (e.g., Collins, 2000; Crenshaw, 1991; Davis, 1983; Lorde, 1984/2007). ISIM puts the criticism of progressive scholars into practice to potentially yield empirically informed solutions. By integrating all levels of social interaction, acknowledging the role of history, and widening our methodological bounds, we are better able to capture the complexities of social lives and disparities in all forms of behaviors. Such understanding will better inform targeted policy solutions at varied levels of society to best serve those that need it most. Applying such a lens will allow us to bring justice to the criminal "justice" system. And this is the call I aim to answer with the formulation of TWC.

Notes

1 This chapter originally appeared in Isom* (2020) and has been revised to contextualize the TWC; used with permission.
2 This is not to say other theories have completely failed to acknowledge the significance of race or gender. Race and gender are common foci of labeling theorists, symbolic interactionists, cultural criminologists, and others. However, of the three leading micro-level orthodox theories of crime – strain, learning, and control – and their modern primary theorists – Agnew, Akers, and Hirschi – only Agnew has attempted to craft racialized and gendered versions of general strain theory.

References

Adler, F. (1975). *Sisters in crime: The rise of the new female criminal.* McGraw-Hill.
Agnew, R. (2011). *Toward a unified criminology: Integrating assumptions about crime, people, and society.* New York University Press.
Anderson, C. (2016). *White rage: The unspoken truth of our racial divide.* Bloomsbury.

Anderson, E. (1999). *Code of the street: Decency, violence, and the moral life of the inner city*. W.W. Norton & Company.

Anzaldúa, G. (1987). *Borderlands/La frontera: The new mestiza*. Spinsters/Aunt Lute Press.

Baca Zinn, M., & Dill, B. T. (1996). Theorizing difference from multiracial feminism. *Feminist Studies, 22*, 321–331.

Baca Zinn, M., & Zambrana, R. E. (2019). Chicanas/Latinas advance intersectional thought and practice. *Gender & Society, 33*(5), 677–701.

Ball, M. (2016). *Criminology and queer theory: Dangerous bedfellows?* Springer Publishing.

Bandura, A. (1977). Self-efficacy: A unifying theory of behavioral change. *Psychological Review, 84*(2), 191–215.

Belknap, J. (1996). *The invisible woman: Gender, crime, and justice*. Wadsworth.

Belknap, J., & Holsinger, K. (2006). The gendered nature of risk factors for delinquency. *Feminist Criminology, 1*(1), 48–71.

Bell, K. (2013). Young adult offending: Intersectionality of gender and race. *Critical Criminology, 21*(1), 103–121.

Berger, J., & Conner, T. L. (1974). Performance expectations and behavior in small groups: A revised formulation. In J. Berger, T. L. Conner, & M. H. Fisek (Eds.), *Expectation states theory: A theoretical program* (pp. 85–109). Winthrop.

Berger, J., & Webster, M., Jr. (2006). Expectations, status, and behavior. In P. J. Burke (Ed.), *Contemporary social psychological theories* (pp. 268–300). Stanford University Press.

Bem, S. (1974). The measurement of psychological androgyny. *Journal of Consulting and Clinical Psychology, 42*(2), 155–162.

Blau, P. M. (1977). A macrosociological theory of social structure. *The American Journal of Sociology, 83*(1), 26–54.

Blee, K. M. (2002). *Inside organized racism: Women in the hate movement*. University of California Press.

Blumer, H. (1969). *Symbolic interactionism: Perspective and method*. University of California Press.

Bohrer, A. J. (2019). *Marxism and intersectionality: Race, gender, class and sexuality under contemporary capitalism*. Transcript Verlag.

Bowleg, L. (2008). When Black + lesbian + woman ≠ Black lesbian woman: The methodological challenges of qualitative and quantitative intersectionality research. *Sex Roles, 59*, 312–325.

Bonilla-Silva, E. (2018). *Racism without racists: Color-blind racism and the persistence of racial inequality in America* (5th ed.). Rowman & Littlefield.

Bourdieu, P., & Wacquant, L. J. D. (1992). *An invitation to reflexive sociology*. The University of Chicago Press.

Briggs, H., Kothari, B., Briggs, A. C., Bank, L., & DeGruy, J. (2015). Racial respect: Initial testing and validation of the racial respect scale for adult African Americans. *Journal of the Society for Social Work and Research, 6*(2), 269–303.

Broidy, L. M. (2001). A test of general strain theory. *Criminology, 30*(1), 9–35.

Broidy, L., & Agnew, R. (1997). Gender and crime: A general strain theory perspective. *Journal of Research in Crime and Delinquency, 34*(3), 275–306.

Buist, C. L., & Lenning, E. (2016). *Queer criminology*. Routledge.

Burgess, R. L., & Akers, R. L. (1966). A differential association-reinforcement theory of criminal behavior. *Social Problems, 14*, 128–147.

Chesney-Lind, M. (1989). Girls, crime and woman's place: Toward a feminist model of female delinquency. *Crime and Delinquency, 35*, 5–29.

Chesney-Lind, M., & Irwin, K. (2008). *Beyond bad girls: Gender, violence and hype*. New Routledge.

Cho, S., Crenshaw, K. W., & McCall, L. (Eds.). (2013). Intersectionality: Theorizing power, empowering theory [Special issue]. *Signs, 38*(4).

Choo, H. Y., & Ferree, M. M. (2010). Practicing intersectionality in sociological research: A critical analysis of inclusions, interactions, and institutions in the study of inequalities. *Sociology Theory, 28*(2), 129–149.

Cole, E. R. (2009). Intersectionality and research in psychology. *American Psychologist, 64*, 170–180.

Collins, P. H. (1993). Toward a new vision: Race, class, and gender as categories of analysis and connection. *Race, Sex, and Class, 1*(1), 25–45.

Collins, P. H. (2000). *Black feminist thought: Knowledge, consciousness, and the politics of empowerment* (2nd ed.). Routledge.

Collins, P. H. (2015). Intersectionality's definitional dilemmas. *Annual Review of Sociology, 41*, 1–20.

Collins, P. H. (2019). *Intersectionality as critical social theory*. Duke University Press.

Collins, P. H., & Bilge, S. (2016). *Intersectionality*. Polity.

Cooley, C. H. (1902). *Human nature and social order*. Pantianos Classics.

Crenshaw, K. (1991). Mapping the margins: Intersectionality, identity, politics, and violence against women of color. *Stanford Law Review, 43*(6), 1241–1299.

Crenshaw, K., Cotanda, N., Peller, G., & Thomas, K. (Eds.). (1995). *Critical race theory: The key writings that formed the movement*. The New Press.

Cuadraz, G. H., & Uttal, L. (1999). Intersectionality and in-depth interviews: Methodological strategies for analyzing race, class, and gender. *Race, Gender & Class, 6*, 156–186.

Daly, K. (1994). Criminal law and justice system practices as racist, white, and racialized. *Washington and Lee Law Review, 51*(2), 431–464.

Daly, K., & Chesney-Lind, M. (1988). Feminism and criminology. *Justice Quarterly, 5*(4), 497–538.

Davis, A. Y. (1983). *Women, race, and class*. Vintage Books.

Davis, K. (2008). Intersectionality as buzzword: A sociology of science perspective on what makes a feminist theory successful. *Feminist Theory, 9*(1), 67–85.

Davis, K. (2020). Who owns intersectionality? Some reflections on feminist debates on how theories travel. *European Journal of Women's Studies, 27*(2), 113–127.

Davis, K., & Zarkov, D. (2017). EJWS retrospective on intersectionality. *European Journal of Women's Studies, 24*(4), 313–320.

DeKeseredy, W. S., & Dragiewicz, M. (Eds.). (2018). *Routledge handbook of critical criminology* (2nd ed.). Routledge.

Delgado Bernal, D. (2002). Critical race theory, Latino critical theory, and critical raced-gendered epistemologies: Recognizing students of color as holders as creators of knowledge. *Qualitative Inquiry, 8*(1), 105–126.

Delgado, R., & Stefancic, J. (2017). *Critical race theory: An introduction* (3rd ed.). New York University Press.

Delgado, R., & Stefancic, J. (Eds.). (2013). *Critical race theory: The cutting edge* (3rd ed.). Temple University Press.

Dill, B. T., & Zambrana, R. E. (2009). *Emerging intersections: Race, class, and gender in theory, policy and practice*. Rutgers University Press.

Du Bois, W. E. B. (1899). *The Philadelphia negro: A social study*. University of Pennsylvania.

Else-Quest, N. M., & Hyde, J. S. (Eds.). (2016a). Intersectionality research and feminist psychology [Special section]. *Psychology of Women Quarterly, 40*(2).

Else-Quest, N. M., & Hyde, J. S. (Eds.). (2016b). Intersectionality research and feminist psychology [Special section]. *Psychology of Women Quarterly, 40*(3).

Farrell, A., Ward, G., & Rousseau, D. (2010). Intersections of gender and race in federal sentencing: Examining court contexts and effects of representative court authorities. *Journal of Gender, Race, and Justice, 14*, 85–125.

Feagin, J. R. (2013). *The white racial frame* (2nd ed.). Routledge.

Felson, R. B. (1985). Reflected appraisal and the development of the self. *Social Psychology Quarterly, 48*, 71–78.

Ferber, A. L. (1998). *White man falling: Race, gender, and white supremacy*. Rowman & Littlefield.

Gabbidon, S. L. (2015). *Criminological perspectives on race and crime* (3rd ed.). Routledge.

Giddens, A. (1991). *Modernity and self-identity*. Stanford University Press.

Goddard, H. H. (1914). *Feeble-mindedness: Its causes and consequences*. The Macmillan Company.

Goffman, E. (1959). *Presentation of self in everyday life*. Doubleday.

Goffman, E. (1963). *Behavior in public places*. Free Press.

Gottfredson, M. R., & Hirschi, T. (1990). *A general theory of crime*. Stanford University Press.

Grzanka, P. R. (Ed.). (2019). *Intersectionality: Foundations and frontiers* (2nd ed.). Routledge.

Hancock, A. M. (2016). *Intersectionality: An intellectual history*. Oxford University Press.

Harris, A. P. (1990). Race and essentialism in feminist legal theory. *Stanford Law Review, 42*(3), 581–616.

Hawkins, D. F. (1995). Ethnicity, race, and crime: A review of selected studies. In D. F. Hawkins (Ed.), *Ethnicity, race, and crime: Perspectives across time and place* (pp. 11–45). State University of New York Press.

Heimer, K., & De Coster, S. (1999). The gendering of violent delinquency. *Criminology, 37*, 277–318.

Herrnstein, R. J. (1961). Relative and absolute strength of response as a function of frequency of reinforcement. *Journal of Experimental Analysis of Behavior, 4*(3), 267–272.

Hochschild, A. R. (2016). *Strangers in their own land: Anger and mourning on the American right*. The New Press.

hooks, b. (1989). *Talking back: Thinking feminist, thinking Black*. South End Press.

Hurtado, A. (2003). *Voicing Chicana feminisms: Young women speak out on sexuality and identity*. New York University Press.

Hurtado, A. (2020). *Intersectional Chicana feminisms*. The University of Arizona Press.

Hysom, S. J. (2009). Status valued goal objects and performance expectations. *Social Forces*, *87*(3), 1623–1648.

Isom*, D. (2018a). Latina fortitude in the face of disadvantaged: Exploring the conditioning effects of ethnic identity and gendered ethnic identity on Latina offending. *Critical Criminology*, *26*, 49–73.

Isom*, D. A. (2018b). Understanding White Americans' perceptions of "reverse" discrimination: An application of a new theory of status dissonance. In S. R. Thye & E. J. Lawler (Eds.), *Advances in group processes* (Vol. 35, pp. 129–157). Emerald Insight.

Isom*, D. A. (2020). Status, socialization, and identities: Central factors to understanding disparities in crime. *Sociology Compass*, *14*(9), e12825.

Isom*, D. A., & Mikell, T. (2019). 'Gender' and general strain theory: Investigating the impact of gender socialization on young women's criminal outcomes. *Journal of Crime and Justice*, *42*(4), 393–413.

James, W. (1890/1950). *The principles of psychology* (Vol. 1). Dover Publications.

Jones, N. (2010). *Between good and ghetto: African American girls and inner-city violence*. Rutgers University Press.

Joseph, J. (2006). Intersectionality of race/ethnicity, class, and justice: Women of color. In A. V. Merlo & J. M. Pollack (Eds.), *Women, law, and social control* (2nd ed., pp. 292–312). Allyn & Bacon.

Kaufman, J. M., Rebellon, C. J., Thaxton, S., & Agnew, R. (2008). A general strain theory of racial differences in criminal offending. *The Australian and New Zealand Journal of Criminology*, *41*(3), 421–437.

♠Kimmel, M. (2017). *Angry white men: American Masculinity at the end of an era*. Nation Books.

Lesane-Brown, C. L. (2006). A review of race socialization with black families. *Developmental Review*, *26*, 400–426.

Lombroso, C. (1876/2007). *Criminal man* (Translated and with a new introduction by Mary Gibson and Nicole Hahn Rafter, 2nd ed.). Duke University Press.

Lombroso, C., & Ferrero, G. (1893/2004). *Criminal woman, the prostitute, and the normal woman* (Translated and with a new introduction Nicole Hahn Rafter and Mary Gibson). Duke University Press.

López, N., Vargas, E., Juarez, M., Cacari-Stone, L., & Bettez, S. (2018). What's your "street race"? Leveraging multidimensional measures of race and intersectionality for examining physical and mental health status among Latinx. *Sociology of Race and Ethnicity*, *4*(1), 49–66.

Lopez, V., & Pasko, L. (2017). Bringing Latinas to the forefront: Latina girls, women, and the justice system. *Feminist Criminology*, *12*(3), 195–198.

Lorde, A. (1984/2007). *Sister outsider*. Crossing Press.

May, V. M. (2015). *Pursuing intersectionality, unsettling dominant imaginaries*. Routledge.

McCall, G. J. (2003). The me and the not-me. In P. J. Burke, T. J. Owens, R. T. Serpe, & P. A. Thoits (Eds.), *Advances in identity theory and research* (pp. 11–25). Springer.

McCall, G. J., & Simmons, J. L. (1978*). Identities and interactions*. Free Press.

McCall, L. (2005). The complexity of intersectionality. *Signs*, *30*(3), 1771–1799.

McCorkel, J. A. (2013). *Breaking women: Gender, race, and the new politics of imprisonment*. New York University Press.

Mead, G. H. (1934). *Mind, self and society*. University of Chicago Press.

Merton, R. K. (1938). Social structure and anomie. *American Sociological Review*, *3*, 672–682.

Messerschmidt, J. W. (2000). *Nine lives: Adolescent masculinities, the body, and violence*. Westview Press.

Messerschmidt, J. W. (2004). *Flesh & blood: Adolescent gender diversity and violence*. Rowman & Littlefield.

Messerschmidt, J. W. (2014). *Crime as structured action: Doing masculinities, race, class, sexuality, and crime* (2nd ed.). Rowman & Littlefield.

Miller, J. (2001). *One of the guys: Girls, gangs, and gender*. Oxford University Press.

Miller, J. (2008). *Getting played: African American girls, urban inequality, and gendered violence*. New York University Press.

Misra, J. (Ed.). (2012). Symposia on the contributions of Patricia Hill Collins [Special issue]. *Gender & Society*, *26*(1).

Mogul, J. L., Ritchie, A., & Whitlock, K. (2011). *Queer (in)justice: The criminalization of LGBT people in the United States*. Beacon Press.

Morin, R. (2014). Phrenology and crime. In J. M. Miller (Ed.), *The encyclopedia of theoretical criminology* (online edition). John Wiley & Sons. http://doi.org/10.1002/9781118517390.wbetc102

Murchison, C. (1926). Mental tests and other concomitants of some Negro women criminals. *The Pedagogical Seminary and Journal of Genetic Psychology*, *33*, 527–530.

Murchison, C., & Nafe, R. (1925). Intelligence of Negro recidivists. *The Pedagogical Seminary and Journal of Genetic Psychology*, *32*, 248–256.

Nash, J. (2019). *Black feminism reimagined: After intersectionality*. Duke University Press.

Parker, K. F., & Hefner, M. K. (2015). Intersections of race, gender, disadvantage, and violence: Applying intersectionality to the macro-level study of female homicide. *Justice Quarterly*, *32*(2), 223–254.

Pérez, D. M., Jennings, W. G., & Gover, A. R. (2008). Specifying general strain theory: An ethnically relevant approach. *Deviant Behavior*, *29*(6), 544–578.

Peterson, R. D. (2012). The central place of race in crime and justice. *Criminology*, *50*, 303–28.

Peterson, R. D. (2017). Interrogating race, crime, and justice in a time of unease and racial tension. *Criminology*, *55*(2), 245–272.

Phinney, J. S. (1992). The multigroup ethnic identity measure: A new scale for use with diverse groups. *Journal of Adolescent Research*, *7*, 156–176.

Phoenix, A., & Pattynama, P. (Eds.). (2006). Intersectionality [Special issue]. *European Journal of Women's Studies*, *13*(3).

Potter, H. (2006). An argument for Black feminist criminology: Understanding African American women's experiences with intimate partner abuse using an integrated approach. *Feminist Criminology*, *1*(2), 106–124.

Potter, H. (2008). *Battle cries: Black women and intimate partner abuse*. New York University Press.

Potter, H. (2015). *Intersectionality and criminology: Disrupting and revolutionizing studies of crime*. Routledge.

Pratt, T. C., & Cullen, F. T. (2000). The empirical status of Gottfredson and Hirschi's general theory of crime: A meta-analysis. *Criminology*, *38*, 931–964.

Pratt, T. C., & Cullen, F. T. (2005). Assessing macro-level predictors and theories of crime: A meta-analysis. *Crime & Justice*, *32*, 373–450.

Pratt, T. C., Cullen, F. T., Sellers, C. S., Winfree, L. T., Jr., Madensen, T. D., Daigle, L. E., Fearn, N. E., & Gau, J. M. (2010). The empirical status of social learning theory: A meta-analysis. *Justice Quarterly*, *27*(6), 765–802.

Richie, B. E. (2012). *Arrested justice: Black women, violence, and America's prison nation*. New York University Press.

Ridgeway, C. (1991). The social construction of status value: Gender and other nominal characteristics. *Social Forces*, *70*, 367–386.

Ridgeway, C. L., & Balkwell, J. W. (1997). Group processes and the diffusion of status beliefs. *Social Psychology Quarterly*, *60*(1), 14–31.

Ridgeway, C., & Berger, J. (1986). Expectations, legitimation and dominance in task groups. *American Sociological Review*, *51*, 603–617.

Ridgeway, C. L., Boyle, E. H., Kuipers, K. J., & Robinson, D. T. (1998). How do status beliefs develop? The role of resources and interactional experience. *American Sociological Review*, *63*, 331–350.

Ridgeway, C., & Correll, S. J. (2006). Consensus and the creation of status beliefs. *Social Forces*, *85*(1), 431–453.

Ridgeway, C., & Erickson, K. G. (2000). Creating and spreading status beliefs. *American Journal of Sociology*, *106*, 579–615.

Rios, V. M. (2011). *Punished: Policing the lives of Black and Latino boys*. New York University Press.

Robertiello, G. (2014). Sheldon, William H. In J. M. Miller (Ed.), *The encyclopedia of theoretical criminology* (online edition). John Wiley & Sons. http://doi.org/10.1002/9781118517390.wbetc047

Robinson, D. T., & Smith-Lovin, L. (1992). Selective interaction strategy for identity maintenance: An affect control model. *Social Psychology Quarterly*, *55*, 12–28.

Rock, P. (1973). Phenomenalism and essentialism in the sociology of deviance. *Sociology*, *7*(1), 17–29.

Rodriguez-Seijas, C., Burton, C. L., Adeyinka, O., & Pachankis, J. E. (2019). On the quantitative study of multiple marginalization: Paradox and potential solution. *Stigma and Health*, *4*(4), 495–502.

Rogers, S. A., Isom, D. A., & Rader, N. E. (2023). Fear of victimization among LGBQ, non-binary, and transgender college and university students in the United States. *Victims & Offenders*, *18*(1), 169–193.

Russell, K. K. (1992). Development of a black criminology and the role of the black criminologist. *Justice Quarterly*, *9*(4), 667–683.

Russell-Brown, K. K. (2009). *The color of crime* (2nd ed.). New York University Press.

Sellers, R. M., Smith, M. A., Shelton, J. N., Rowley, S. A. J., & Chavous, T. M. (1998). The multidimensional model of racial identity: A reconceptualization of African American racial identity. *Personality and Social Psychology Review*, *2*, 18–39.

Sharp, S. F., & Hefley, K. (2007). This is a man's world… or least that's how it looks in the journals. *Critical Criminology*, *15*, 3–18.

Shaw, C. R., & McKay, H. D. (1942). *Juvenile delinquency and urban areas*. University of Chicago Press.

Simpson, S. S. (1989). Feminist theory, crime, and justice. *Criminology*, *27*, 605–631.

Sprague, J. (2016). *Feminist methodologies for critical researchers* (2nd ed.). Rowman & Littlefield.

Steffensmeier, D., & Allan, E. (1996). Gender and crime: Toward a gendered theory of female offending. *Annual Review of Sociology, 22*, 459–487.

Stockard, J. (2006). Gender socialization. In J. S. Chafetz (Ed.), *Handbook of the sociology of gender* (pp. 215–227). Springer.

Stryker, S. (1980). *Symbolic interactionism.* The Blackburn Press.

The White House Office. (2016, April 6). *Fact sheet: Breaking down gender stereotypes in media and toys so that our children can explore, learn, and dream without limits.* Office of the Press Secretary, Washington, DC. https://obamawhitehouse.archives.gov/the-press-office/2016/04/06/factsheet-breaking-down-gender-stereotypes-media-and-toys-so-our

Taylor, P. J., Russ-Eft, D. F., & Chan, D. W. L. (2005). A meta-analytic review of behavior modeling training. *Journal of Applied Psychology, 90*(4), 692–709.

Thoits, P. A. (1986). Multiple identities: Examining gender and marital status differences in distress. *American Sociological Review, 51*, 259–272.

Thoits, P. A. (1992). Identity structures and psychological well-being: Gender and marital status comparisons. *Social Psychology Quarterly, 55*, 236–256.

Tulchin, S. H. (1939). *Intelligence and crime: A study of the penitentiary and reformatory offenders.* The University of Chicago Press.

Turner, J. C. (1999). Some current issues in research in social identity and self categorization theories. In N. Ellemers, R. Spears, & B. Dossje (Eds.), *Social identity* (pp. 6–34). Blackwell.

Unnever, J. D., & Gabbidon, S. L. (2011). *A theory of African American offending.* Routledge.

Unnever, J. D., Gabbidon, S. L., & Chouhy, C. (2018). *Building a Black criminology: Race, theory, and crime.* Routledge.

Valdez, Z., & Golash-Boza, T. (2017). Towards an intersectionality of race and ethnicity. *Ethnic and Racial Studies, 40*(13), 2256–2261.

Webster, M., Jr., & Hysom, S. J. (1998). Creating status characteristics. *American Sociological Review, 63*, 351–378.

Wuthnow, R. (2018). *The left behind: Decline and rage in small-town America.* Princeton University Press.

8
MAKING THE INVISIBLE VISIBLE

The past decade has been full of social and political strife – a rise in racial tensions as numerous people of Color lost their lives at the hands of law enforcement and those emboldened by "stand your ground" mandates; the election of a man known for his sexist, racist, and xenophobic behaviors largely in response to the tenure of America's first president of Color; a rise in hate crimes against Muslim, Jewish, Asian, and other communities following the prejudicial, derogatory, and hateful rhetoric – and countless lies – of Donald Trump; increased polarization, ignorance, and fear as more and more people are inundated with misinformation and lack the ability to decipher falsehoods from facts – all topped off with the political weaponization of a global pandemic and an attempted insurrection on the US Capitol. Many of us thought the tensions would wane following the election of Joe Biden over a second term of Trump and that we would return to some sense of "normalcy." Yet, that did not happen as the increasing number of mass shootings, the attacks on critical infrastructure, and the continued weaponizing of politics and laws against marginalized and oppressed groups have shown. But, we also know this current moment is not new; just the latest iteration of the myths of white supremacy in action.

While this book is not about the current political and social moment, it does provide insight into what is happening. More often than not, the United States fails to not only *not learn* from its history, but to not even tell the truth about it. Instead of dealing with the horrors of the founding of America on the backs of enslaved labor stolen from Africa on land that was taken from Indigenous people, we continue to teach children whitewashed narratives of great explorers, kind slaveowners, and the end of racial inequality with the passing of the Civil Rights Acts in the 1960s. We continue to fight against restorative justice

DOI: 10.4324/9781003167877-9

and retributions for the atrocities of our foundation, and instead perpetuate the dismissal and erasure of not only white people's sins, but the vast stories of survival, endurance, and excellence of those who were oppressed that contributed to the greatness of America. America stands on the shoulders of great visionaries, intellectuals, and heroes of Color that are rarely, if ever, acknowledged. The perpetuation of the silencing of marginalized voices and stories is a manifestation of white fear, their habitus angst, their aggrieved entitlement. The myth of white supremacy is held together by a single thread – the idea of not being the "Other" – and when that thread begins to unravel, those held up by it get scared and grasp at whatever they can to hold on to it.

Thus, whiteness has been weaponized by those in power to intimidate, marginalize, and control people of Color and oppressed Others while manipulating working and lower-class, heterosexual, cisgender whites, particularly men, into being agents of social control, the police of the white supremacist, patriarchal, capitalist status quo. The Founding Fathers' great "experiment" has not only succeeded as they intended – to manipulate and dominate the masses for their gain – but has evolved and improved into a more precise and deadly weapon (much like their beloved firearms – from muskets to AR-15s). The white habitus' roots are so deeply embedded throughout society, it is almost impossible to destroy. The myth of white supremacy – the true cornerstone of the real "American ideals" – is a virus with the intent on feeding off its host – the American people. It evolves to become more resistant to treatment and vaccines to ensure its survival. The myths of white supremacy and the emergent white habitus – released by the Founding Fathers – have infected all of American society and is virtually treatment resistant. Just as we begin to make progress toward eradicating the sicknesses of racism, sexism, bigotry, and the like, they evolve again and expand their reach. Technology, and especially the internet, have exacerbated the spread through increased polarization and division, radicalization, perpetuation of falsehoods, and reinforcement of hate-fueled ideologies. Thus, those in power maintain their positions and influence while the masses tear each other down through perpetual infighting. So, yes, our society is sick – not from a strong, just civilization being infiltrated by a few bad apples – no, *we are the virus*. A virus brought to this land by European colonizers – a virus that spreads racism, sexism, homophobic, xenophobic, and other bigoted beliefs to perpetuate the myths of white patriarchal supremacy. Thus, the pillars of American society, institutions, and orthodox ideals are infected, and the disease is just getting worse. Some even believe we are on the edge of another civil war (Kaufman, 2022; Nance, 2022), and unless something changes, they may not be wrong.

To disrupt and dismantle our unjust, inequitable, and toxic social norms that create and perpetuate social disparities, we must first take an honest and complete look at our past. Recognizing our full history, countering the myths of white supremacy, and questioning the creation, perpetuation, and use of whiteness are central components of critical whiteness studies. The current strife (and potentially impending civil war if nothing is done) is why the theory of whiteness and crime (TWC) is so timely and vitally important. By grounding itself in an integrative structural identities model (ISIM) framework, TWC applies an intersectional, socio-historically informed, critical whiteness lens to the racial disparities in deviant and criminal behaviors and criminal legal entanglements within the United States. Such a perspective centers the role of the myth of white supremacy and resultant white habitus on individuals' sense of self and identity. The varied degrees of internalization of such orthodox referential structures then provide a lens through which one sees, interprets, and interacts with the social world. This lens is either reinforced and exacerbated or countered and mitigated through broadcast processes, particularly through media consumption – and due to the advances in technology and the polarization of media, one's internalized lens is more than likely further entrenched. The resultant perspectives fuel habitus angst, or unwarranted fear, anger, and animosity, toward people of Color and other marginalized and oppressed groups, those somehow different from one's self. These perspectives also spark feelings of aggrieved entitlement when things don't work out for one's benefit or go counter to how one believes they should. Habitus angst and aggrieved entitlement reinforce and feed off one another until one is driven to action to relieve their stress and strain – they vote for MAGA Republicans; they join clandestine online forums; they get involved in pro-white organizations; they go off on persons of Color in public; or they attack the US Capitol, just for example. Yet, despite (sometimes) engaging in criminal behavior to cope, they are less likely to pay the legal price for their actions. Instead of being arrested, some are thanked by police for "helping" control the crowd at protest (or are the police themselves); they are given a warning instead of sanctions; they are provided leniency from a judge; and/or, they are represented by a competent attorney that gets their charges dropped.

This is white privilege in action – allowing whites, particularly cisgender, heterosexual men, privileged pathways to deviant and criminal behaviors as well as privileged protections from entanglements within the criminal legal system. And, applying a socio-historical lens allows us to realize this is nothing new and to better understand how the law, politics, and social institutions have perpetuated this process. This is the essence of TWC, and it explains the vast variation within white people's responses to changes to society as well as their likelihood of behaving in deviant, criminal, and violent ways. Furthermore, TWC highlights how vast the reach of the myth of white supremacy truly is and why we need to focus more broadly than solely on those deemed "white supremacists." As Ferber (1998) states, "(T)he narrow attention to organized hate groups is insufficient. They are clearly simply one manifestation of a more widespread problem. Focusing on only one small segment of the continuum, and treating it as an isolated, exceptional movement, distorts the problem, erases from view the rest of the continuum, and hinders our understanding of the organized hate movement itself…White supremacist discourse gains power precisely because it rearticulates mainstream racial and gender narratives once taken for granted" (pp. 149–150). TWC sheds light on this notion and provides a framework to begin to counter it.

This theoretical perspective flips the focus away from the marginalized onto the powerful to answer the question – why are white folks treated differently? When we understand the complexity of this answer, we not only begin to better understand the varied pathways to and from criminal and deviant behaviors and entanglements with the legal system within whites and between them and other groups, but to also start thinking about real solutions, at all levels of society and social interactions. Laws and policies must change; institutions and practices, especially within law enforcement and prosecutors' offices, must change; businesses and education must change; news media and technology, particularly social forums and networks, must change; but most importantly, individual ideologies must change. If this is all rooted in the myth of white supremacy, then it must be refuted and eradicated at all levels. In other words, we must abolish the cornerstones of our American culture and reimagine a society that is truly just for all.

While it is extremely difficult, social psychology has proven orthodox referential structures *can* be countered – through cross-group, meaningful interactions; through more people of Color and other oppressed groups being in positions of power and influence; by making their presence, perspectives, and lived experiences a part of normative interactions and social spaces (e.g., Goar & Sell, 2005; Pettigrew & Tropp, 2006; Ridgeway, 1997; Walker et al., 2014; Webster & Driskell, 1978). Thus, we must have more diverse and inclusive leadership; we need more accurate and broad representation in books, television, and movies; and we need full, inclusive education of all histories and cultures – in other words, *we must undo the whitewashing*. Furthermore, we must change the orthodox standard of society – wealth gaps most be eradicated, and healthcare and education must be free and accessible to all – only when *everyone's* basic human needs are met can we begin to form a true and just democracy.

These things are easily fixed with legislation – just as we've changed our norms around seat belts and smoking – so too can basic equalities of income, healthcare, and education be met by political leaders being willing to act. We must also radically change who and what we fear and how we approach social control. In other words, we must reimagine our criminal legal system. We must *honestly* answer what are the purposes of law enforcement and incarceration. We must create better ways to meet citizens' needs in times of distress as well as establish ways to deal with those that truly do harm to society, so they face accountability without losing their dignity or humanity. Other societies provide examples of how all of these can be accomplished, we just must be bold enough to follow others' lead.

Pushed largely to action in response to the 2016 election of Trump, renowned progressive scholars, Walter DeKeseredy and Elliott Currie (2019), edited a volume of works from leading researchers on strategies for challenging the rise of the radical right. Within it, there are informed discussions around countering toxic masculinity and patriarchy, radical police reform, recognizing the significance of place – globally, regionally, and contextually (i.e., rural, suburban, urban spaces), understanding the harm of white-collar crimes, the impacts of climate change, and particularly countering the rise of right-wing populism. Overall, they aim, as Currie (2016) called for, "… ways of fostering a criminology that is more than a relative passive witness to the destruction wrought by contemporary global forces – much less an accomplice – an instead vigorously steps up to take on the job of combatting those forces and dedicating itself unapologetically to the reduction of needless pain, fear, and injustice around the world" (p. 29). This book further adds to such a criminology.

The solutions proposed earlier are all big general asks, but there are some steps we can take as individuals to move us toward a more just and equitable society. First off, I echo Winlow and colleagues (2019) (to a degree) that we must find a way to come together and unite around shared concerns if we are ever going to make truly just changes. Yet, this – nor any of the boarder goals suggested prior – cannot be done without first countering the myth of white supremacy's hold on all of us, particularly white people. Aligned with status dissonance theory, research suggests exposure to concepts of white privilege can shift people's perceptions of racism, even if one holds more conservative beliefs (Cooley et al., 2019). Thus, the messages received through broadcast processes and exposure to dissimilar others is vital to begin dismantling the hold white supremacist ideologies have on our society (see Chapter 2). Hence, I suggest exposure to knowledge and getting out of one's comfort zone are fruitful battlegrounds.

We must fight the banning of books in schools and libraries and the prohibition of teaching the complete and full history of our country. Topics that are distinctly under attack are issues of race and racism, LGBTQ experiences and issues, non-Christian religious traditions, women's rights, and general themes of activism (Friedman & Johnson, 2022). Restrictions on these topics and threats posed to people of Color, the LGBTQ community, women, immigrants, religious minorities, and other marginalized and oppressed groups are growing across the United States (e.g., Chamlee, 2023; Cohen & Barajas, 2023; Guttmacher Institute, 2023; Human Rights Campaign, 2023; NAACP, 2023; Najarro, 2023; Romo, 2023; Southern Poverty Law Center, n.d.) under the guise of "protecting freedoms" (e.g., Brownstein, 2022; Friedersdorf, 2023). This "whitewashing" of history does nothing but silence the oppressed and marginalized and maintain the status quo of the white, cisgender, heterosexual, male power majority.

In addition to exposing children early to the full and complete history of the United States (and the world) and all its people, as well as creating space for them to interact with various others, we must also find ways to counteract the disinformation in the media. In attention to the spreading of polarizing rhetoric and falsehoods through conservative news outlets and social media discussed earlier (see Chapter 1), the rapidly growing use of artificial intelligence (AI) technology is making it ever more difficult to know what is real and what is not. Companies are now working on ways to create "lie detectors" for deepfakes (i.e., manipulations of photos and videos; Pogue & Morgan, 2023). I propose a worthwhile endeavor would be to create software that can verify the validity of information and provide references for primary sources of information posted online. If AI can scan the internet, learn from it, and provide a simple assessment (and produce a validation check mark) if a video has been manipulated or not, why can't we find a way to assess information provided by a news source or social media platform for its validity and reliability? I'm definitely not a computer scientist, but this seems like a social good AI could potentially serve. This is the type of out-of-the-box, innovative, interdisciplinary thinking and research we need. In the interim, we all can do our part to be conscious consumers of information – question what you hear and read, validate the information, and seek out the full story from primary sources.

Scholars must also do their part to produce not only empirically sound, but inclusive and meaningful knowledge. We must do the research to inform socially just reforms that serve and protect the most vulnerable. It is hard work, but we must push the methodological and theoretical bounds to further expose and fill our gaps in knowledge around the experiences of those too-oft forgotten as well as the powerful hiding in plain sight. It is only through this type of disruptive scholarship that we can begin to imagine new policies, systems, institutions, and structures grounded in true equity and justice to establish a real democracy "for the people, by the people" and where *all* are fully "equal under the law."

Most of all, none of us can stay silent, especially us white folks. White people must deal with their own white fragility and learn to use their white privilege for the good of others. We cannot sit complicitly by and continue to allow the ideologies of white supremacy, patriarchy, and capitalism to flourish. The easiest way to use your voice is to vote. Yes, our pseudo-democracy is set up against us (Anderson, 2018; Crump, 2019; Glaude, 2016), but that doesn't mean we give up the fight. We must exercise (and protect) our right to vote and encourage others to do the same. We must understand and get involved in local and state politics, because that is where true change always begins – just look at the recent "Minnesota Miracle" (Dionne, 2023). It is through these personal action steps – learning more, stepping out of our comfort zones, and getting involved – that will lead to change, especially if enough of us do it.

This book builds upon and integrates a substantial amount of modern progressive theoretical and empirical work. *Gratuitous Angst* and TWC recognize that *The White Racial Frame* (Feagin, 2013) informs the belief in an *Exceptional America* (Jouet, 2017) and a society where there is *Racism without Racists* (Bonilla-Silva, 2018) because of *How the Word is Passed* (Smith, 2021) down through history. Such beliefs result in many whites feeling as if they are *The Left Behind* (Wuthnow, 2018) or *Strangers in Their Own Land* (Hochschild, 2016), and feeling *Mediocre* (Oluo, 2021), experiencing *White Fragility* (DiAngelo, 2018) or *White Rage* (Anderson, 2016), or are labeled *Angry White Men*[*] when society no longer looks like the "good ole days." Such sentiments lead to *White Identity Politics* (Jardina, 2019) and explain *Why We're Polarized* (Klein, 2020), in addition to providing insight into why Blacks are more likely than whites to end up in a *Chokehold* (Butler, 2017), why *The Rich Get Richer and the Poor Get Prison* (Reiman & Leighton, 2020), and why, for so many whites, *They Want to Kill Americans* (Nance, 2022), and thus *Everything You Love Will Burn* (Tenold, 2018). We, therefore, must start *Thinking About Crime* (Tonry, 2004) differently and stop *Punishing Race* (Tonry, 2011) because *We Are Not Yet Equal* (Anderson, 2018). We must be *Unapologetic* (Carruthers, 2018) about our *Eloquent Rage* (Cooper, 2018), for it's time to answer for *America's Original Sin* (Wallis, 2016) and stop *The Violence of Hate* (Levin & Nolan, 2017). This is *The Hill We Climb* (Gorman, 2021) in pursuit of a truly just society. These are only some of the countless works (and a suggested starting point for an intrigued reader) that touch on the varied components integrated here and hopefully inspire action.

The TWC provides a framework to begin to empirically assess these disparate pathways as well as investigate possible solutions. It lays a foundation that may be reassessed and revised as we gain more knowledge about the varied and complex associations between whiteness and crime. I hope researchers are motivated to deeply examine racialization, gendering, economic exploitation, and power (Choo & Ferree, 2010) through this lens over continued surface-level looks at differences between races and ethnicities, gender identities, and social classes. Only through deeper exploration may we find real avenues for social change.

As stated repeatedly here, America was founded on racial inequality, and the myth of white supremacy is firmly rooted in that history (Anderson, 2016; Hannah-Jones et al., 2021; Kendi, 2016; McGhee, 2021; Mills, 1997; Rothstein, 2017; Smith, 2021; Wallis, 2016). While political and racial tensions have ebbed and flowed over time, the 2016 presidential election of Donald Trump set off a firestorm that continues to burn uncontrollably in the wake of numerous deaths at the hands of police, two presidential impeachment hearings, controversial

Supreme Court Justices appointments, a global pandemic, and the insurrection of the Capitol on January 6, 2021. While beliefs in the status quo and racial hierarchies have always been tied to animosity toward social progress (e.g., Bobo & Hutchings, 1996; Craig & Richeson, 2014; Eitle et al., 2002; Giles & Hertz, 1994; Liska, 1992; Morrison et al., 2009; Tajfel & Turner, 1979), such sentiments have arguably never been as strong as the current moment. America has not healed its racial divisions and social inequities it was founded upon. We must understand the root causes and complexities that perpetuate such divisions to ever know how to remedy them. Understanding the complexities and intricacies of these associations is vital to reveal legitimate ways to bridge social gaps. The TWC provides a framework to explore these links empirically. Scholars such as Du Bois (1920) have long called for the critical assessment of the myth of white supremacy and whiteness for over a century. While the sentiments around the racial hierarchy in America have shifted over time (Anderson, 2016; Kaufmann, 2019), TWC shines a light on distinct experiences and behaviors of white Americans, particularly in regard to their unique pathways to deviant and criminal behaviors and privileged protections from punishment by the criminal legal system. This is just one step toward answering the call of Du Bois and other progressive scholars (e.g., Bell, 1995; Collins, 2019; Delgado & Stefancic, 2013), and the beginning of bringing critical whiteness studies into the field of criminology. I hope this will serve as a catalyst for the pursuit of knowledge that can inform socially just change and lead America into an age where its reality is an accurate reflection of its just and equal ideals for all – before it is too late.

References

Anderson, C. (2016). *White rage: The unspoken truth of our racial divide*. Bloomsbury.

Anderson, C. (2018). *We are not yet equal: Understanding our racial divide*. Bloomsbury.

Bell, D. A. (1995). Who's afraid of critical race theory? *University of Illinois Law Review, 4*, 893–910.

Bobo, L., & Hutchings, V. L. (1996). Perceptions of racial group competition: Extending Blumer's theory of group position to a multiracial social context. *American Sociological Review, 61*, 951–972.

Bonilla-Silva, E. (2018). *Racism without racists: Color-blind racism and the persistence of racial inequality in America* (5th ed.). Rowman & Littlefield.

Brownstein, R. (2022, July 8). The glaring contradiction of Republicans' rhetoric of freedom. *The Atlantic*. https://www.theatlantic.com/politics/archive/2022/07/democrats-republicans-rhetoric-freedom-rollback/661519/

Butler, P. (2017). *Chokehold: Policing Black men*. The New Press.

Carruthers, C. A. (2018). *Unapologetic*. Beacon Press.

Chamlee, V. (2023, June 6). Anti-drag legislation is sweeping the nation: Here's where each state stands on drag bans. *People*. https://people.com/politics/anti-drag-legislation-united-states/

Choo, H. Y., & Ferree, M. M. (2010). Practicing intersectionality in sociological research: A critical analysis of inclusions, interactions, and institutions in the study of inequalities. *Sociology Theory, 28*(2), 129–149.

Cohen, J., & Barajas, J. (2023, April 24). How many book bans were attempted in your state? Use this map to find out. *PBS News Hour.* https://www.pbs.org/newshour/arts/how-many-book-bans-were-attempted-in-your-state-use-this-map-to-find-out

Collins, P. H. (2019). *Intersectionality as critical social theory.* Duke University Press.

Cooley, E., Brown-Iannuzzi, J., & Cottrell, D. (2019). Liberals perceive more racism than conservatives when police shoot Black men – but, reading about White privilege increases perceived racism, and shifts attributions of guilt, regardless of political ideology. *Journal of Experimental Psychology, 85,* 103885.

Cooper, B. (2018). *Eloquent rage.* St. Martin's Press.

Craig, M. A., & Richeson, J. A. (2014). On the precipice of a "majority-minority" America: Perceived status threat from the racial demographic shift affects white Americans' political ideology. *Psychological Science, 25*(6), 1189–97.

Crump, B. (2019). *Open season: Legalized genocide of colored people.* Amistad/HarperCollins Publishers.

Currie, E. (2016). The violence divide: Taking 'ordinary' crime seriously in a volatile world. In R. Matthews (Ed.), *What is to be done about crime and punishment? Towards a "public criminology* (pp. 9–30). Palgrave Macmillan.

DeKeseredy, W. S., & Currie, E. (Eds.). (2019). *Progressive justice in an age of repression.* Routledge.

Delgado, R., & Stefancic, J. (Eds.). (2013). *Critical race theory: The cutting edge* (3rd eds.). Temple University Press.

DiAngelo, R. (2018). *White fragility: Why it's so hard for white people to talk about racism.* Beacon Press.

Dionne, E. J. Jr. (2023, June 4). The 'Minnesota Miracle' should serve as a model for democrats. *The Washington Post.* https://www.washingtonpost.com/opinions/2023/06/04/democratic-party-minnesota-legislature-progressives/

Du Bois, W. E. B. (1920/1999). *Darkwater: Voices from within the veil.* Dover Publications, Inc.

Eitle, D., D'Alessio, S. J., & Stolzenberg, L. (2002). Racial threat and social control: A test of the political, economic, and threat of black crime hypotheses. *Social Forces, 81*(2), 557–576.

Feagin, J. R. (2013) *The White racial frame* (2nd ed.), Routledge.

Ferber, A. L. (1998). *White man falling: Race, gender, and white supremacy.* Rowman & Littlefield.

Friedman, J., & Johnson, N. F. (2022, September 19). *Banned in the USA: The growing movement to censor books in schools.* PEN America. https://pen.org/report/banned-usa-growing-movement-to-censor-books-in-schools/

Friedersdorf, C. (2023, April 30). Ron DeSantis's Orwellian redefinition of freedom. *The Atlantic.* https://www.theatlantic.com/ideas/archive/2023/04/desantis-disney-lawsuit-free-speech-florida/673903/

Giles, M. W., & Hertz, K. (1994). Racial threat and partisan identification. *American Political Science Review, 88*(2), 317–326.

Glaude, E. S. Jr. (2016). *Democracy in black: How race still enslaves the American soul.* Crown Publishers.

Goar, C., & Sell, J. (2005). Using task definition to modify racial inequality within task groups. *The Sociological Quarterly, 46*, 525–543.

Gorman, A. (2021). *The hill we climb*. Viking.

Guttmacher Institute. (2023, June 6). *Interactive map: US abortion policies and access after Roe*. https://states.guttmacher.org/policies/

Hannah-Jones, N., Roper, C., Silverman, I., & Silverstein, J. (Eds.). (2021). *The 1619 project: A new origin story*. One World.

Hochschild, A. R. (2016). *Strangers in their own land: Anger and mourning on the American right*. The New Press.

Human Rights Campaign. (2023, June 1). *Map: Attacks on gender affirming care by state*. https://www.hrc.org/resources/attacks-on-gender-affirming-care-by-state-map

Jardina, A. (2019). *White identity politics*. Cambridge University Press.

Jouet, M. (2017). *Exceptional America: What divides Americans from the world and from each other*. University of California Press.

Kaufman, S. J. (2022). Is the U.S. heading for a civil war? Scenarios for 2024-25. *Studies in Conflict & Terrorism*. Advance online publication. https://doi.org/10.1080/10576 10X.2022.2137892

Kaufmann, E. (2019). *Whiteshift: Populism, immigration, and the future of white majorities*. Abrams Press.

Kendi, I. X. (2016). *Stamped from the beginning*. Bold Type Books.

♠Kimmel, M. (2017). *Angry white men: American masculinity at the end of an era*. Nation Books.

Klein, E. (2020). *Why we're polarized*. Avid Reader Press.

Levin, J., & Nolan, J. (2017). *The violence of hate* (4th eds.). Rowman & Littlefield.

Liska, A. E. (Ed.). 1992). *Social threat and social control*. Suny Press.

McGhee, H. (2021). *The sum of us: What racism cost everyone and how we can prosper together*. One World.

Mills, C. (1997). *The racial contract*. Cornell University Press.

Morrison, K. R., Fast, N. J., & Ybarra, O. (2009). Group status, perceptions of threat, and support for social inequality. *Journal of Experimental Social Psychology, 45*(1), 204–10.

NAACP. (2023, May 20). *NAACP issues travel advisory to Florida*. https://naacp.org/articles/naacp-issues-travel-advisory-florida

Najarro, I. (2023, February 1). College Board releases AP African American studies framework, runs into anti-CRT laws. *Education Week*. https://www.edweek.org/teaching-learning/college-board-releases-ap-african-american-studies-framework-runs-into-anti-crt-laws/2023/02

Nance, M. (2022). *They want to kill Americans: The militias, terrorists, and deranged ideology of the Trump insurgency*. St. Martin's Press.

Oluo, I. (2021). *Mediocre: The dangerous legacy of white male America*. Seal Press.

Pettigrew, T. F., & Tropp, L. R. (2006). A meta-analytic test of intergroup contact theory. *Journal of Personality and Social Psychology, 90*(5), 751–783.

Pogue, D., & Morgan, D. (2023, January 29). Creating a "lie detector" for deepfakes. *CBS News Sunday Morning*. https://www.cbsnews.com/news/creating-a-lie-detector-for-deepfakes-artificial-intelligence/

Reiman, J., & Leighton, P. (2020). *The rich get richer and the poor get prison: Thinking critically about class and criminal justice* (12th eds.). Routledge.

Ridgeway, C. (1997). Interaction and the conservation of gender inequality: Considering employment. *American Sociological Review*, *62*, 218–235.

Romo, V. (2023, May 30). Why Florida's new immigration law is troubling businesses and workers alike. *NPR*. https://www.npr.org/2023/05/30/1177657218/florida-anti-immigration-law-1718-desantis

Rothstein, R. (2017). *The color of law*. Liveright Publishing Company/W.W. Norton & Company.

Smith, C. (2021). *How the word is passed: A reckoning with the history of slavery across America*. Little, Brown and Company.

Southern Poverty Law Center. (n.d.). *Tracking anti-Muslim legislation across the U.S.* https://www.splcenter.org/data-projects/tracking-anti-muslim-legislation-across-us

Tajfel, H., & Turner, J. (1979). An integrative theory of intergroup conflict. In M. J. Hatch, & M. Schultz (Eds.), *Organizational identity: A reader* (pp. 56–65). Oxford University Press.

Tenold, V. (2018). *Everything you love will burn: Inside the rebirth of white nationalism in America*. Nation Books.

Tonry, M. (2004). *Thinking about crime: Sense and sensibility in American penal culture*. Oxford University Press.

Tonry, M. (2011). *Punishing race: A continuing American dilemma*. Oxford University Press.

Walker, L. S., Doerer, S. C., & Webster, M. Jr. (2014). Status, participation, and influence in task groups. *Sociological Perspectives*, *57*(3), 364–381.

Wallis, J. (2016). *America's original sin: Racism, white privilege, and the bridge to a new America*. Brazos Press.

Webster, M. Jr., & Driskell, J. E. Jr. (1978). Status generalization: A review and some new data. *American Sociological Review*, *43*, 220–236.

Winlow, S., Hall, S., & Treadwell, J. (2019). Why the left must change: Right-wing populism in context. In W. S. DeKeseredy, & E. Currie (Eds.), *Progressive justice in an age of repression* (pp. 26–41). Routledge.

Wuthnow, R. (2018). *The left behind: Decline and rage in small-town America*. Princeton University Press.

INDEX

Note: *Italic* page numbers refer to figures and page numbers followed by "n" refer to end notes.

people of Color 1, 3–8, 10n1, 11n8, 26,
45, 49, 52, 55, 64, 66–68, 81–83,
86–88, 91, 93–94, 107–108, 111–
113, 115–116, 128, 151–155
performance expectations 47–48, 56n5
Plessy v. Ferguson 4
policing 94–95
Potter, H. 25–26, 131, 140–143
power 1–4, 7, 11n6, 25–27, 29, 34, 45–46,
50, 62, 64, 67–72, 73n4, 82–83,
85–88, 91, 94, 111, 115–117, 125,
129, 134, 137–140, 142, 152, 154,
156–157
privileged protections 93–95, 108–109,
111–112, 117, 125, 128, 153, 158
progressive scholars 9, 11n8, 11n10

race 11n8, 22, 25–28, 35n3, 35n5, 46–48,
50–51, 56n4, 66–69, 72, 84, 87–
88, 94, 96n3, 113, 115, 117, 125,
127, 133–134, 136, 140, 143n2,
155, 157
racial: attitudes and significant events
29, *30*, 31; disparities 128–129;
socialization 136
racism 2–4, 8–9, 23, 26–27, 29, 66–67,
70, 88–89, 108, 132, 152, 155
The Red Lily (France) 111
Reed, S. M. 90
reflected appraisals 49, 56n7
reverse discrimination 64–66
reward expectations theory 56n5
Ridgeway, C. L. 46–49, 51–52
Ritchie, A. J. 113
Rittenhouse, K. 93
Robinson, D. T. 137
rural 66, 72n2

Samson, F. L. 25
Scaptura, M. N. 90
SDT *see* status dissonance theory (SDT)
Sell, J. 48
sex/sexuality 8, 50, 70, 87, 89–92, 94, 107,
112, 126–127, 129, 132–135, 140
Shaw, C. R. 132
small dick problems (Rowland) 90
Smart, C. 11n7
Smith, D. N. 23
Smith-Lovin, L. 137
social capital 115–116
socialization 34, 63, 71, 126, 131,
133–141

social media 6, 32–33, 90, 156
social psychology 55, 62, 64, 135, 154
Sommers, S. R. 27
status construction theory 46–49, 51–52,
56n4–56n5, 135
status dissonance theory (SDT) 46, 49,
126–127, 140, 155; broadcast
process 51–52; characteristics
50; contact with dissimilar others
51–52; justice principles 52;
and positional lens 52–53, *54*;
referential structures 51; white
crime 55; and whites' perceptions
and outlook 53, 55
status value 46–52, 55, 56n4–56n5, 68,
138, 140
Stevenson, B. 114
stratification 134
Stryker, S. 137
symbolic interactionism 137

theory of whiteness and crime (TWC)
9–10, 34–35, 46, 95, 108,
125–129, *126*, 140, 142–143,
153–154, 157–158; aggrieved
entitlement 127; habitus angst
127; racial disparities 128–129;
status dissonance 126–127; white
privilege 127–128
threat: reverse discrimination and
victimhood 64–66; white America
and far-right 66–67; white women
67–69
Trump, D. 3, 6, 11n11, 22–29, 31–33,
66–67, 71, 83, 92–93, 129, 151,
155, 157
TWC *see* theory of whiteness and crime
(TWC)

Unite the Right rally 23

violence 5, 22, 24–25, 28, 33–35, 35n3,
52, 55, 63–65, 71, 83–85, 89–95,
108, 113–114, 118n8, 126–129
Voting Rights Act 4

Walker, L. S. 48
Webster, M. Jr. 48
white habitus 63, 67–69, 71, 94, 126, 136,
152–153
white male 11n8, 51, 107, 113, 127;
supremacy 86–87, 90, 93